Patricia Smith's
DOLL VALUES
Antique to Modern
Eighth Series

COLLECTOR BOOKS
A Division of Schroeder Publishing Co., Inc.

Searching For A Publisher?

We are always looking for knowledgeable people considered to be experts within their fields. If you feel that there is a real need for a book on your collectible subject and have a large comprehensive collection, contact us.

COLLECTOR BOOKS
P.O. Box 3009
Paducah, Kentucky 42002-3009

Additional copies of this book may be ordered from:

COLLECTOR BOOKS
P.O. Box 3009
Paducah, KY 42002-3009

@ $12.95 add $2.00 for postage and handling.

CREDITS

Our thanks go to the following for sharing their dolls and knowledge. Collectors helping each other sure make a better world!

Vickie Andings, Etta Anderson, Gloria Anderson, Alice Arthur, Shirley Bertrand, Arthur Boulette, Billyboy™ (Paris, France), Joanne Brunkin, Sylvia Bryant, Stan Buler, Barbara Earnshaw-Cain (P.O. Box 14381, Lenexa, KS, 66215), Bessie Carson, Lee Crane, Sandra Cummins, Ellen Dodge, Durham Art Studios (36429 Row River Rd., Cottage Grove, OR), Marie Ernst, Frasher Doll Auctions (Rt. 1, Box 72, Oak Grove, MO, 64075), Maureen Fukushima, Green Madame Alexander Museum (Chatworth, GA), Karen Geary, O.D. Gregg, Virginia Jones, Mimi Hiscox, Kris Lindquist, Margaret Mandel, Patty Martin, Jeanne Mauldin (Mauldin Doll Museum, 2238 Whitefield Place, Kennesaw, GA, 30144), Jay Minter, Sharon McDowell, Chris McWilliams, Helen & Bill Moore (Photo by Mike Krambeck), Ellen Petersen, Peggy Pergande, Bonnie Stewart, Henri & John Startzel, Violette Steinke, Turn of Century Antiques (Photos by Neal Eisaman), Carol Turpin, Ann Wencel, Glorya Woods, Jeannette & Robert Woodall.

COVER PHOTO CREDIT

Frasher Doll Auctions
Rt. 1, Box 72; Oak Grove, MO 64075.

PRICES

This book is divided into "Antique" and "Modern" sections, with the older dolls in the first section and the newer dolls in the second section. Each section lists the dollmaker, type of material or name of doll alphabetically. (Example: Bye-lo or Kewpie.) This is done to try to make a quick reference for the reader. An index is provided for locating a specific doll.

The condition of the doll is the uppermost concern in pricing. An all original modern doll in excellent condition will bring a much higher price than listed in a price guide. A doll that is damaged or without original clothes, is soiled and dirty, will bring far less than the top price listed. The cost of doll repairs and cleanup has soared, and it is wise to judge the damage and estimate the cost of repairs before you attempt to sell or buy a damaged doll.

With antique dolls, the condition of the bisque, or material the head is made from, is of uppermost importance, as is the body in that it does not need repairs and is correct to the doll. Antique dolls must be clean, nicely dressed and ready to place into a collection and have no need of repair in any way for them to bring book price. An all original doll with original clothes, marked shoes and original wig will bring a lot more than any price listed. Boxes are very rare, so here again, the doll will have a higher price.

It is very important to show the "retail" price of dolls in a price guide and to try to be as accurate as possible for insurance reasons. This can be referred to as "replacement cost" as an insurance company or a postal service must have some means to appraise a damaged or stolen doll for the insuree, and the collector must have some means to judge their own collections to be able to purchase adequate amounts of insurance.

No one knows your collection better than yourself and in the end, in relation to what to pay for a doll, you must ask yourself if the doll is affordable to you and whether you want it enough to pay the price. You will buy the doll, or pass it up — it is as simple as that!

Prices shown are for dolls that are clean, undamaged, well-dressed and in overall excellent condition with many prices listed for soiled, dirty, redressed dolls also.

ANTIQUE AND OLDER DOLLS

Left, rear row: 33" marked "DEP." Right, rear row: 34"
S&H/K*R 85. Left, middle row: 20" Tete Jumeau with
closed mouth. Right, middle row: 24" Jules Steiner with
closed mouth. Front row: 18½" marked "E. 8. J." by
Jumeau. (See photo in Series 7, pg. 5.)

French all bisque dolls will be jointed at the necks, shoulder and hips. They have slender arms and legs, glass eyes and most have kid-lined joints. The majority of the heads have a sliced pate with a tiny cork insert. French all-bisque dolls have finely painted features with outlined lips, well tinted bisque, and feathered eyebrows. They can have molded-on shoes, high top boots with pointed toes, high top buttoned boots with four or more painted straps. They can also be barefooted or just have stockings painted onto the legs. Any French bisque should be in very good condition, not have any chips, breaks, nor should there be any hairline cracks to bring the following prices:

Swivel Neck: (Socket head.) Molded shoes or boots. 5" - $850.00; 7" - $1,200.00.

Bare Feet: 5-6" - $1,000.00; 8-9" - $1,700.00; 11" - $2,700.00.

With Jointed Elbows: 5½-6" - $2,500.00.

With Jointed Elbows and Knees: 5½-6" - $3,500.00.

S.F.B.J., UNIS, or other late French all bisques: 5-6" - $550.00; 7" - $700.00.

Left: 9½" all bisque marked "150-11." Sleep eyes, smiling open mouth with tiny dimples, jointed shoulders and hips, painted-on shoes and socks, maybe original clothes. Right: 5½" all bisque French type. Unmarked, painted-on long stockings, thin limbs, jointed neck, shoulders and hips. Open mouth and original wig over cork pate, glass eyes. 9½" - $775.00; 5½" - $900.00.

German-made all bisque dolls run from excellent to moderate quality. Prices are for excellent quality and condition with no chips, cracks, breaks or hairlines. Dolls should be nicely dressed and can have molded hair or wig. They generally have painted-on shoes and socks. Ca. 1880's-1930's.

Swivel Neck, Glass Eyes: Open or closed mouth, good wig, nicely dressed, painted-on shoes and socks. *Allow more for unusual colored boots (orange, gold or yellow) 5" - $465.00; 6" - $550.00; 8" - $775.00; 10" - $975.00 up. Jointed knees or elbows: 6" - $2,000.00; 8" - $3,000.00.

Swivel Neck, Painted Eyes: Open or closed mouth, one-strap shoes and painted socks. Nice clothes and wig. 4" - $250.00; 6" - $350.00; 8" - $500.00; 10" - $800.00 up.

One-Piece Body and Head, Glass Eyes: Excellent bisque, open or closed mouth with good wig and nicely dressed. 4" - $285.00; 7" - $500.00; 9" - $700.00; 11" - $1,200.00. Bent knees: 6" - $250.00.

One-Piece Body and Head, Painted Eyes: Open or closed mouth with good wig or molded hair and nicely dressed. 2" - $85.00; 5" - $200.00; 6" - $250.00; 8" - $350.00; 10" - $950.00.

Marked: 155, 156, 158, 162: Smiling, closed or open/closed mouth, glass eyes and swivel head. 5½" - $600.00; 7" - $850.00. Same, with one-piece body and head: 6" - $400.00; 7" - $500.00.

Molded-on Clothes or Underwear: Jointed at shoulders only or at shoulders and hips. No cracks, chips or breaks. 4" - $165.00; 5" - $225.00; 7" - $425.00. (See photo in Series 5, pg. 11.) Molded clothes or underwear, glass eyes: 5" - $365.00; 7" - $525.00.

Marked: 100, 125, 161, 225: (Made by Alt, Beck and Gottschalck.) Closed mouth or open/closed, sleep or inset glass eyes, chubby body and limbs and molded-on one-strap shoes with painted socks. No chips, cracks or breaks. Has one-piece body and head: 5" - $245.00; 6½" - $385.00; 8" - $550.00; 10" - $900.00.

Marked 130, 150: (Made by Kestner or Bonn.) One-piece body and head, painted-on one strap shoes with painted socks. Glass eyes, not damaged and nicely dressed. 4" - $275.00; 6" - $385.00; 7" - $425.00; 8" - $550.00; 9" - $750.00; 10" - $950.00; 11" - $1,000.00; 12" - $1,250.00.

Marked 130, 150, 160, 184, 208: Kestner, with painted eyes and molded hair. 4" - $250.00; 7" - $325.00; 11" - $1,200.00. With wig: 4" - $195.00; 7" - $300.00.

Marked 130, 150, 160, 184, 208: With swivel neck and glass eyes. 5" - $500.00; 9" - $1,100.00 up.

3" German all bisque with glass eyes, one-piece body and head, ribbed stockings and painted-on shoes. 3" - $285.00. Courtesy Stan Buler Collection.

Marked 184: Kestner, swivel neck, sweet face, glass eyes. Outlined, solid colored boots. 5" - $450.00; 8" - $550.00.

Molded Hair: One-piece body and head, painted eyes, painted-on shoes and socks. Excellent quality bisque and artist workmanship. No chips, cracks, and nicely dressed: 5" - $250.00; 6½" - $375.00.

Marked: 881, 886, 890: (Simon and Halbig) Or any all bisque marked S&H. Painted-on high-top boots with four or five straps. No damage and nicely dressed. 6" - $975.00; 8" - $1,500.00.

Black or Brown All Bisque: see Black Section.

Molded-on Hat or Bonnet: All in perfect condition. 6" - $450.00 up; 8" - $600.00 up.

7" rare Kestner all bisque, marked "111" on head. Extra joints at elbows and knees. Sleep googly eyes. Painted-on shoes and socks. 7" - $2,400.00.
Courtesy Ellen Dodge.

With Long Stockings: (To above the knees.) Glass eyes, open or closed mouth; jointed at neck and stockings will be black, blue or green. Perfect condition: 6" - $650.00; 8" - $850.00.

Hertel, Schwab: see that section.

Flapper: One-piece body and head, wig, painted eyes, painted-on long stockings and has thin limbs, fired-in tinted bisque, one-strap painted shoes. 6" - $365.00; 8" - $485.00. Same, but with molded hair: 6" - $325.00; 8" - $425.00. Same, but medium quality bisque and artist workmanship: 6" - $185.00; 8" - $275.00.

Marked With Maker: (S&H, JDK, A.B.G., etc.) Closed mouth, early fine quality face. 8" - $1,400.00; 11" - $1,700.00 up. Same, with open mouth and later quality bisque: 6" - $700.00; 8" - $1,200.00; 10" - $1,700.00. K*B: 8" - $1,500.00

Pink Bisque: 1920's and 1930's. Jointed shoulders and hips with painted features, can have molded hair or wig. All in excellent condition: 3" - $80.00; 5" - $100.00; 7" - $185.00.

Bathing Dolls: see that section.

Mold 415: Aviator with molded-on goggles and cap. 3½" - $225.00; 5" - $300.00; 7" - $450.00.

Figurines: Called "Immobilies" (no joints). Child: 3" - $85.00 up. Adults: 5" - $150.00 up. Bride & groom cake top: 6" - $300.00.

Left to right: 4" boy with molded hair, eyes to side and jointed at shoulders and hips. 5½" baby, jointed at shoulders and hips, painted eyes and hair. 3¾" baby, jointed at shoulders and hips, painted hair, and open/closed mouth. Marked **"830/0."** All figures made in Germany. 4" - $300.00; 5½" - $185.00; 3¾" - $100.00. Courtesy Frasher Doll Auctions.

ALL BISQUE – BABIES

All bisque babies were made in both Germany and Japan, and dolls from either country can be excellent quality or poor quality. Prices are for excellent workmanship to the painting and quality of bisque. There should be no chips, cracks, or breaks. Dressed or nude - 1900; bent limbs - after 1906.

Germany (Jointed Necks, Shoulders and Hips): Can have glass eyes or painted eyes, wigs or painted hair. 3½" - $185.00; 6" - $300.00; 8½" - $450.00.

Germany (Jointed at Shoulders and Hips Only): Well-painted features, free-formed thumbs and many have molded bottle in hand. Some have molded-on clothes. 3½" - $95.00; 6" - $185.00.

Germany (Character Baby): Jointed shoulders and hips, molded hair, painted eyes with character face. 4" - $185.00; 6" - $400.00. Glass eyes: 4" - $450.00; 6" - $550.00. **Mold #833:** 8" - $850.00 up; 11" - $1,400.00 up. Swivel neck, glass eyes: 6" - $600.00; 10" - $1,200.00 up.

Germany (Toddler): Jointed neck, glass eyes, perfect condition. 7" - $700.00; 9" - $1,000.00; 11" - $1,600.00.

"Candy Babies": (Can be either German or Japanese.) Generally poorly painted with high bisque color. Were given away at candy counter with purchase. 1920's. 4" - $60.00; 6" - $80.00.

Pink Bisque Baby: Jointed at shoulders and hips, painted features and hair, bent baby legs. 1920's and 1930's. 2" - $50.00; 4" - $75.00; 8" - $135.00.

Mold #231: (A.M.) Toddler. Open mouth, glass eyes. 8½" - $1,200.00 up.

Left to right: 5" character made by Heubach and marked with Heubach in square and "9748." 4¾" character with molded-on clothes and side glance eyes. Jointed at shoulders only. 4" molded one-piece with wide spread legs and hands, looks as if he is calling to someone. All made in Germany. 5" - $600.00; 4¾" - $400.00; 4" - $185.00. Courtesy Frasher Doll Auctions.

ALL BISQUE CHARACTERS

All bisque with character faces or stances were made both in Germany and Japan. The German dolls have finer bisque and workmanship of the painted features. Most character all bisque dolls have jointed shoulders only, with some having joints at the hips and a very few have swivel heads. They can have molded-on shoes or be barefooted. Prices are for dolls with no chips, cracks, hairlines or breaks.

Annie Rooney, Little: 4" - $350.00; 7" - $475.00.

Baby Bo Kaye: Made by Alt, Beck & Gottschalck. Marked with mold number **1394**. 4½" - $1,275.00; 6½" - $1,675.00.

Baby Bud: Glass eyes, wig: 6-7" - $575.00.

Baby Darling: Mold #497; Kestner #178. Swivel neck, glass eyes: 6" - $550.00; 8" - $850.00. One-piece body, painted eyes: 6" - $450.00; 8" - $650.00; 10" - $950.00 up.

Baby Peggy Montgomery: Made by Louis Amberg and marked with paper label. 6" - $550.00.

Bonnie Babe: Made by Georgene Averill. Has paper label. 5" - $750.00; 7" - $1,000.00. Molded-on clothes: 6" - $1,300.00.

Bye-Lo. Made J.D. Kestner. Has paper label. Jointed neck, glass eyes, solid dome. 4" - $525.00; 6" - $700.00. Jointed neck, wig, glass eyes: 5" - $700.00;

7-8" - $1,200.00. Painted eyes, molded hair and one-piece body and head: 5" - $385.00; 7-8" - $650.00. Immobile: "Salt" and "Pepper" on back or stomach. 3-3½" - $400.00.

Campbell Kids: Molded-on clothes, "Dutch" hairstyle. 5" - $285.00.

Chi Chi: Made by Orsini. 5-6" - $1,600.00. Painted eyes: $950.00.

Chin-Chin: Made by Heubach. 4½" - $325.00. Poor quality: 4½" - $250.00.

Didi: Made by Orsini. 5-6" - $1,600.00. Painted eyes: $950.00.

Fefe: Orsini. 5-6" - $1,600.00. Painted eyes: $950.00.

Googly: 1911-on. Glass eyes: 6" - $650.00. Painted eyes: 4" - $300.00; 6" - $485.00. Glass eyes, swivel neck: 6" - $775.00; 8" - $1,200.00. Jointed elbow and/or knees: 6" - $2,100.00; 7-7½" - $2,400.00. Marked with maker (example K*R): 6½-7" - $2,600.00 up.

Grumpy Boy: Marked "Germany": 4" - $185.00. Marked "Japan": 4" - $85.00.

Happifats: Boy or girl. 5" - $365.00 each and up.

Hebee or Shebee: 4½" - $450.00-$475.00. (See photo in Series 5, pg. 11; Series 7, pg. 9.)

Heubach: Molded hair, side glance eyes: 6½" - $775.00. Molded ribbon: 6½" - $850.00. Wigged: 7" - $925.00.

Bunny Boy or Girl figurine: 5" - $600.00.

Little Imp: Has hooved feet. 6½" - $600.00.

Kestner: Marked mold number **257, 262,** etc. 10" - $1,200.00 up; 12" - $1,400.00 up.

Max and Moritz: Kestner. 6" - $2,000.00 up each. (See photo in Series 7, pg. 12.)

Medic: One piece, molded-on uniform, carries case. 3½-4" - $250.00. (See photo in Series 7, pg. 9.)

Mibs: Made by Louis Amberg. May be marked "1921" on back and have paper label with name. 3½" - $250.00; 5" - $375.00.

Mimi: Made by Orsini. 6" - $1,600.00. Painted eyes: $950.00.

Molded-on Clothes: Made in Germany. Unjointed, painted features. 4" - $200.00; 7" - $400.00. Jointed at shoulders: 4" - $300.00; 7" - $650.00. (See photo in Series 5, pg. 11.)

Orsini: Head tilted to side, made in one piece and hands hold out dress. 2½-3" - $450.00; 6" - $700.00.

Our Fairy: Molded hair and painted eyes. 9" - $1,600.00. Wig and glass eyes: 9" - $1,900.00.

Our Mary: Has paper label. 4½" - $475.00.

5½" all bisque "Bonnie Babe" with sleep eyes, open mouth with two lower teeth, painted-on shoes and socks. Swivel neck and jointed at shoulders and hips. 5½" - **$850.00.** Courtesy Ellen Dodge.

Peek-a-boo: By Drayton. 4" - $325.00.

Peterkin: 9" - $450.00.

Peterkin, Tommy: Horsman. 4" - $275.00.

Queue San Baby: Various poses. 5" - $300.00. Japan: 4" - $85.00-100.00.

Scootles: Made by Cameo. 6" - $950.00 up.

Sonny: Made by Averill. 5" - $850.00.

Teenie Weenie: Made by Donahey. Painted one-piece eyebrows and features. 4½" - $250.00.

Tynie Baby: Made by Horsman. Glass eyes: 9" - $1,700.00. Painted eyes: 9" - $1,100.00.

Wide Awake Doll: Germany. 7½" - $325.00. Japan: 7½" - $125.00.

Veve: Made by Orsini. 6" - $1,600.00. Painted eyes: $950.00.

"Wrestler": (so called) Fat legs, painted high-top boots, glass eyes, closed or open mouth, no damage. (See photo in Series 7, pg. 10.) Excellent bisque: 8" one-piece body and head - $1,000.00. 8" swivel neck - $1,800.00 up. Bare feet: 8"- $2,300.00 up; 11" - $3,200.00 up.

ALL BISQUE – NODDERS

"Knotters" are called "Nodders" as when their heads are touched, they "nod." The reason they should correctly be called "knotters" is due to the method of stringing. The string is tied through a hole in the head, and they can also be made with cutouts on the bodies to take a tiny rod that comes out of the side of the neck. Both styles were made in Germany and Japan.

Santa Claus or Indian: 6" - $175.00.

Teddy Bear: 6" - $185.00.

Other Animals: (Rabbit, dog, cat, etc.) 3½-5" - $40.00-85.00. Molded-on clothes: 4-4½" - $145.00 up.

Comic Characters: 3½-5" - $145.00 up.

Children/Adults: Made in Germany. 4½-5½" - $65.00-165.00.

Japan/Nippon: 4½" - $25.00; 5½" - $45.00.

Sitting Position: 6" - $200.00 up; 8" - $300.00.

ALL BISQUE – JAPAN

All bisque dolls from Japan vary a great deal in quality. They are jointed at shoulders and may have other joints. Good quality bisque and well painted with no chips or breaks. (Also see all bisque characters and nodder sections.)

Marked Nippon: The mark "Nippon" ceased in 1923. 4" - $40.00; 6" - $85.00.

"Betty Boop": Style with bobbed hair, large painted eyes to side and one-piece body and head. 4" - $30.00; 7" - $50.00.

Child: With molded clothes. 4½" - $45.00; 6" - $60.00.

Comic Characters: See "All bisque – Comic Characters" section.

Occupied Japan: 3½" - $20.00; 5" - $30.00; 7" - $45.00.

Figurines: Called "Immobilies" (no joints). Bride & groom cake top: 6-6½" - $125.00. Children: 3" - $45.00.

Teddy Bears: 3" - $60.00. Indians, Dutch, etc: 2½" - $35.00. Santa Claus: 3½" - $95.00. Adults: 5" - $95.00. Child with animal on string: 3½" - $95.00.

Bent Leg Baby: May or may not be jointed at hips and shoulders. Very nice quality: 3½-5" - $20.00-75.00.

Bye-Lo Copy: (See photo in Series 6, pg. 12.) 3½" - $95.00, 5" - $145.00. Medium to poor quality: 3½-5" - $6.00-45.00.

5" and 5½" all bisque dolls, jointed only at shoulders, molded hair and painted features. All made in Japan. Girls: **$45.00** each; Boy: **$55.00.** Courtesy Gloria Anderson.

ALL BISQUE – COMIC CHARACTERS

Annie Rooney: Made in Germany. 4" - $350.00; 7" - $475.00.

Betty Boop: With musical instrument. Made in Japan. 3½" - $60.00 up.

Betty Boop: Fleisher Studios. Made in Japan. 3½" - $55.00 up.

Dick Tracy: Made in Germany. 4" - $265.00.

Jackie Coogan: Japan. 6½" - $145.00.

Johnny: "Call for Phillip Morris." Made in Germany. 5" - $135.00.

Katzenjammer: Mama: 4" - $40.00; 8" - $90.00. **Uncle Ben:** 4" - $45.00, 8" - $95.00. **Kids:** 4" - $50.00; 6" - $60.00. **Papa:** 4" - $55.00; 8" - $70.00.

Max or Moritz (K*R): 5-5½", each - $2,000.00 up.

Mickey Mouse: Walt Disney. 5", each - $250.00 up.

Mickey Mouse: With musical instrument. $250.00 up.

Minnie Mouse: Walt Disney. $250.00 up.

ALL BISQUE – COMIC CHARACTERS

Moon Mullins and Kayo: 4" - $95.00.

Orphan Annie: 3½" - $70.00. Nodder - $90.00 up.

Mr. Peanut: Made in Japan. 4" - $45.00.

Our Gang: Boys: 3½" - $80.00. Girls: 3½" - $90.00.

Popeye: 3" - $95.00 up.

Seven Dwarfs: Walt Disney. 3½", each - $85.00 up.

Skeezix: 3½" - $95.00.

Skippy: 5" - $125.00. (See photo in Series 6, pg. 13.)

Snow White: 5½" - $100.00. In box with Dwarfs: $800.00 up. (See photo in Series 6, pg. 13.)

Three Bears/Goldilocks: Boxed set: $600.00 up.

ALL BISQUE – PAINTED BISQUE

Painted bisque has a layer of paint over the bisque which has not been fired. Molded hair, painted features, painted-on shoes and socks. Jointed at shoulder and hips. All in good condition with no paint chips.

Boy or Girl: 4" - $55.00; 6" - $85.00.
Baby: 4" - $70.00; 6" - $90.00.

ALT, BECK & GOTTSCHALCK

Alt, Beck & Gottschalck was located near Ohrdruf at Nauendorf, Germany as a porcelain factory from 1854. It is not known when they started making dolls. The firm was the maker of both the "Bye-lo" baby and "Bonnie Babe" for the distributor, George Borgfeldt. The leading authorities in Germany, and now the United States, have assigned nearly all the turned-head dolls as being made by Alt, Beck & Gottschalck, with the bodies being made by Wagner & Zetzsche. It is claimed that this firm produced dolls with tinted bisque and molded hair (see that section of this book), as well as wigged turned head and shoulder head dolls and also dolls made of china. There is a vast variation to the eyebrows among these dolls, which is just one variation listed here, but "officially" almost all these dolls are being lumped under Alt, Beck & Gottschalck. *Also see All Bisque section.

Marks:

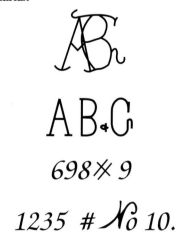

Babies: After 1909. Open mouth, some have pierced nostrils, bent leg baby body and are wigged. Prices will be higher if on toddler body or has flirty eyes. Allow more for toddler body. Clean, nicely dressed and with no cracks, chips or hairlines. 12-13" - $425.00; 17" - $600.00; 21" - $850.00; 25" - $1,500.00.

Child, #1361, 1367, etc.: Socket head on jointed composition body, sleep or set eyes. No crack, chips or hairlines. Clean and nicely dressed. 12" - $425.00; 14" - $450.00; 17" - $500.00; 21" - $625.00; 25" - $775.00; 31" - $1,100.00; 36" - $1,800.00; 40-42" - $2,700.00.

Character Child or Baby: Ca. 1910 on. Socket head on jointed composition body, sleep or set eyes, open mouth. Nicely dressed with good wig or molded hair with no hairlines, cracks or chips. **#630:** 22" - $2,300.00. **#911:** Closed mouth. 19" - $2,500.00. **#1322:** 15" - $525.00; 19" - $750.00. **#1352:** 12" - $450.00; 16" - $575.00; 21" - $850.00. **#1357:** 14" - $650.00; 18" - $900.00. **#1358, 1359, 1362:** 14" - $2,000.00; 18" - $3,200.00. **#1361:** 12" - $395.00; 16" - $495.00; 21" - $750.00. **#1367:** 16" - $550.00; 20" - $800.00.

Turned Shoulder Head: Bald head or plaster pate, closed mouth, glass eyes, kid body with bisque lower arms. All in good condition with no chips, hairline and nicely dressed. Ca. 1870's and 1880's. If marked "DEP" or "Germany," dates after 1886. Some have the Wagner & Zetzsche mark on head or paper label inside top of body. Some mold numbers include: **639, 698, 870, 890, 911, 912, 916, 990,**

22" marked "A.B.G. 1361 55 Germany." Composition bent limb baby body, sleep eyes, pierced nostrils and open mouth with two upper teeth, tremble tongue. 22" - $775.00. Courtesy Frasher Doll Auctions.

16" marked "#639." Attributed to Alt, Beck & Gottschalck. Turned head on kid body with bisque lower arms, closed mouth and glass eyes. 16" - $800.00. Courtesy Frasher Doll Auctions.

1000, 1008, 1028, 1032, 1044, 1064, 1123, 1127, 1142, 1234, 1235, 1254, 1288, 1304. 16" - $800.00; 20" - $950.00; 24" - $1,400.00.

Turned Shoulder Head: Same as above, but with open mouth. 16" - $485.00; 20" - $650.00; 24" - $800.00.

Mold #784, 1000, 1008, 1028, 1046, 1142, 1210, etc.: 1880's-1890's. China glaze, black or blonde molded hair, cloth or kid body, china limbs. 17" - $350.00; 21" - $465.00; 25" - $675.00.

AMBERG, LOUIS & SONS

Louis Amberg & Sons were in business from 1878 to 1930 in New York City and Cincinnati, Ohio.

Marks:

L.A. & S. 1926

AMBERG
DOLLS
THE WORLD
STANDARD
MADE
IN
U.S.A.

AMBERG
L.A. & S. 1928

Prices for dolls in perfect condition, no cracks, chips or breaks, clean and nicely dressed.

Baby Peggy (Montgomery): 1923 and 1924. Closed mouth, socket head. **Mold # 973 or 972:** 18" - $3,000.00; 22" - $3,300.00.

Baby Peggy: Shoulder head. **Mold #983 or 982:** 18" - $3,000.00; 22" - $3,300.00.

Baby Peggy: All bisque. See "All Bisque" section.

Baby Peggy: Composition head and limbs with cloth body, painted eyes, closed mouth, molded brown short bobbed hairdo. 1923. 12" - $375.00; 16" - $575.00; 19" - $850.00.

Right: 16" "Baby Peggy" marked "1924/L.A. & Sons - N.Y. Germany." Bisque shoulder head, sleep eyes, closed mouth and original wig. Cloth body with composition limbs. Left: 22" marked "F.G. 9." Early white bisque, closed mouth and on fully jointed body. 16" - $2,900.00; 22" - $3,700.00.
Courtesy Frasher Doll Auctions.

Baby, Mold #88678: Cloth body. 20" - $1,500.00; 25" - $1,900.00.

Charlie Chaplin: Marked "Amberg. Essamay Film Co."1915-1920's. Portrait head of composition with painted features, composition hands, cloth body and legs. Black suit and white shirt. Cloth tag on sleeve or inside seam of coat. 13-14" - $500.00; 20" - $765.00.

Newborn Babe: Bisque head with cloth body and can have celluloid, composition or rubber hands. Lightly painted hair, sleep eyes, closed mouth with protruding upper lip. 1914 and reissued in 1924. Marks: "L.A.&S. 1914/**G45520** Germany." Some will be marked "L. Amberg and Son/**886**" and some will be marked "Copyright by Louis Amberg." (See photo in Series 7, pg. 15.) 9-10" - $475.00; 14" - $650.00; 18" - $1,300.00.

Newborn Babe: Open mouth version. Marked "L.A.&S. **371**." 9-10" - $375.00; 14" - $600.00.

Mibs: Marked "L.A.&S. 1921/Germany" and can have two different paper labels with one "Amberg Dolls/Please Love Me/I'm Mibs," and some with the same label, but does not carry the name of Amberg. Molded hair with long strand down center of forehead. Composition head and limbs with cloth body, painted eyes. All in good condition. (See photo in Series 6, pg. 17.) 12" - $550.00; 16-17" - $850.00.

Mibs: All bisque. See All Bisque section.

Sue (or Edwina): All composition with painted features, molded hair and with a waist that swivels on a large ball attached to the torso. Jointed shoulders, neck and hips. Molded hair has side part and swirl bangs across forehead. Marked "Amberg/Pat. Pen./L.A.&S." 1928. (See photo in Series 6, pg. 17.) 14" - $475.00

Twist Bodies: (Tiny Tots) 1926, 1928. All composition with swivel waist made from large ball attached to torso. Boy or girl with molded hair and painted

features. Tag attached to clothes: "An Amberg Doll/Body Twist/Pat. Pend. #32018." 7½"-8½" - $200.00.

Vanta Baby: Marked "Vanta Baby-Amberg (or L.A.&S.)" Composition head and limbs with fat legs. Cloth body, spring strung, sleep eyes, open/closed mouth with two teeth. Made to advertise Vanta baby garments. 1927. 18" - $285.00; 24" - $375.00.

Vanta Baby: Same as above, but with bisque head. (See photo in Series 6, pg. 17.) Glass eyes, open mouth. 22" - $1,500.00; 26" - $1,900.00. Glass eyes, closed mouth: 25" - $1,600.00.

14" all composition with molded hair, painted eyes, and closed smiling mouth. Marked "Amberg & Sons." 14" - $475.00.

Prices are for perfect dolls with no chips, cracks, breaks or hairline cracks, and need to be clean and nicely dressed.

Armand Marseille made the majority of their dolls after the 1880's and into the 1920's, so they are some of the most often found dolls today. The factory was at Kopplesdorf, Germany. A.M. marked dolls can be of excellent to very poor quality. The finer the bisque and artist workmanship, the higher the price. This company made a great many heads for other companies also, such as George Borgfeldt, Amberg (Baby Peggy,) Hitz, Jacobs & Kassler, Otto Gans, Cuno & Otto Dressel, etc. They were marked with "A.M." or full name "Armand Marseille."

Mold #370, 326, 309, 273, 270, 375, 376, 920, 957: Kid or kidaleen bodies, open mouths. 15" - $265.00; 21" - $375.00; 26" - $600.00.

Mold #390, 266, 300, 310, (not "Googly"), 384, 390N, 391, 395: Socket head, jointed body and open mouth. 6" (closed mouth) - $250.00; 10" (crude 5-piece body) - $175.00; 10" (good quality jointed body) - $285.00; 14" - $300.00; 16" - $350.00; 18" - $425.00; 22" - $500.00; 24" - $575.00; 26" - $600.00; 28" - $675.00; 32" - $975.00.

Large Sizes Marked Just A.M.: Jointed bodies, socket head and open mouths. 36"- $1,600.00; 38" - $1,900.00; 42" - $2,600.00.

Mold Number 1776, 1890, 1892, 1893, 1894, 1896, 1897 (which can be a shoulder head or have a socket head); **1898, 1899, 1901, 1902, 1903, 1908, 1909, 3200:** Kid or kidaleen body, open mouth. (See below for prices if on composition bodies.) 10" - $165.00; 14" - $245.00; 19" - $425.00; 23" - $450.00; 27" - $650.00.

Same as above, on composition jointed bodies: 10" - $300.00; 14" - $400.00; 19" - $600.00; 23" - $725.00; 28" - $875.00; 31" - $925.00; 35" - $1,450.00; 39" - $1,800.00.

34" marked "A. 11 M." Made in Germany. Shoulder head, cloth body with bisque lower arms, open mouth. 34" - $1,500.00. Courtesy Frasher Doll Auctions.

Alma, Floradora, Mabel, Lilly, Darling, My Playmate, Sunshine, Dutchess, #2000, 3700, 14008: 1890's. Kid or kidaleen body. 10" - $185.00; 14" $250.00; 17" - $300.00; 21" - $400.00; 24" - $500.00; 29" - $900.00.

Same as above, on composition body: 15" - $325.00; 19" - $475.00; 23" - $500.00; 27" - $675.00; 30" - $1,000.00.

Queen Louise, Beauty, Columbia, Jubilee, Majestic, Princess, Rosebud: Kid or kidaleen body. 13" - $265.00; 17" - $350.00; 21" - $450.00; 25" - $550.00; 28" - $865.00; 32" - $1,100.00.

Same as last listing, on composition body: 15" - $350.00; 19" - $450.00; 26" - $750.00; 29" - $900.00; 32" - $1,000.00; 36" - $1,300.00.

Babies (infant style): Some from 1910; others from 1924. Can be on composition bodies, or have cloth bodies with curved or straight cloth legs. (Add $100.00-150.00 more for toddler babies.)

Mold #340, 341: With closed mouth (My Dream Baby, also called "Rock-A-Bye Baby.") Made for the Arranbee Doll Co. 6-7" - $185.00; 9" - $250.00; 12" - $365.00; 14" - $575.00; 16" - $650.00; 20" - $775.00; 24" - $1,100.00; 28" - $1,500.00.

Mold #345, 351: With open mouth. Same as above, but some will also be marked "Kiddiejoy" or "Our Pet." 7-8" - $195.00; 10" - $265.00; 14" - $575.00; 20" - $750.00; 28" - $1,400.00.

Mold #340, 341 or 345, 347, 351: Twin puppets in basket - $850.00 up. Hand puppet, single doll - $350.00.

Mold #341, 345, 351 ("Kiddiejoy" or "Our Pet"): With fired-on black or brown color. See Black section.

Babies: 1910 on. (Add $100.00-150.00 for toddler bodies.) **Mold #256, 259, 326, 327, 328, 329, 360, 750, 790, 900, 927, 971, 975, 980, 984, 985, 990, 991, 992, 995, 996, 1321, 1330, 1330A, 1333:** 9" - $300.00; 12" - $350.00; 15" - $450.00; 20" - $625.00; 23" - $725.00; 27" - $1,000.00. **Same mold numbers as above, but painted bisque:** 13" - $225.00; 17" - $350.00; 20" - $450.00; 25" - $600.00

Character Babies: 1910 on. (Add $100.00-150.00 for toddler body.) Composition jointed body. Can have open mouth or open/closed mouth.

Mold #233: 9" - $300.00; 13" - $565.00; 17" - $850.00.

Mold #248: With open/closed mouth: 15" - $1,800.00. With open mouth: 15" - $900.00.

Mold #251: With open/closed mouth. 15" - $1,600.00; 17" - $1,700.00. With open mouth, 16" - $900.00.

Mold #327, 328: 9" - $250.00; 13" - $400.00; 17" - $575.00; 21" - $750.00.

20" toddler marked "Armand Marseille Germany 990 A. 9 M." Five-piece toddler body, open mouth with two upper teeth. 20" - $775.00. Courtesy Frasher Doll Auctions.

Mold #346: 16" - $600.00; 21" - $725.00; 26" - $900.00.

Mold #352: (See photo in Series 7, pg. 18.) 9" - $250.00; 13" - $375.00; 17" - $575.00; 24" - $900.00.

Mold #355: A. Eller/3K. Closed mouth, sweet face. 11" - $785.00; 16" - $975.00.

Mold #362: 9" - $245.00; 16" - $600.00; 22" - $900.00.

Mold #410: Two rows of teeth, some are retractable. 14" - $950.00; 16" - $1,300.00.

Mold #518: 15" - $575.00; 21" - $700.00.

Mold #506A, 560A: 14" - $550.00; 19" - $850.00.

Mold #570: Open/closed mouth. 16" - $1,600.00; 20" - $1,900.00.

Mold #550, 580: Has open/closed mouth. 12-13" - $1,300.00; 18" - $1,700.00; 22" - $2,000.00.

Mold #590: Has open/closed mouth. (See photo in Series 7, pg. 19.) 17" - $1,700.00; 23" - $2,200.00. Open mouth: 12-13" - $600.00; 16" - $950.00.

Mold #920: Cloth body, shoulder head. 20" - $925.00.

Mold #970: 18" - $600.00; 22" - $875.00; 27" - $1,100.00.

Baby Gloria: Mold #240: (See photo in Series 5, pg. 18.) 10" - $400.00; 14" - $600.00; 18" - $1,000.00; 24" - $1,400.00.

Baby Phyllis: Heads by Armand Marseille. Painted hair, closed mouth. 12" - $450.00; 16" - $700.00; 20" - $1,200.00.

Baby Florence: 12" - $500.00; 20" - $1,400.00.

Baby Betty: 1890's. Jointed composition child body, but few heads found on bent limb baby body. 14-15" - $485.00; 17" - $600.00; 21" - $800.00.

Fany Baby: Mold #231 along with incised "Fany." Can be baby, toddler or child. With wig: 15" - $4,200.00; 19" - $6,800.00.

Fany Baby: Mold #230 along with incised "Fany." Molded hair. 15" - $4,000.00; 19"- $6,5000.00; 25" - $8,000.00.

Just Me: Mold #310. See Googly section.

Melitta: Baby: 16" - $600.00; 20" - $850.00. Toddler: 20" - $1,000.00.

Character Child: 1910 on. May have wig, molded hair, glass or intaglio painted eyes and some will have fully closed mouths while others have open/closed mouth. For these prices, doll must be in excellent condition and have no damage.

Mold #250: 14-15" - $775.00; 18" - $1,200.00.

Mold #340: 14" - $2,700.00.

Mold #345: (See photo in Series 5, pg. 17.) 10" - $1,000.00; 18" - $2,000.00.

19" marked "A.M. Baby Betty 1 D.R.G.M." Shoulder head with kid body and bisque lower arms. Sleep eyes with lashes, open mouth. 19" - $725.00.

23" character baby incised "Melitta." Made by Armand Marseille. Sleep eyes and open mouth. 23" - $1,300.00.

Mold #350: Socket head, glass eyes, closed mouth. 9" - $1,200.00; 15" - $2,200.00; 22" - $3,800.00.

Mold #360: 14" - $465.00; 18" - $850.00.

Mold #372: "Kiddiejoy." Kid body, molded hair, glass eyes. (See photo in Series 5, pg. 18.) 13" - $625.00; 18" - $995.00; 22" - $1,400.00.

Mold #400: Glass eyes, socket head and closed mouth. 15" - $2,700.00; 18" - $3,300.00.

Mold #449: Painted eyes, socket head and closed mouth. 9" - $450.00; 17" - $1,200.00; 19" - $1,550.00.

Mold #450: Socket head, glass eyes and closed mouth. 21" - $2,100.00 up.

Mold #500, 520: Molded hair, intaglio eyes, open/closed mouth. 9" - $425.00; 17" - $1,000.00; 22" - $1,600.00.

Mold #500, 520, 620, 640: Wigged, glass eyes and open/closed mouth. Compo. jointed body. 9" - $675.00; 17" - $1,200.00; 22" - $2,000.00. Same, with kid body. 16" - $975.00; 20" - $1,600.00.

Mold #550, 600, 640: Molded hair, painted eyes. (See photo in Series 7, pg. 19.) 11" - $1,300.00; 15" - $2,100.00. Glass eyes: 12" - $1,750.00; 17" - $3,400.00; 22" $4,000.00. Closed mouth, dimples. 14" - $1,450.00.

Mold #570, 590: Open mouth: 10" - $500.00; 15" - $875.00. Open/closed mouth: 17" - $1,800.00.

Mold #700: Glass eyes. 12" - $2,000.00; 14-15" - $3,000.00; 18" - $3,600.00. Painted eyes: 13-14" - $2,500.00.

Left to right: 12½" with sleep eyes, closed mouth, slender limbs and jointed body, marked "400 A 4/0 M." 9½" googly marked "200 A 3/0 M Germany/ DRGM 243" with glass eyes and five-piece toddler body. 12½" with sleep eyes, closed mouth, dimples and on fully jointed body, marked "550 A.1 M/ DRGM." "400" - $1,450.00; "200" - $1,900.00; "550" - $1,750.00. Courtesy Frasher Doll Auctions.

Left: 13½" marked "700 3/0." Sleep eyes, closed pouty mouth. On fully jointed body. Right: 13½" marked "800 A. 2 M." Bisque shoulder head with glass eyes, open/closed mouth with molded gums and tongue and dimples. Kid toddler body and composition lower limbs. "700" - $3,000.00; "800" - $1,500.00. Courtesy Frasher Doll Auctions.

Mold #701, 709, 711: Glass eyes, closed mouth, sweet expression. 9" - $1,200.00; 17" - $2,900.00.

Mold #800, 820: Glass eyes, open/closed mouth. (See photo in Series 6, pg. 21.) 18" - $2,100.00; 22" - $2,800.00.

Mold #950: Painted hair and eyes, open mouth. 10" - $400.00; 15" - $900.00.

Character with Closed Mouth Marked only "A.M.": Intaglio, 19" - $4,900.00. Glass eyes, 19" - $5,200.00.

Googly: See Googly section.

Black or Brown Dolls: See that section.

Adult Lady Dolls: 1910-1920's.

Adult face with long, thin jointed limbs. Knee joint is above knee area.

Mold #300: 10" - $1,000.00.

Mold #400, 401: Closed mouth. 10" - $1,400.00; 15" - $1,900.00; 17" - $2,400.00.

Mold #400, 401: Open mouth. 15" - $1,000.00; 17" - $1,300.00.

Painted Bisque: Mold #400, 401: 15" - $825.00; 17" $1,100.00.

Painted Bisque: Mold #242, 244, 246, etc. 15" - $350.00; 19" - $600.00; 28" - $850.00.

Biscoloid: Like painted bisque but material under paint more plastic type.

Mold #378, 966, etc. 16" - $500.00; 18" - $750.00.

A.T.

A. Thuillier made dolls in Paris from 1875 to 1893 and may be the maker of the dolls marked with "A.T." A.T. marked dolls can be found on wooden, jointed composition or kid bodies and can range in sizes from 14" to 30". The dolls can have closed mouths or open mouths with two rows of teeth. The following prices are for marked A.T. dolls on correct body, clean, beautiful face, dressed nicely and with no damage, such as a hairline cracks, chips or breaks. (See photos in Series 7, pp. 21-22.)

Closed Mouth: Jointed composition body. 13" - $49,000.00 up; 19" - $58,000.00 up; 23" - $68,000.00 up. Same but with kid body, bisque lower arms. 13" - $60,000.00 up; 19" - $70,000.00 up; 23" - $80,000.00 up.

Open Mouth: Jointed composition body. 15" - $14,000.00; 19" - $18,000.00; 26" - $22,000.00.

Marks:

A.T. N°3

A N°6 T

A. 8 T.

11" marked "A 3 T." Closed mouth with tiny modeled tongue, pierced ears, set glass eyes and on jointed body with straight wrists. Original wig and costume may be original. Rare, tiny size 3: $40,000.00 up. Courtesy Frasher Doll Auctions.

Left: 14" marked "A.T." Beautiful child doll on jointed composition/wood body with straight wrists. Large expressive eyes, closed mouth and all original including marked shoes. Head marked "A. 6 T." Above: Close-up of doll. 14" - $49,000.00 up. Courtesy Private Collection.

Georgene Averill used the business names of Madame Georgene Dolls, Averill Mfg. Co., Georgene Novelties and Madame Hendron. Averill began making dolls in 1913 and designed a great many for George Borgfeldt.

First prices are for extra clean dolls and second for dolls with chips, craze lines, dirty or soiled or with part of or none of the original clothes.

Baby Georgene or Baby Hendron: 1918 on. Composition/cloth and marked with name on head. 16" - $225.00, $80.00; 22" - $350.00, $100.00; 24" - $425.00, $150.00.

Baby Yawn: Composition with closed eyes and yawn mouth. 14" - $425.00, $150.00; 17" - $500.00, $200.00.

13" French folk doll made by Georgene Averill called "Becassine," which in French means "little goose." Arm tag says copyright 1953. Cloth with striped legs. 13" - $385.00 up. Courtesy Mimi Hiscox.

Body Twist Dolls: 1927. Composition with large ball joint at waist, painted hair and features. 15" - $450.00, $100.00.

Bonnie Babe: Mold #1368-140 or 1402. 1926. Bisque head, cloth body, open mouth/two lower teeth, molded hair and composition arms/or hands. 14" - $875.00, $350.00; 22" - $1,500.00 up, $500.00. Celluloid head: 15-16" - $575.00 up, $100.00. Composition body, bisque head: 8-9" - $1,300.00.

Bonnie Babe: All bisque. See "All Bisque" section.

Cloth Dolls: 1930's. Mask face with painted features, yarn hair, cloth body. First price for clean dolls; second for soiled dolls.

Characters: Such as Becassine, etc. 1950's. 13-14" - $385.00.

International: 12" - $95.00, $20.00; 15" - $150.00, $60.00.

Children: 15" - $165.00, $50.00; 20" - $225.00, $60.00; 25" - $275.00, $75.00. Musical: 15" - $225.00, $70.00. Brownies: 15" - $200.00, $70.00. Scout: $250.00, $80.00.

Tear Drop Baby: One tear painted on cheek. 16" - $300.00, $65.00.

Animals: 1930's on. B'rer Rabbit, Fuzzy Wuzzy, Nurse Jane, Uncle Wiggley, etc. 18" - $500.00.

Children: Composition, cloth body. Perfect and original. 15" - $350.00, 18" - $500.00; less than mint - $200.00. **Scout, Pirate, Brownie, Storybook:** 15" - $425.00, $165.00; 18" - $600.00, $225.00.

Comic Characters: 1944-1951. All cloth with mask faces and painted features. Includes **Little Lulu, Nancy, Sluggo, Tubby Tom.** 12" - $465.00; 14" - $550.00, $200.00.

Dolly Dingle (for Grace Drayton): All cloth. 11" - $425.00, $125.00.

Fangel, Maude Tousey: All cloth. Marked "M.T.F." on tag. 12" - $485.00, $125.00.

Dolly Record: 1922. Composition with record player in back. 26" - $600.00, $250.00.

Googly: Composition/cloth. 14" - $325.00, $95.00; 16" - $375.00, $125.00; 19" - $600.00, $185.00.

Indian, Cowboy, Sailor, Soldier, Scout, Pirate: Composition/cloth, molded hair or wig, sometimes yarn hair, painted features. 14" - $400.00, $125.00.

Krazy Kat: Felt, unjointed, 1916. (See photo in Series 6, pg. 27.) 14" - $300.00, $85.00. 18" - $500.00, $125.00.

Snookums: 1927. Composition/cloth. Smile face, character from George McManus's "The Newlyweds." 14" - $400.00, $150.00.

Vinyl Head, Laughing Child: With oil cloth body. 28" - $175.00, $60.00.

Whistling Dan: Sailor, cowboy, policeman, child, etc. 1925-1929. (See photo in Series 6, pg. 26.) 14" - $250.00, $85.00; 16" - $300.00, $100.00.

Whistling Rufus: Black doll. 14" - $425.00, $125.00.

Whistling Dolly Dingle: 14" - $425.00, $125.00.

Babies, Infant Types: 1920's. Composition/cloth, painted hair, sleep eyes. 14-16" - $200.00, $70.00; 22-23" - $285.00, $100.00.

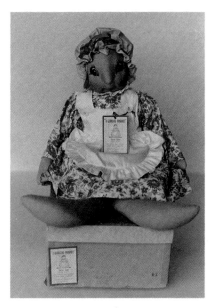

18" "Nurse Jane - Fuzzy Wuzzy" made by Georgene Averill. Tag says copyright 1943. Mint in the box. 18" - $500.00. Courtesy Mimi Hiscox.

BABY BELLE

Barclay Baby Belle: Germany. Open mouth, jointed body. By Bawo & Dotter, 1908-1910. (See photo in Series 6, pg. 28.) 18" - $850.00; 24" - $1,050.00; 30" - $1,900.00.

BABY BO-KAYE

Bisque heads were made by Alt, Beck & Gottschalck in 1925. Celluloid heads were made in Germany, and composition heads were made in the U.S. by Cameo Doll Company. Designer of the doll was Joseph L. Kallus, owner of Cameo Doll Co. (See photo in Series 6, pg. 29.)

Bisque Head: Molded hair, open mouth, glass eyes, cloth body, composition limbs. **Mold #1307-124, 1394-30.** In overall good condition with no damage. 17" - $2,800.00; 20" - $3,000.00.

Celluloid Head: Same as "Bisque Head" description. 16" - $900.00.

Composition Head: Same as above description. 16" - $700.00. Light craze: 16" - $500.00. Cracks and/or chips: 16" - $200.00.

All Bisque: 4½" - $1,275.00; 6½" - $1,675.00.

Right: 20" marked "Copr. by J.L. Kallus/ Germany 1394/30. Baby Bo-Kaye." Sleep eyes, open mouth with two lower teeth and molded hair. Cloth body with composition limbs. Left: 32" Kestner with open mouth, sleep eyes and on fully jointed body. 20" - $3,000.00; 32" - $1,800.00. Courtesy Frasher Doll Auctions.

BAHR & PROSCHILD

Bahr & Proschild operated at Ohrdruf, Germany from 1871 into late 1920's. They also made dolls with celluloid (1910).

Marks:

Character Baby: 1909 on. Bent limbs, sleep eyes, wigged and open mouths. Allow $100.00-150.00 more for toddler body. Clean, nicely dressed and no damage.

Mold #592: Baby: 12" - $675.00. Toddler: 12" - $875.00.

Mold #585, 586, 587, 604, 620, 624, 678, 619, 641: 14" - $575.00; 17" - $650.00; 20" - $725.00; 24" - $1,150.00. Toddler: 10" - $575.00; 14" - $650.00; 17" - $750.00.

Mold #169: 10" - $450.00; 18" - $750.00; 22" - $925.00.

Character Child: Can be on fully jointed composition body or toddler body. Ca 1910. Nicely dressed, clean and no damage. Can have molded hair or be wigged.

Mold #526, 2072, or marked B.P: 1910. Open/closed mouth. 14" - $3,900.00; 18" - $4,900.00.

Mold # in 200 and 300 Series: Now attributed to Bahr & Proschild. Can be on French bodies. Open mouth, jointed composition bodies. Ca. 1880's. Prior to recent findings, these dolls were attributed to Kestner.

Mold #204, 224, 239, 246, 273, 274, 275, 277, 281, 286, 289, 293, 297, 309, 325, 332, 340, 379, 394, etc.: 1880's. As described above. 14" - $700.00; 20" - $900.00; 24" - $1,200.00.

Same as above, on kid bodies: Open mouth. 18" - $500.00; 26" - $750.00; 30" - $1,200.00.

Same as above, closed mouth: Dome head or "Belton type," socket head on composition or kid body with bisque shoulder plate. 16" - $2,100.00; 21" - $2,650.00; 25" - $3,000.00.

Mold #2025: Painted eyes, closed mouth. 16" - $1,200.00 up.

Mold #2072: Closed mouth, glass eyes. 22" - $4,300.00 up.

23" beautiful child made by Bahr & Proschild with mold #224. Open mouth and on jointed body with straight wrists. Shown with two fine 4½" and 5" half dolls and a 3½" German bathing beauty with pebble textured bathing suit. 23" - $1,200.00; 4½" - $265.00; 5" - $300.00; 3½" - $225.00. Courtesy Frasher Doll Auctions.

Lower right: 11" Bahr & Proschild marked "B.P." in heart, "Made in Germany." Open mouth, sleep eyes, and on five-piece baby body. Lower left: 13½" baby, Heubach Koppelsdorf, mold #300. Standing: 18" molded hair bisque by Kling. Marked "Germany 275" with "K" inside a bell. Cloth body, bisque lower limbs. Baby: $325.00; 13½" - $385.00; 18" - $500.00. Courtesy Frasher Doll Auctions.

Bathing dolls of the 1920's can be in any position, including standing on a base. They are all bisque and will have painted-on bathing costumes or be nude. They were made in Germany and some in the United States. Prices are for ones with no damage, chips or breaks. Must be clean.

Excellent quality bisque and artist workmanship, painted eyes: 3" - $225.00; 5-6" - $525.00; 8-9" - $800.00 up.

With animal: 5½" - $1,400.00 up. Two modeled together: 6" - $1,300.00 up. Glass eyes: 4½" - $450.00; 6" - $650.00. Swivel neck: 5" - $675.00; 6" - $725.00.

Fair quality of bisque and workmanship or marked Japan: 3" - $85.00; 5-6" - $125.00; 9" - $185.00.

Ederle, Gertrude: In diving pose. (See photo in Series 7, pg. 26.) 8" - $700.00; 13" - $1,450.00; 18" - $1,850.00.

Group of bathing beauties that are porcelain bisque. All made in Germany except doll with orange cap and shoes that was made in Japan. Standing doll is china glazed and has beautiful modeling detail. Standing, Germany: 5½" - $525.00. Lying down, Germany: 6" - $195.00 up. Lying down, Japan: 3" - $85.00 up.
Courtesy Glorya Woods.

BELTON-TYPE

"Belton-type" dolls are not marked or will just have a number on the head. They have a concave top to a solid uncut head with one to three holes for stringing and/or plugging in wig. The German dome heads have a full round solid uncut head, but some of these may even have one or two holes in them. (See photo in Series 7, pg. 28.)

This style doll was made from 1875 on, and most likely a vast amount of these dolls were actually German made, although they must be on a French body to qualify as a "Belton-type." But since these dolls are found on French bodies, it can be assumed the German heads were made for French firms.

Prices are for dolls with excellent quality bisque, bodies that are French and have a straight wrist, closed or open/closed mouth, nicely dressed and no damage.

French Style Face: 8" on five-piece body - $800.00; 8" on jointed body - $975.00; 13" - $2,450.00; 16" - $2,650.00; 19" - $3,800.00; 22" - $3,300.00; 25" - $4,000.00.

Bru Look: 18" - $3,500.00; 22" - $3,400.00. (* See Bahr & Proschild #200 series for open mouth dolls.)

German Style Face: 10" - $1,200.00; 14" - $1,600.00; 17" - $1,900.00; 21" - $2,300.00; 25" - $2,600.00.

Right: "Belton type" with a Bru look. Incised "124." Closed mouth and on French jointed body with straight wrist. Left: 20" marked "JDK 215." Open mouth, fur eyebrows and fully jointed body that is marked "Germany 6." Belton: 16" - $2,650.00. JDK 215: 20" - $575.00. Courtesy Frasher Doll Auctions.

16" "Belton type" with closed mouth, skin tones to bisque and on jointed French body with straight wrist. 16" - $2,600.00. Courtesy Barbara Earnshaw-Cain.

Charles M. Bergmann made dolls from 1889 at both Waltershausen and Friedrichroda, Germany. Many of the Bergmann heads were made by other companies for him, such as Simon & Halbig, Kestner, Armand Marseille and others.

Marks:

C.M. BERGMANN

S. & H
C.M. BERGMANN
Waltershausen
Germany

Child: 1880's into early 1900's. On fully jointed composition bodies and open mouth. (Add $100.00 more for heads by Simon & Halbig.) 10" - $350.00; 14" - $400.00; 19" - $500.00; 23" - $725.00; 29" - $900.00; 31" - $1,200.00; 39" - $2,400.00.

Character Baby: 1909 and after. Socket head on five-piece bent limb baby body. Open mouth. 10" - $365.00; 14" - $550.00; 18" - $675.00.

Mold #612 Baby: Open/closed mouth. 15" - $1,300.00; 19" - $1,900.00.

Lady Doll: Adult-style body with long thin arms and legs. "Flapper-style" doll. 15" - $975.00; 19" - $1,900.00; 22"- $2,300.00.

Left: 29½" Kley and Hahn marked "Walkure." Sleep eyes, open mouth. Right: 30" marked "Simon & Halbig" along with "C.M. Bergmann." Head made for Bergmann by Simon & Halbig. Open mouth, sleep eyes. Both dolls on fully jointed bodies. 29½" - $1,000.00; 30" - $1,200.00. Courtesy Turn of Century Antiques.

23" marked "C.M.B. Halbig. S&H." Sleep eyes, open mouth and on fully jointed body. Shown with French pyramid blocks, ca. 1920. 23" - $725.00. Courtesy Frasher Doll Auctions.

The French dolls marked "B.F." were made by Ferte (Bébé Ferte), and some collectors refer to them as Bébé Française by Jumeau. They are now being attributed to Danel & Cie who also used the Bébé Française trademark. They have closed mouths and are on jointed French bodies with most having a straight wrist.

Marks:

Child: 14" - $2,800.00; 16" - $4,000.00; 19" - $4,600.00; 23" - $4,900.00; 25" - $5,500.00. 27" - $6,000.00.

Dolls marked "B.L." are referred to as "Bébé Louvre," but they most likely were made by Alexandre Lefebvre, who made dolls from 1890 and by 1922 was part of S.F.B.J. (See photo in Series 7, pg. 30.) This is a very beautiful example of the French doll, marked "B 10 L." 22" tall with open/closed mouth and fully jointed French body. 22" - $4,850.00. Other prices: 12" - $1,900.00; 18" - $2,800.00; 21" - $3,200.00; 25" - $4,200.00; 27" - $4,800.00. Courtesy Turn of Century Antiques.

Black or brown dolls can have fired-in color or be painted bisque, composition, cloth, papier maché and other materials. They can range from very black to a light tan and also be a "dolly" face or have Negroid features. The quality of these dolls varies greatly and prices are based on this quality. Both the French and German made these dolls. Prices are for undamaged, nicely dressed and clean dolls.

Alabama: See Cloth Doll section.

All Bisque: Glass eyes, one-piece body and head. 4-5" - $450.00.

All Bisque: Glass eyes, swivel head. 4-5" - $950.00.

All Bisque: Painted eyes, one-piece body and head. 5" - $250.00. Swivel head: 5" - $450.00.

A.M. 341 or 351: 10-11" - $400.00; 14" - $585.00; 17" - $950.00; 21" - $1,200.00.

A.M. 362: 15" - $725.00.

A.M. 390: (See photo in Series 6, pg. 39.) 12" - $425.00, 16" - $600.00; 20" - $850.00.

A.M. 390n: 15" - $550.00; 23" - $850.00.

A.M. 518, 362, 396, 513: 15"- $700.00; 21" - $1,000.00.

A.M. 451, 458 (Indians): 9" - $325.00; 12" - $475.00.

A.M. 971, 992, 995 Baby or Toddler: 9" - $285.00; 13" - $575.00; 18" - $975.00.

A.M 1894, 1897, 1912, 1914: 10" - $400.00; 16" - $700.00.

Baby Grumpy: Made by Effanbee. 10" - $250.00; 16" - $450.00. Craze, dirty: 10" - $90.00; 16" - $100.00.

Bahr & Proschild #277: Open mouth. 12" - $700.00; 16" - $1,700.00.

Left: 15" marked "A.M. Germany 341." Made by Armand Marseille. Sleep eyes and closed mouth. Right: 18" marked "Heubach Koppelsdorf 399.1 D.R.G.M. Germany." Set eyes and closed mouth. 15" - $685.00; 18" - $900.00. Courtesy Frasher Doll Auctions.

Left back: 11" bisque head marked "A.M. Germany 351." Composition bent limb baby body. Right: 18" German papier maché head, bent limb baby body, glass eyes to side and open mouth. Front: 12" "A.M. 351." 11" - $400.00; 18" - $650.00; 12" - $450.00. Courtesy Frasher Doll Auctions.

Bruckner: See Cloth Section.

Bru Jne: 18" - $30,000.00 up; 24" - $44,000.00 up.

Bru, Circle Dot or Brevette: 16" - $30,000.00 up; 20" - $38,000.00 up.

Bubbles: Made by Effanbee. 17" - $425.00; 21" - $650.00. Craze, dirty: 17" - $100.00; 20" - $200.00.

Bye-Lo: 14" - $2,900.00 up.

Candy Kid: 12" - $325.00. Craze, dirty: 12" - $145.00.

Celluloid: All celluloid (more for glass eyes.) 16" - $325.00; 19" - $600.00. Celluloid shoulder head, kid body (more for glass eyes): 16" - $300.00; 19" - $425.00.

Chase: 24" - $6,200.00; 28" - $6,900.00.

Cloth: See cloth section.

Composition: Made in Germany. 15" - $550.00; 19" - $725.00; 25" - $1,000.00.

E.D.: Open mouth: 17" - $2,200.00; 23" - $2,800.00.

F.G.: Open/closed mouth. 17" - $3,700.00.

Fashion: Swivel neck. Original: 17" - $14,600.00. Redressed: 17" - $9,200.00.

French, Unmarked or Marked "DEP": Closed mouth, bisque head: 15" - $3,200.00; 19" - $4,300.00. Painted bisque: 15" - $975.00; 19" - $1,200.00.

French, Unmarked or Marked "DEP": Open mouth, bisque head: 10" - $500.00; 15" - $1,200.00; 22" - $1,900.00. Painted bisque: 15" - $500.00; 20" - $800.00. With Negroid features: 18" - $4,400.00 up.

Frozen Charlotte or Charlie: 3" - $200.00; 6" - $365.00; 8" - $425.00. Jointed shoulder: 3" - $250.00; 6" - $450.00.

Left: "Baby Bumps." Composition head, stuffed cloth, jointed shoulders and hips. Original clothes. Made by Horsman, 1910. Right: 9½" black "Puss & Boots" on "Patsyette" body. All composition, made by Effanbee. 10" - $275.00; 9½" - $300.00. Courtesy Frasher Doll Auctions.

Right: 15½" brown child marked "DEP." Open mouth, jointed body with straight wrists. Left: 23" toddler marked "K*R Simon & Halbig 126." Open mouth, tremble tongue with four lower teeth, two upper teeth. 15½" - $1,200.00; 23" - $1,300.00. Courtesy Frasher Doll Auctions.

German, Unmarked: Closed mouth, bisque head: 10" - $565.00; 13" - $850.00; 16" - $1,000.00. Painted bisque: 14" - $350.00; 20" - $600.00.

German, Unmarked: Open mouth, bisque head. 10-11"-$375.00; 14"-$450.00; 17" - $625.00; 21" - $1,000.00. Painted bisque: 16" - $400.00; 19" - $600.00.

Heinrich Handwerck: Open mouth. 18" - $900.00; 22" - $1,000.00; 26" - $1,500.00.

Hanna: Made by Schoenau & Hoffmeister. 9" - $450.00; 14" - $725.00; 17" - $1,100.00.

Heubach, Gebruder Mold #7668, 7671: Wide smile mouth. 9" - $1,400.00; 11" - $2,000.00; 13" - $2,400.00.

Heubach, Gebruder: (Sunburst mark) Boy, eyes to side. 12" - $2,100.00.

Heubach Koppelsdorf Mold #320, 339: 10" - $425.00; 13" - $550.00; 18" - $750.00; 21" - $950.00.

Heubach Koppelsdorf Mold #399: Allow more for toddler. 10" - $550.00; 14" - $675.00; 18" - $900.00. Celluloid: 14" - $300.00; 17" - $600.00.

Heubach Koppelsdorf Mold #414: 14" - $775.00; 17" - $1,300.00.

Heubach Koppelsdorf Mold #418: (Grin) 9" - $700.00; 14" - $1,100.00.

Heubach Koppelsdorf Mold #463: 12" - $600.00; 16" - $950.00.

Heubach Koppelsdorf Mold #444, 451: 9" - $450.00; 13" - $800.00.

Heubach Koppelsdorf Mold #452: 10" - $400.00; 14" - $650.00.

Heubach Koppelsdorf Mold #458: 10" - $450.00; 15" - $700.00.

Heubach Koppelsdorf Mold #1900: 14" - $475.00; 17" $675.00.

Hottentot: (Kewpie) All bisque. 5" - $500.00 up. Maché: 8" - $165.00.

Kestner #134: 10-11" - $675.00; 13-14" - $975.00.

Kestner #245, 237: Hilda. 15" - $5,600.00; 19" - $6,900.00.

Kestner: Child, no mold number. 12" - $525.00; 16" - $800.00. Five-piece body: 12" - $400.00.

Jumeau: Open mouth. 14" - $2,300.00; 17" - $2,900.00; 22" - $3,500.00.

Jumeau: Closed mouth. 14" - $4,500.00; 17" - $5,000.00; 22" - $6,400.00.

Jumeau Type: Unmarked/number only. (See photo in Series 7, pg. 33.) 12" - $2,600.00; 15" - $3,200.00; 19" - $4,000.00.

Jumeau: Marked "E.J." 14" - $7,000.00; 18" - $8,000.00.

K Star R: Child, no mold number. 14" - $675.00.

K Star R #100: (See photo in Series 6, pg. 38.) 10" - $700.00; 14" - $1,100.00; 17" - $1,800.00.

K Star R #101: 16" - $5,400.00.

K Star R #114: (See photo in Series 7, pg. 35.) 13" - $3,200.00

K Star R #116, 116a: 15" - $3,000.00; 19" - $3,500.00.

K Star R #126: (See photo in Series 5, pg. 28.) Baby. 10" - $750.00; 17" - $1,300.00.

Kewpie: Composition. 12" - $400.00. Toddler, 12" - $650.00; 16" - $975.00.

KW/G (Konig & Wernicke) 18" - $700.00.

Papier Maché: Negroid features: 10" - $300.00; 14" - $675.00. Others: 14" - $300.00; 24" - $800.00.

Paris Bébé: 15" - $4,400.00; 18" - $5,500.00.

Parson-Jackson: Baby: 13-14" - $475.00.

Recknagel: Marked "R.A." May have mold **#138**. 15" - $950.00; 21" - $1,900.00.

Schoenau & Hoffmeister, "Hanna": 8" - $300.00; 10" - $485.00; 13" - $685.00.

Schoenau & Hoffmeister #1909: (See photo in Series 5, pg. 29.) 15" - $600.00; 19" - $900.00.

Scowling Indian: (See photo in Series 6, pg. 41.) 10" - $375.00; 13" - $500.00.

Scootles: Composition: 15" - $725.00 up. Vinyl: 14" - $250.00; 19" - $425.00; 27" - $585.00.

Simon & Halbig #729: Open mouth and smiling. 17" - $4,150.00.

Simon & Halbig #739: (See photo in Series 6, pg. 38.) Closed mouth: 18" - $3,200.00; 21" - $4,000.00.

Simon & Halbig #939: Closed mouth: 18" - $3,200.00; 21" - $4,300.00. Open mouth. (See photo in Series 7, pg. 34.): 18" - $1,800.00.

25" marked "Simon & Halbig 1079." Open mouth and beautiful skin tones. 25" - $2,000.00. Courtesy Turn of Century Antiques.

6" African doll made of papier maché. Painted features and decorations. Remains of original skirt. Pin jointed at elbows, knees and the legs are fitted down into wooden feet. Ca. 1880's–1890's. 6" - $225.00. Courtesy Shirley Bertrand.

Simon & Halbig #949: Closed mouth: 18" - $2,700.00; 21" - $3,200.00. Open mouth: 18" - $1,500.00.

Simon & Halbig #969: Open mouth, puffed cheeks. 17" - $1,100.00.

Simon & Halbig #1039, 1079: Open mouth: 16" - $1,300.00; 19" - $1,600.00. Pull string, sleep eyes: 19" - $2,400.00.

Simon & Halbig #1248: Open mouth. 14" - $750.00; 17" - $1,000.00.

Simon & Halbig #1302: Closed mouth, glass eyes, very character face. Black: 18" - $6,400.00. Indian: 18" - $7,500.00.

Simon & Halbig #1303: Indian: 18" - $7,800.00.

Simon & Halbig #1339, 1358: 16" - $6,000.00; 20" - $7,600.00.

Simon & Halbig #1368: (See photo in Series 6, pg. 37.) 15" - $5,800.00; 18" - $6,900.00.

S.F.B.J. #301 or 60: Open mouth. 10" - $450.00; 14" - $625.00.

S.F.B.J. #235: Open/closed mouth. 15" - $2,600.00; 17" - $2,900.00.

S.F.B.J. 34-29: (See photo in Series 5.) Open mouth. 17" - $4,000.00 up; 23" - $5,400.00.

Sarg, Tony: Mammy Doll. Composition/cloth. 18" - $575.00.

S.P. mark: Toddler, glass eyes, open mouth: 16" - $600.00.

Steiner, Jules: Open mouth. "A" series: 16" - $4,400.00; 19" - $5,100.00.

Steiner, Jules: Closed mouth. "A" series: 17" - $5,600.00; 21" - $6,300.00. "C" series: 17" - $5,200.00; 19" - $6,000.00.

Stockenette: Oil painted features. 18" - $2,800.00 up.

S & Q #251: 9" - $600.00; 16" - $2,100.00. **#252:** 14" - $1,700.00.

Unis #301 or 60: Open mouth. 13" - $425.00; 16" - $785.00.

Standing: 18" Tony Sarg's "Mammy." Composition head and limbs with cloth body. All original. Sitting: 14" marked "Germany G 329 BA 3 M." Made for George Borgfeldt by Armand Marseille. Open mouth with two lower teeth. 18" - $575.00; 14" - $565.00. Courtesy Frasher Doll Auctions.

11½" stitch jointed, needle sculpted face, wire and celluloid spectacles. Felt eyes, sewn-on caracul wig, felt lips and ears. Carved wooden legs and feet. Tin pail marked "McKessions" (bottle cap). Original clothes. Ca. 1930's. 11½" - $185.00. Courtesy Margaret Mandel.

Bonnet Dolls date from the 1880's to the 1920's. They can be all bisque or have cloth or kid bodies. The lower limbs can be china, leather, or stone bisque. Most were made in Germany, but some were made in Japan. Also see under Goebel, Googly, and Recknagel sections.

All Bisque: 4½-5" - $375.00; 7" - $500.00 up.

Stone Bisque: 8-9" - $165.00; 12" - $225.00; 15" - $385.00; 18" - $850.00; 21" - $975.00.

Stone Bisque with Molded Bonnet: 8" - $175.00; 10" - $265.00; 13" - $385.00.

Japan: 8-9" - $95.00; 12" - $135.00.

Bisque Head: Five-piece papier maché body. 7" - $200.00; 9" - $325.00; 12" - $450.00.

Bisque Head: Fully jointed composition body. 7" - $300.00; 9" - $425.00; 12" - $550.00.

Right: 10" stone bisque bonnet head with molded hair and modeled on bonnet. Cloth body with stone bisque lower limbs, painted-on boots. Left: Stone bisque child, same as other but without bonnet. 10" with bonnet - $265.00; 10" - $165.00. Courtesy Gloria Anderson.

The "Bonnie Babe" was designed by Georgene Averill in 1926 with the bisque heads being made by Alt, Beck & Gottschalck and the cloth bodies made by the K & K Toy Co. (NY). The dolls were distributed by George Borgfeldt. The doll can have cloth body and legs or can have composition arms and legs.

Marks: "Copr. by Georgene Averill/ Germany/1005/3652" and sometimes "1368."

Bisque head, open, crooked smile mouth: 16" - $850.00; 24" - $1,700.00.

Celluloid head: 10" - $400.00; 16" - $700.00.

All Bisque: See the All Bisque section.

14½" head circumference, life-size "Bonnie Babe." Bisque head with flange neck, open mouth with crooked smile and two lower teeth. Cloth body with composition arms, straight composition baby legs. Marked "Copy. by/Georgene Averill/1005/3652/Germany." Costumed in owner's childhood clothes. 24" - $1,700.00 up. Courtesy Margaret Mandel.

BORGFELDT, GEORGE

George Borgfeldt imported, distributed and assembled dolls in New York, and the dolls that he carried or had made ranged from bisque to composition. He had many dolls made for him in Germany.

Marks:

G.B.

Child: Mold #325, 327, 329, etc. 1910-1922. Fully jointed composition body, open mouth. No damage and nicely dressed. 13" - $385.00; 16" - $465.00; 19" - $575.00; 21" - $625.00; 23" - $725.00; 27" - $900.00.

Baby: 1910. Five-piece bent limb baby body, open mouth. 10" - $300.00; 14" - $565.00; 17" - $675.00; 22" - $900.00; 28" - $1,500.00 up.

Back right: Marked "C.M. Bergmann." Open mouth and on fully jointed body. Back left: 24" marked "G.B." and made for George Borgfeldt. Front right: 23" Armand Marseille "Mabel" on kid body with bisque lower arms. Open mouth. Front left: 25" Armand Marseille "Floradora" on kid body with bisque lower arms. Open mouth. Bergmann - $750.00; G.B. - $725.00; A.M "Mabel" - $475.00; A.M. "Floradora" - $475.00. Photo by Neal Eisaman.

BOUDOIR DOLLS

Boudoir dolls are also called "Flapper" dolls and were most popular during the 1920's and early 1930's, although they were made through the 1940's. Very rarely is one of these dolls marked with the maker or country of origin, but the majority were made in the United States, France and Italy.

The most desirable Boudoir dolls are the ones from France and Italy (Lenci, especially. See that section.) These dolls will have silk or cloth painted face mask, have an elaborate costume, and are of overall excellent quality.

The least expensive ones have a full or half-composition head, some with glass eyes, and the clothes will be stapled or glued to the body.

Boudoir Dolls: With excellent quality, finely painted features and excellent clothes. 28" - $485.00; 32" - $575.00. Average quality: 28" - $225.00; 32" - $350.00. Undressed: 28-32" - $90.00.

Boudoir Dolls: With composition head, stapled or glued-on clothes. No damage, and original clothes. 28" - $145.00; 32" - $185.00.

Lenci: See that section.

Smoking Doll: Cloth: 25" - $550.00 up. Composition: 25" - $350.00; 28" - $425.00.

27" Boudoir doll with portrait-style head that is a silk covered mask face with oil-painted features. All original. 27" - $485.00. Courtesy Bonnie Stewart.

26" in original box that is marked "Dream Girl." Came in yellow, pink, lavender, and blue. Soft mohair wig. Maker and date unknown. Celluloid head and limbs with cloth body. Inset glass eyes. Mint in box - $300.00; Doll only - $165.00. Courtesy Gloria Anderson.

BRU

Bru dolls will be marked with the name Bru or Bru Jne, Bru Jne R. Some will have a circle and dot (⊙) or a half circle and dot (◡). Some have paper labels – see marks. Prices are for dolls with no damage at all, very clean, and beautifully dressed. Add $2,000.00 up for all original clothes and marked shoes.

Closed Mouth Dolls: All kid body. Bisque lower arms. 15" - $10,000.00; 17" - $13,000.00; 23" - $25,000.00; 25" - $29,000.00.

Marks:

BEBE BRU BTE SGDG

BEBE
BREVEE SDGD
PARIS

Bru Jne: Ca. 1880's. Kid over wood, wood legs, bisque lower arms. 12-13" - $23,000.00; 15" - $19,000.00; 18" - $24,500.00; 21" - $27,500.00; 24" - $32,000.00; 27" - $39,000.00.

Bru Jne: All wood body. 17" - $16,000.00; 20" - $22,000.00.

Circle Dot or Half Circle: Ca. 1870's. 15" - $22,000.00; 20" - $27,000.00; 24" - $30,000.00; 27" - $34,000.00.

Brevette: Ca. 1870's. 13" - $17,000.00; 18" - $26,000.00; 23" - $31,000.00.

Bru Jne R., Closed Mouth: 18" - $8,500.00; 22" - $9,200.00.

Bru Jne R., Open Mouth: 1890's. Jointed composition body. First price for excellent quality bisque and second for poor quality bisque. 16" - $6,500.00, $4,000.00; 19" - $7,400.00, $5,200.00; 24" - $8,300.00, $6,400.00; 29" - $10,000.00, $7,600.00.

Walker Body, Throws Kiss: 16" - $4,900.00; 20" - $6,000.00; 24" - $7,000.00.

Nursing Bru: 1878-1899. Operates by turning key in back of head. Early, excellent quality: 14" - $7,600.00; 17" - $9,500.00. Not as good quality: 14" - $5,400.00; 17" - $6,200.00. High color, late S.F.B.J. type: 14" - $2,600.00; 17" - $3,200.00.

Shoes: Marked "Bru Jne." Size 3 - $900.00 up; Size 6 - $1,100.00 up; Size 9 - $1,800.00 up.

Breathing, Crying, Kissing: (See photo in Series 7, pg. 41.) 19" - $15,000.00; 23-24" - $18,500.00.

24" Bru Jne 11. Bisque shoulder plate, kid body with kid over wood upper arms and legs, wooden lower legs and arms. Marked on head, shoulder, and has paper label on body. 24" - $30,000.00 up. Courtesy Frasher Doll Auctions.

Very beautiful 37" Bru Jne 16. Shown with her is a 13" Bru Breveté Bébé with swivel head on bisque shoulder plate, pierced ears, closed mouth, kid body with bisque lower arms. 37" - $44,000.00 up; 13" - $17,000.00. Courtesy Frasher Doll Auctions.

17" Bru "Breveté" that is all original. Bisque swivel head on bisque shoulder plate and bisque lower arms. Kid thin-waisted body. A 17" doll with head marked #1 is a "fashion" doll; if marked "5" it is a child/baby. 17" - $25,000.00. Private Collection.

21½" Bru Jne 9 with Bru walker body, talker (pull strings) and arms come up to mouth to blow kiss. Open mouth. 21½" - $6,800.00. Courtesy Turn of Century Antiques, Photo by Neal Eisaman.

22" Bru Jne R with closed mouth. Wood and composition jointed body with straight wrists. 22" - $9,200.00. Courtesy Frasher Doll Auctions.

The Bye-Lo baby was designed by Grace Storey Putnam, distributed by George Borgfeldt, and the cloth bodies were made by K & K Toy Co. of NY. The bisque heads were made by Kestner, Alt, Beck & Gottschalck and others. The all bisque dolls were made by Kestner. The dolls date from 1922. Celluloid or composition hands. Prices are for undamaged, clean and nicely dressed dolls.

Marks:

1923 by
Grace S. Putnam
Made in Germany
7372145

Copy. By
Grace S. Putnam

Bye-Lo Baby
Pat. Appl'd For

Bisque Head: 8" - $485.00; 10" - $525.00; 12"- $625.00; 15" - $1,000.00; 18" - $1,600.00.

Mold #1415, Smiling Mouth: Bisque – very rare, painted eyes. 14" - $4,900.00 up. Composition head: 13-14" - $900.00 up.

Socket Head: Bisque head on five-piece bent limb baby body. 14" - $1,700.00; 17" - $2,200.00.

Composition Head: 10" - $345.00; 12" - $425.00; 15" - $550.00.

Painted Bisque: With cloth body, composition hands. 10" - $300.00; 13" - $450.00; 15" - $650.00.

8" all bisque "Bye-lo" on five-piece bent limb baby body. Neck joint lined with kid. Brown sleep eyes. Marked on back "6-20/Copr. By/Grace S Putnam/G Germany." Has "Bye-lo" sticker on chest. 8" - $800.00. Courtesy Joanna Brunken.

Schoenhut, wood: Cloth body, wooden hands. 13" - $1,900.00 up.

Celluloid: All celluloid: 6" - $200.00. Celluloid head/cloth body: 10" - $425.00.

All Bisque: See All Bisque section, Characters.

Vinyl Heads: Early 1950's. Cloth/ stuffed limbs. Marked "Grace Storey Putnam" on head. 16" - $350.00.

Honey Child: Bye-lo look-a-like made by Bayless Bros. & Co. in 1926. 16" - $365.00; 20" - $475.00.

Wax Bye-lo: Cloth or sateen body. 15-16" - $3,800.00 up.

Basket with blanket and extra clothes: Five babies in basket, bisque heads: 12" - $4,400.00 up. Composition heads: 12" - $2,700.00 up.

Mold # 1418, Fly-Lo Baby (Baby Aero): Bisque head, cloth body, celluloid hands, glass eyes. Closed mouth, deeply molded hair. Very rare. 10" - $3,800.00; 12" - $4,900.00; 16" - $6,000.00.

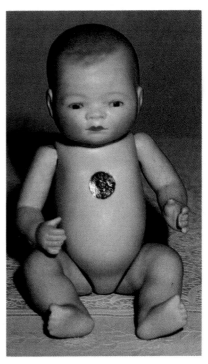

23" "Bye-lo" with 17" head circumference. Marked "Copr. by Grace S.
Putnam." Flange neck on cloth body
with celluloid hands. 23" - $1,850.00.
Courtesy Frasher Doll Auctions.

8½" all celluloid "Bye-lo" with open/closed
mouth and painted eyes. 8½" - $400.00.
Courtesy Shirley Bertrand.

Twin "Bye-lo" dolls in original
box, original clothes, pins, and
tags. The blanket is also
imprinted "Bye-lo." One has
blue sleep eyes; the other has
brown. Twins - $1,800.00.
Courtesy Turn of Century Antiques,
photo by Neal Eisaman.

Catterfelder Puppenfabrik of Germany made dolls from 1902 until the late 1930's. The heads for their dolls were made by various German firms, including Kestner.

Marks:

$$\frac{\underset{219}{CP}}{5} \quad \begin{array}{c} C\ P \\ 201/40 \\ Deponiert \end{array}$$

Catterfelder
Puppenfabrik
45

Child: Ca. 1900's. Composition jointed body. Open mouth. **Mold #264:** Or marked "C.P." 19" - $685.00; 25" - $975.00.

Character Child: 1910 or after. Composition jointed body, closed mouth and can be boy or girl, with character face. **Mold #207:** 15" - $3,200.00. **Mold #215:** 16" - $4,200.00; 20" - $4,800.00 **Mold #219:** 15" - $3,400.00; 19" - $4,200.00.

Babies: 1909 or after. Wig or molded hair, five-piece bent limb baby body, glass or painted eyes.

Mold #262, 263, 264: 10" - $425.00; 14" - $550.00; 20" - $800.00; 24" - $1,000.00.

Mold #200, 201: 17" - $775.00.

Mold #207, 208, 209, etc.: 15" - $600.00; 20" - $825.00; 24" - $1,000.00.

CELLULOID DOLLS

Celluloid dolls date from the 1880's into the 1940's when they were made illegal in the United States because they burned or exploded if placed near an open flame or heat. Some of the makers were:

United States – Marks Bros., Irwin, Horsman, Averill, Parsons-Jackson, Celluloid Novelty Co.

France – Societe Industrielle de Celluloid (Sisoine), Petitcolin (eagle symbol), Societe Nobel Francaise (SNF in diamond), Jumeau/Unis (1950's), Neumann & Marx (dragon symbol).

Germany – Rheinische Gummi and Celluloid Fabrik Co. (turtle mark), Minerva (Buschow & Beck) (helmet symbol), E. Maar & Sohn (3 M's mark), Adelheid Nogler Innsbruck Doll Co. (animal with spread wings and a fish tail, in square), Cellba (mermaid symbol).

Poland – P.R. Zask ("ASK" in triangle).

Prices for perfect, undamaged dolls.

All Celluloid Baby: 1910 on. Painted eyes: 7" - $85.00; 10" - $145.00; 14" - $200.00; 16" - $250.00; 19" - $300.00; 22" - $375.00; 26" - $500.00. Glass inset eyes: 14" - $200.00; 16" - $325.00; 19" - $400.00; 22" - $485.00.

All Celluloid Dolls: (Germany) Jointed at neck, shoulders and hips. Painted eyes: 5" - $65.00; 9" - $95.00; 12" - $175.00; 16" - $275.00; 19" - $400.00. Jointed at neck and shoulders only: 5" - $35.00; 7" - $50.00; 9" - $70.00.

All Celluloid Dolls: Same as above, but with glass eyes: 12" - $200.00; 16" - $300.00. Jointed at neck and shoulders only: 12" - $150.00; 16" - $225.00.

All Celluloid Dolls: Same as above, but marked "France": 7" - $150.00; 9" - $200.00; 12" - $265.00; 19" - $425.00.

All Celluloid, Molded on Clothes: Jointed at shoulders only. 5" - $65.00; 7" - $95.00; 9" - $135.00. Immobilies (no joints): 4" - $35.00.

All Celluloid - Black Dolls: See Black Doll section.

Celluloid Shoulder Head: 1900-1912. Germany. Molded hair or wigged, painted eyes, open or closed mouth, kid or kidaleen bodies, cloth bodies and can have any material for arms. 14" - $200.00; 17" - $275.00; 20" - $350.00.

Celluloid Shoulder Head: Same as above, but with glass eyes: 14" - $250.00; 17" - $325.00; 20" - $400.00.

Celluloid Socket Heads: (Germany.) Glass eyes (allow more for flirty eyes). Ball-jointed body or five-piece bodies. Open or closed mouths. 15" - $365.00; 18" - $550.00; 22" - $625.00; 25" - $750.00.

Jumeau: Marked on head, jointed body. 12" - $400.00; 15" - $600.00.

Heubach Koppelsdorf Mold #399: Brown or Black. See Black section.

5½" all celluloid "Max/Moritz" German comic character. Jointed shoulders only. Clothes modeled on. Marked with turtle mark. 5½" - $900.00. Courtesy Shirley Bertrand.

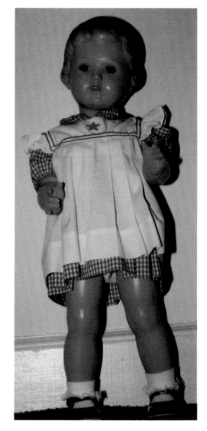

Unusual 28" tall all celluloid with sleep eyes, open/closed mouth with two upper teeth, molded hair. Doll is strung and unusually large for all celluloid. "Turtle mark/70." 28" - $600.00. Courtesy Jeannie Mauldin.

Kruse, Käthe: All original. 14" - $500.00; 17" - $800.00.

Kammer & Reinhardt: (K star R) Mold #406, 700: Child or baby. 14"- $575.00. **Mold #701:** 12" - $800.00. **Mold #714 or 715:** 15" - $750.00. **Mold #717:** 20" - $900.00; 25" - $1,400.00. **Mold #728, 828:** 15" - $550.00; 19" - $750.00. **Mold #826, 828, 406, 321, 255, 225:** Baby: 12" - $265.00; 15" - $565.00; 18" - $675.00; 22" - $825.00. Child: 14" - $385.00; 17" - $700.00; 21" - $985.00.

Kewpie: See that section.

Konig & Wernicke: (K&W) Toddler: 14" - $450.00; 20" - $700.00.

Japan: 5" - $30.00; 8" - $45.00; 12" - $75.00; 16" - $145.00; 19" - $250.00; 22" - $325.00; 26" - $400.00.

Parson Jackson: Baby: 13-14" - $285.00. Toddler: 14-15" - $365.00. Black: 13-14" - $475.00.

17" celluloid socket head with glass eyes, open mouth, and two upper teeth. On five-piece bent limb baby body. Marked "K&W/2-298/9" with turtle mark. Made for Konig & Wernicke. 17" - $400.00. Courtesy Frasher Doll Auctions.

2" and 2½" tall celluloid rabbits and bear. Jointed at hips and shoulders. Original, made in Germany. Bear - $100.00; Rabbits - $45.00 each. Courtesy Shirley Bertrand.

CELLULOID DOLLS

Above: 6" all celluloid clown, with fez style hat, hanging onto balloon. Unmarked. Below: 6" all celluloid swimming boy. Modeled in one piece and will float in water. Made in Germany. Clown - $100.00; Swimming boy - $125.00. Courtesy Shirley Bertrand.

CHAD VALLEY

Chad Valley dolls usually will have a felt face and all velvet body that is jointed at the neck, shoulders and hips. They can have painted or glass eyes and will have a mohair wig. First prices are for those in mint condition and second price for dolls that are dirty, worn or soiled and/or do not have original clothes.

Marks: "Hygienic Toys/Made in England by/Chad Valley Co. Ltd."

"The Chad Valley Hygienic Textile/Toys/Made in England."

Child With Painted Eyes: 9" - $165.00, $45.00; 12" - $350.00, $100.00; 16" - $550.00, $200.00; 18" - $675.00, $300.00.

Child With Glass Eyes: 14" - $600.00, $150.00; 16" - $750.00, $225.00; 18" - $900.00, $400.00.

Child Representing Royal Family: Four in set: Princess Elizabeth, Princess Margaret Rose, Prince Edward, Princess Alexandria. All four have glass eyes. (See photos in Series 5, pgs. 39-40.) Prince Edward as Duke of Kent: 15" - $1,700.00, $600.00; 18" - $1,900.00, $700.00. As Duke of Windsor: 15" - $1,700.00, $600.00; 18" - $1,900.00, $700.00. Others: 15" - $1,500.00 up, $500.00; 18" - $1,600.00, $500.00.

Long John Silver, Captain Bly, Policeman, Train Conductor, Pirates: (See photo in Series 6, pg. 56.) 20" - $1,000.00 up, $400.00.

Ghandi/India: 16" - $800.00 up, $350.00.

Martha Jenks Chase of Pawtucket, Rhode Island began making dolls in 1893, and they are still being made by members of the family. They all have oil painted features and are made of stockinette and cloth. They will be marked "Chase Stockinette" on left leg or under the left arm. There is a paper label (often gone) on the backs with a drawn head:

The older Chase dolls are jointed at the shoulders, hips, knees and elbows where the newer dolls are jointed at the shoulders and hips with straight arms and legs. Prices are for very clean dolls with only minor wear.

OLDER DOLLS:

Babies: 16" - $600.00; 20" - $800.00; 24" - $985.00. Hospital used: 23" - $550.00; 29" - $850.00.

Child: Molded bobbed hair: 12-13" - $1,300.00; 16" - $1,650.00; 21-22" - $2,300.00.

Lady: 15-16" - $2,700.00; 17" - $2,850.00; 25" - $3,250.00. Life size (Hospital): $2,600.00.

Man: 17" - $2,800.00; 25" - $3,000.00. Life size: $2,800.00.

Black: 24" - $6,200.00; 28" - $6,900.00.

NEWER DOLLS:

Babies: 14" - $185.00; 16" - $250.00; 20" - $400.00.

Child, boy or girl: 14" - $250.00; 16" - $350.00.

Chase Type: 15" - $1,600.00; 20-22" - $2,100.00.

16-16½" early Chase boy and girl characters. Unusual faces and hairdos. Boy has modeled fat cheeks and is dressed in original romper suit. Boy - $1,700.00; Girl - $1,650.00.

Almost all china heads were made in Germany between 1840 and the 1900's. Most have black hair, but blondes became popular by the 1880's and by 1900, one out of every three were blonde. China dolls can be on a cloth or kid body with leather or china limbs. Generally, these heads are unmarked, but a few will have a number and/or "Germany" on the back shoulder plate. Prices are for clean dolls with no cracks, chips, or repairs on a nice body and nicely dressed. Also see Huret/Rohmer under "Fashions" and Alt, Beck & Gottschalck.

Alice In Wonderland: Snood, head band: 17" - $650.00; 21" - $950.00. With swivel neck: 8" - $950.00; 12" - $1,400.00; 16" - $2,800.00.

Adelina Patti: 1860's. Center part, roll curl from forehead to back on each side of head and "spit" curls at temples and above exposed ears. 16" - $365.00; 20" - $485.00.

Bald Head/Biedermeir: Ca. 1840. Has bald head, some with top of head glazed black, takes wigs.

Excellent quality: 12" - $775.00; 16" - $950.00; 23" - $1,400.00.

Medium quality: 10-12" - $365.00; 15" - $525.00; 22" - $950.00.

Glass eyes: 16" - $1,600.00; 21" - $2,500.00.

Bangs: Full across forehead, 1870's. Black hair: 14" - $250.00; 18" - $475.00; 22" - $600.00. Blondes: 15" - $275.00; 22" - $575.00; 27" - $650.00.

Brown eyes: Painted eyes, can be any hairstyle and date, but usually has short, "flat top" Civil War hairdo. 14" - $650.00; 17" - $1,100.00; 20" - $1,200.00.

Brown hair: Early hairdo with flat top or long sausage curls around head. Center part and smooth around face. 18" - $3,200.00; 22" - $4,000.00.

Bun: China with bun, braided or rolled and pulled to back of head. Usually has pink luster tint. 1830's & 1840's.

Rear left: 7" "Pet Name" with common hairdo, modeled on blouse top with name "Ruth." Right rear: 7" center part "apple cheek" Civil War-era china head. Front left: Kling girl with full bangs. Front center: 8" large breast plate Civil War head. Front right: "Common" hairdo, 1900. Pet Name: $250.00; Apple cheek Civil War - $250.00; Kling - $365.00; 8" Civil War - $285.00; Common - $225.00. Courtesy Turn of Century Antiques.

Cloth body, nicely dressed and undamaged. Prices depend upon rarity of hairdo and can run from $700.00 - 3,800.00.

Early Hairdo: Also see "Wood Body." 7" - $825.00 up; 14" - $1,600.00 up; 17" - $2,100.00 up; 23" - $2,800.00 up.

Common Hairdo: Called "Lowbrow" or "Butterfly." Made from 1890, with most being made after 1900. Black or blonde hair. Wavy hairdo, center part with hair that comes down low on forehead. Also see "Pet Names." 8" - $85.00; 14" - $150.00; 17" - $225.00; 21" - $300.00; 25" - $385.00. Jewel necklace: 14" - $200.00; 20" - $450.00.

Child: Swivel neck, china shoulder plate and may have lower torso and limbs made of china. 12" - $2,400.00.

Child or Boy: Short black or blonde hairdo, curly with partly exposed ears. 16" - $400.00; 22" - $585.00.

Currier & Ives: 13" - $500.00; 18" - $700.00.

Covered Wagon, Civil War: 1840-1870's. Hair parted in middle with flat hairstyle and has sausage-shaped curls around head. 8" - $300.00; 14" - $485.00; 18" - $675.00; 22" - $925.00.

Curly Top: 1845-1860's. Ringlet curls that are loose and over entire head. 18" - $700.00; 22" - $800.00.

Dolly Madison: 1870-1880's. Loose curly hairdo with modeled ribbon and bow in center of the top of the head. Few curls on forehead. 16" - $365.00; 19" - $525.00; 23" - $625.00; 27" - $800.00.

Early Marked China (Nurenburg, Rudustat, etc.): 14" - $2,800.00; 17" - $3,600.00 up.

Flat Top, Civil War: Also called "High Brow." 1850-1870's. Black hair parted in middle, smooth on top with short curls around head. 12" - $165.00; 15" - $245.00; 18" - $325.00; 21" - $375.00; 23" - $425.00; 25" - $475.00; 32-34" - $825.00. Swivel neck: 14" - $800.00; 21" - $1,500.00.

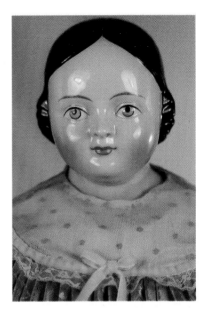

Large 30" pink luster china with rare painted lower lashes. Flat top with sausage curls around head. Cloth body with china limbs. 30" - $900.00 up. Courtesy Frasher Doll Auctions.

24" brown eye china with "flat top" hairdo, twelve sausage curls around head, cloth body with china limbs, blue boots. 24" - $1,400.00. Courtesy Turn of Century Antiques.

Glass eyes: Can have a variety of hairdos. 1840-1870's. 16" - $1,900.00; 19" - $2,800.00; 23" - $3,200.00.

Hat or Bonnet: Molded on. 13" - $3,300.00; 17" - $4,500.00.

Highbrow: Like Covered Wagon, but has very high forehead, smooth on top with a center part, curls over ears and around base of neck, and has a very round face. 1860-1870's. 15" - $450.00; 21" - $750.00; 26" - $900.00.

Japanese: 1910 - 1920's. Can be marked or unmarked. Black or blonde and can have a "common" hairdo, or have much more adult face and hairdo. 12" - $125.00; 15" - $185.00.

Jenny Lind: Hair pulled back in bun. 19" - $3,600.00.

Kling: Number and bell. 14" - $365.00; 17" - $475.00; 21" - $675.00.

Man or Boy: Excellent quality, early date, side part hairdo. Brown hair. 15" - $2,300.00; 17" - $2,900.00; 21" - $3,500.00 up.

Man or Boy: Glass eyes. 15" - $2,500.00; 17" - $3500.00; 21" - $4,000.00.

Open Mouth: Common hairdo. 16" - $750.00; 20" - $1,000.00.

Pet Names: 1905, same as "Common" hairdo with molded shirtwaist with the name on front: Agnes, Bertha, Daisy, Dorothy, Edith, Esther, Ethel, Florence, Helen, Mabel, Marion, Pauline. 6-7" - $115.00; 13" - $195.00; 15" - $225.00; 17" - $275.00; 19" - $325.00; 21" - $275.00; 25" - $450.00.

Pierced Ears: Can have a variety of hairstyles (ordinary hairstyle, flat top, curly, covered wagon, etc.) 15" - $575.00; 20" - $900.00.

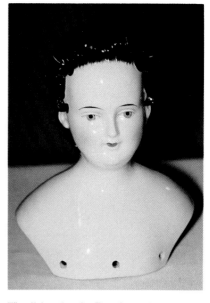

21" china head that is also seen often as a "parian." Pierced ears, fancy hairdo with brush strokes around face, excellent facial and hair details. Cloth body, china lower limbs. 21" - **$1,200.00.** Courtesy Turn of Century Antiques.

7" tall head only. Brush strokes around face, exposed ears, snood with spill curls over ears and hair pulled back into bun. Head only - **$650.00.** Courtesy Shirley Bertrand.

Pierced Ears: Rare hairstyles. 16" - $1,200.00 up; 20" - $1,800.00 up.

Snood, Combs: Applied hair decoration. 16" - $750.00; 19" - $900.00. Grapes in hairdo: 19" - $1,600.00 up.

Spill Curls: With or without headband. Many individual curls across forehead and over shoulders. Forehead curls continued to above ears. 16" - $525.00; 19" - $800.00; 21" - $900.00.

Swivel neck: 8-9" - $1,000.00; 14" - $2,600.00.

Whistle: Has whistle holes in head. 16" - $700.00; 20" - $950.00.

Wood Body: Articulated with slim hips, china lower arms. 1840-1850's. Hair pulled back in bun or coiled braids. 6" - $1,200.00; 8" - $1,400.00; 12" - $2,800.00 up; 15" - $3,100.00 up; 18" - $4,500.00 up. Same with Covered Wagon hairdo: 8" - $975.00; 12" - $1,400.00; 16" - $1,900.00.

6" china with tinted porcelain, china lower limbs, wood body, original clothes, and unusual hairstyle. 6" - $1,000.00. Courtesy Ellen Dodge.

CLOTH DOLLS

Alabama Indestructible Doll: All cloth with head molded and painted in oils, painted hair, shoes and stockings. Marked on torso or leg "Pat. Nov. 9, 1912. Ella Smith Doll Co." or "Mrs. S.S. Smith/Manufacturer and dealer/ The Alabama Indestructible Doll/ Roanoke, Ala./Patented Sept. 26, 1905 (or 1907)."

Prices are for clean dolls with only minor scuffs or soil.

Child: 19" - $2,600.00; 24" - $3,300.00.

Baby: 20" - $2,500.00.

Black Child: 19" - $6,000.00; 24" - $6,800.00.

Black Baby: 20" - $6,400.00.

Art Fabric Mills: See Printed Cloth Dolls.

Babyland: Made by E.I. Horsman from 1904 to 1920. Marked on torso or bottom of foot. Oil painted features, photographic features or printed features. With or without wig. All cloth, jointed at shoulders and hips. First price for extra clean, original dolls; second price for dolls in fair condition that show wear and have slight soil.

Oil Painted Features: 14" - $900.00, $400.00; 17" - $1,100.00, $500.00; 26" - $1,700.00, $800.00; 29" - $2,000.00, $950.00.

Black Oil Painted Features: 14" - $975.00, $450.00; 17" - $1,200.00, $550.00; 26" - $2,000.00, $950.00; 29" - $2,400.00; $1,000.00.

Photographic Face: 17" - $850.00, $400.00.

Black Photographic Face: 17" - $1,000.00, $500.00.

Printed: 18" - $600.00, $250.00; 21" - $800.00, $375.00; 26" - $950.00, $425.00.

Black printed: 18" - $800.00, $400.00; 21" - $1,000.00, $500.00; 26" - $1,200.00, $600.00.

Beecher: 1893–1910. Stuffed stockinette, painted eyes, needle sculptured features. Originated by Julia Jones Beecher of Elmira, N.Y., wife of Congregational Church pastor. Dolls made by sewing circle of church and all proceeds used for missionary work, so dolls can also be referred to as "Missionary Babies." Have looped wool hair. Extra clean: 15" - $2,800.00; 22" - $6,200.00. Slight soil and wear: 15" - $1,400.00; 22" - $2,500.00. Black: Extra clean: 15" - $3,300.00; 22" - $7,000.00 up. Soil and wear: 15" - $1,500.00; 22" - $3,500.00.

Bing Art: By Bing Werke; Germany, 1921–1932. All cloth, all felt, or composition head with cloth body.

17" all cloth Popeye. Original (missing corncob pipe.) Excellent detail, most likely made by Gund. 17" - $850.00 up. Courtesy Shirley Bertrand.

Molded face mask, oil painted feature, wig or painted hair, can have pin joints on cloth body, seams down front of legs, mitt hands with free formed thumbs. Painted hair, cloth or felt: 10" - $625.00; 15" - $850.00. Wig: 10" - $325.00; 15" - $500.00. Composition head: 8" - $125.00; 13" - $285.00.

Bruckner: Made for Horsman, 1901 on. Marked on shoulder "Pat'd July 8, 1901." Cloth with mask face stiffened and printed. Clean: 12-14" - $325.00; Soil and wear: 12-14" - $125.00. **Black:** Clean: 12-14" - $485.00; Soil and wear: 12-14" - $200.00.

Columbian Doll: Ca. 1890's. Sizes 15-29". Stamped "Columbian Doll/Manufactured by/Emma E. Adams/Oswego Centre/N.Y." After 1905–1906, the mark was "The Columbian Doll/ Manufactured by/ Marietta Adams Ruttan/Oswego, NY." All cloth with painted features and flesh-painted hands and feet. Stitched fingers and toes. Extra clean: 16" - $4,000.00; 21" - $6,500.00. Fair, with slight scuffs or soil: 16" - $2,000.00; 21" - $3,000.00. Columbian type: 22" - $2,800.00 up, $1,200.00.

Comic Characters: Extra clean: 15" - $500.00-600.00. Soil and wear: 15" - $165.00-200.00.

Deans Rag Book Dolls: Golliwogs (black): (See photo in Series 6, pg. 65.) 12" - $225.00; 14" - $300.00. **Child:** 10" - $300.00; 16" - $625.00; 18" - $825.00. Printed face: 10" - $100.00; 16" - $165.00; 18" - $225.00.

Drayton, Grace: Dolly Dingle. 1923 by Averill Mfg. Co. Cloth with printed features, marked on torso. 12" - $450.00; 16" - $650.00. **Chocolate Drop:** 1923 by Averill. Brown cloth with printed features and three tufts of yarn hair. 12" - $400.00; 16" - $600.00. **Hug Me Tight:** By Colonial Toy Mfg. Co. in 1916. One-piece printed cloth with boy standing behind girl: 12" - $300.00; 16" - $500.00. **Peek-A-Boo:** Made by

Horsman in 1913–1915. All cloth with printed features: 12" - $300.00; 14" - $475.00.

Embroidered Features (Primitive): Home made, all cloth, yarn, lamb's wool or painted hair. White: 16" - $265.00 up; 20" - $485.00 up. Black: 16" - $450.00 up; 20" - $950.00 up.

Fangel, Maud Toursey: 1938 on. All cloth, printed features. Can have printed cloth body or plain without "undies clothes." Mitt-style hands with free-formed thumbs. Child: 9" - $425.00; 12" - $625.00; 15" - $775.00; 20" - $950.00. Baby: 14" - $600.00; 17" - $875.00.

Farnell's Alpha Toys: Marked with label on foot "Farnell's Alpha Toys/Made in England." (See photo in Series 6, pg. 58.) **Child:** 15" - $465.00; 17" - $575.00. **Baby:** 14" - $500.00; 17" - $550.00. **King George VI:** 17" - $1,200.00. **Palace Guard/Beefeater:** 17" - $750.00.

Georgene Novelties: See Averill, Georgene section.

Kamkins: Made by Louise Kampes. 1928–1934. Marked on head or foot, also has paper heart-shaped label on chest. All cloth with molded face mask and painted features, wigs, boy or girl. Extra clean: 20" - $1,700.00; 25" - $2,600.00. Slight wear/soil: 20" - $800.00; 25" - $1,000.00.

Kewpie Cuddles: See Kewpie section.

Lenci: See Lenci section.

Liberty of London Royal Dolls: Marked with cloth or paper tag. Flesh-colored cloth faces with stitched and painted features. All cloth bodies. 1939 Royal Portrait dolls are 10" and include Queen Mary, King George VI, Queen Victoria and Queen Elizabeth. (See photo in Series 7, pg. 53) Extra clean: 10" - $200.00. Slight wear/soil: 10" - $95.00. Other Historical or Coronation figures - Extra clean: 10" - $200.00. Slight wear/soil: 10" - $95.00.

Kruse, Käthe: See Kruse section.

Madame Hendron: See Averill section.

Mammy Style Black Dolls: All cloth with painted or sewn features. Ca. 1910–1920's. 15" - $365.00; 18" - $425.00. Ca. 1930's: 15" - $185.00 up.

Missionary Babies: See Beecher in this section.

Mollye: See Mollye in Modern section.

Mother's Congress Doll: Patented Nov. 1900. All cloth, printed features and hair. Mitt-style hands without formed thumbs. Designed and made by Madge Mead. Marked with cloth label "Mother's Congress Doll/Children's Favorite/Philadelphia, Pa./Pat. Nov. 6, 1900." Extra clean: 18" - $975.00 up; 23" - $1,000.00 up. Slight soil: 18" - $400.00; 23" - $475.00. Oil painted faces and hair, unidentified. Cloth body and limbs, 24" - $600.00; 29" - $900.00.

Tiny ½" miniature doll made on a wire armature covered with embroidery floss and very detailed clothes. A tiny work of art made for Marshall Fields by Elaine Cannon, 1930's. $185.00 up.

Old Cottage Doll: England, 1948 on. Cloth and English composition. Later versions have hard plastic heads. Hand painted features. 8" - $145.00 up; 12" - $185.00 up.

Philadelphia Baby: Also called "Sheppard Doll" as made by J.B. Sheppard in late 1890's and early 1900's. Stockinette covered body with painted cloth arms and legs. Head is modeled and painted cloth. Extra clean: 21" - $3,600.00; 26" - $4,300.00. Slight soil and wear: 21" - $2,000.00; 26" - $2,500.00. Very worn: 21" - $950.00; 26" - $1,400.00.

Petzold, Dora: Germany, 1920's. Pressed paper head, painted old features, wig, stockinette body filled with sawdust, short torso. Soft stuffed arms, free formed thumbs, stitched fingers. Legs have formed calves. (See photo in Series 7, pg. 139.) 20" - $850.00; 24" - $950.00; 27" - $1,000.00.

Poir, Eugenie: 1920's, made in New York and France. All cloth body with felt face and limbs or can be all felt. Painted features, majority of eyes are painted to the side, mohair wig. Stitched four fingers together with free-standing thumb. Unmarked except for paper label. Extra clean: 18" - $775.00; 25" - $1,000.00. Slight soil and wear: 18" - $350.00; 25" - $500.00. Photographic faces: (also see Babyland in this section) - Extra clean: 16" - $750.00. Slight soil and wear: 16" - $350.00.

Printed Cloth Dolls: 1903 on. All cloth with features and/or underwear/clothes printed. These dolls are cut and sew types. **Rastus, Cream of Wheat:** 18" - $145.00. **Aunt Jemima:** Set of four dolls. $100.00 each; **Printed-on underwear (Dolly Dear, Merry Marie, etc.)** Cut: 6" - $95.00; 15" - $250.00; 18" - $300.00. Uncut: 6" - $145.00; 15" - $265.00; 18" - $325.00. **Boys and girls with printed outer clothes:** Cut: 6" - $100.00; 15" - $175.00; 18" - $245.00. Uncut: 6" - $145.00; 15" - $250.00; 18" - $325.00. **Black boy or girl:** 18" -

"Ceresota Flour" boy with a brimmed hat, uncut. Made for the Northwestern Consolidated Milling Co., ca. 1899. The very first one was made in 1895 had a plain cap. Uncut panel - $200.00 up. Courtesy Shirley Bertrand.

$550.00; 22" - $700.00. **Brownies:** By Palmer Cox, 1892. 8" - $125.00; 14" - $200.00. **George and Martha Washington:** 1901 by Art Fabric - Cut: $450.00, set of four; Uncut: $850.00, set of four. **St. Nicholas/Santa Claus:** Marked "Pat. Dec. 28, 1886. Made by E.S. Peck, NY." One arm stuffed with toys and other arm holds American flag. Cut: 15" - $450.00. Uncut: 15" - $800.00

Raynal: Made in France by Edouard Raynal. 1920's. Cloth body and limbs (sometimes has celluloid hands), felt mask face with painted features. Eyes painted to side. Marked on soles of shoes or will have necklace imprinted "Raynal." Original clothes generally are felt, but can have combination felt/organdy or just organdy. Extra clean: 16" - $575.00; 21" - $875.00. Slight soil and wear: 16" - $200.00; 21" - $400.00.

Russian: 1920–1930's. All cloth with stockinette hands and head. Molded face mask with painted features. Dressed in regional costumes. Marked "Made in Soviet Union." Extra clean: 10" - $95.00, 14" - $165.00. Slight soil and wear: 10" - $30.00; 14" - $75.00. **Tea Cozies:** Doll from waist up and has full skirt that is hollow to be placed over

pot to keep contents warm. 17" - $165.00; 22" - $265.00; 28" - $350.00.

Rollinson Dolls: Molded cloth with painted features, head and limbs. Molded hair or wig. Designed by Gertrude F. Rollinson, made by Utley Doll Co. Marked with a stamp of doll in a diamond and printed around border "Rollinson Doll Holyoke, Ma." Molded hair, extra clean: 21" - $1,200.00 up. Molded hair slight soil and wear: 21" - $500.00. Wigged by Rollinson - Extra clean: 20" - $1,600.00 up, 26" - $2,300.00. Wigged, slight soil and wear: 20" - $700.00; 26" - $950.00. Toddler: With wig. 17" - $1,850.00.

Smith, Mrs. S.S.: See Alabama in this section.

Steiff: See Steiff section.

Walker, Izannah: Made in 1870's and 1880's. Modeled head with oil painted features. Ears are applied. Cloth body and limbs. Hands and feet are stitched and can have painted on boots. Marked "Patented Nov. 4, 1873." Brushstroke or corkscrew curls around face over ears. Very good condition: 16-17" - $21,000.00; 20" - $26,000.00. Fair condition: 16-17" - $9,500.00; 20" - $12,000.00. Poor condition: 16-17" -

20" and 11" Russian tea cosy dolls. Covers tea pot to keep contents warm. Character oil painted features. 20" - $265.00; 11" - $145.00. Courtesy Shirley Bertrand.

$2,500.00; 20" - $3,400.00. Two vertical curls in front of ears. Very good condition: 20" - $23,000.00 up; 26" - $28,000.00 up. Fair condition: 20"- $14,000.00; 26" - $18,000.00.

Wellington: 1883 on. Label on back: "Pat. Jan. 8, 1883." All stockinette, oil painted features, lower limbs. Features are needle-sculpted. Hair is painted. Has distinctive buttocks; rounded. Excellent condition: 22-23" - $14,500.00 up. Fair to poor condition: 22-23" - $3,700.00 up.

23" W.P.A. doll, all cloth, oil painted. Tag marked "W.P.A. Wisconsin State University." Unique mitt formed hands, very pointed chin. Wig pinned on, no ears. Doll filled with sand. 23" - $600.00 up.

CLOWNS

14" unmarked clown. White bisque head with fired-in color on face. Glass eyes, five-piece body and original clothes. 14" - $565.00.
Courtesy Arthur Bouliette.

Group of clown dolls. Taller dolls (left to right): Marked S.F.B.J. 301; German head on all cloth body, unmarked; "A" series Steiner (see close-up below). Smaller dolls (left to right): "A" Herm Steiner; German marked "210." All clowns are original. S.F.B.J. - $1,200.00; H. Steiner - $650.00; German "210" - $700.00. Courtesy Ellen Dodge.

13" marked Jules Steiner body. Head marked "Fire A." Paperweight eyes, closed mouth with paint between lips. Painted features and original. 13" - $3,600.00. Courtesy Ellen Dodge.

Most German makers made composition-headed dolls as well as bisque and other materials. Composition dolls were made in Germany before World War I, but the majority were made in the 1920's and 1930's. They can be all composition or have a composition head with cloth body and limbs. Prices are for excellent quality and condition.

Child Doll: All composition with wig, sleep/flirty eyes, open or closed mouth and jointed composition body. Unmarked or just have numbers. 16" - $250.00; 19" - $385.00; 22" - $500.00; 25" - $650.00.

Child: Same as above, but with name of company (or initials): 16" - $325.00; 19" - $525.00; 24" - $685.00; 27" - $875.00.

Baby: All composition, open mouth. 14" - $185.00; 17" - $350.00; 19" - $450.00. Toddler: 23" - $600.00; 26" - $700.00.

Baby: Composition head and limbs with cloth body, open mouth, sleep eyes. 15" - $165.00; 19" - $285.00; 27" - $400.00.

Painted Eyes: Child: 13" - $125.00; 17" - $185.00. Baby: 15" - $135.00; 19" - $265.00.

Shoulder Head: Composition shoulder head, glass eyes, wig, open or closed mouth, cloth or kidaleen body with composition arms (full arms or lower arms only with cloth upper arms), and lower legs. May have bare feet or modeled boots. Prices for dolls in extra clean condition and nicely dressed. Unmarked.

Excellent Quality: Extremely fine modeling. 15-16" - $450.00; 20" - $525.00; 23-24" - $675.00; 29-30" - $785.00.

Average Quality: May resemble a china head doll. 11-12" - $165.00; 14" - $200.00; 17" - $250.00; 22" - $325.00; 25" - $365.00; 29" - $485.00.

Painted Hair: 10" - $185.00; 15" - $265.00; 19" - $425.00.

Swivel Neck: On composition shoulder plate. 14" - $425.00; 17" - $550.00; 23" - $700.00.

Gebruder Heubach all composition, ca. 1909. Painted-on high top boots with tan painted socks. Five-piece body, molded hair and ribbon, painted features, original. 14" mint - $375.00; 14" fair condition - $185.00. Courtesy Vickie Andings.

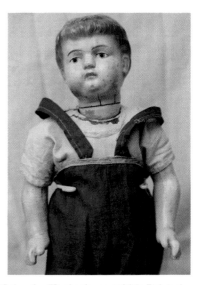

Gebruder Heubach, ca. 1909. Painted-on black shoes. Five-piece body, all composition except wood at neck joint, original. 15" mint - $400.00; 14" fair condition - $195.00. Courtesy Vickie Andings.

Many French and German dolls bear the mark "DEP" as part of their mold marks, but the dolls referred to here are marked *only with the* DEP *and a size number*. They are on French bodies with some bearing a Jumeau sticker. The early 1880's DEP dolls have fine quality bisque and artist workmanship, and the later dolls of the 1890's and into the 1900's generally have fine bisque, but the color will be higher, and they will have painted lashes below the eyes with most having hair eyelashes over the eyes. The early dolls will have outlined lips where the later ones will not. Prices are for clean, undamaged and nicely dressed dolls.

Marks:

26" marked "DEP." Open mouth, sleep eyes and on fully jointed French body. 26" - $2,400.00. Courtesy Turn of Century Antiques.

Open Mouth: 12" - $675.00; 15" - $875.00; 17" - $975.00; 21" - $1,300.00; 26" - $1,900.00; 32" - $2,600.00. Open mouth, very Jumeau looking, red check marks: 17" - $1,500.00; 21" - $1,900.00; 25" - $2,400.00.
Closed Mouth: 15" - $1,650.00; 19" - $2,650.00; 23" - $2,900.00; 28" - $3,300.00.
Walking, Kissing, Open Mouth: 16" - $1,200.00; 19" - $1,550.00; 23" - $1,800.00; 27" - $2,400.00.

18" marked "DEP." Paperweight eyes, closed mouth, and on fully jointed French body. 18" - $2,650.00. Courtesy Barbara Earnshaw-Cain.

30" marked "DEP." She is in her original box marked "Eden Bebe Articlado." Open mouth and fully jointed French body with pull strings to operate "Mama/Papa" cryer. Original clothes. 30" - $2,600.00. Courtesy Frasher Doll Auctions.

DOLL HOUSE DOLLS

3½ - 4" doll house chinas. All pre-1890's with one on far left being original. All have early hairstyles. 3½ - 4" - $300.00-385.00 each. Courtesy Shirley Bertrand.

Doll House Man or Lady: With molded hair/wig and painted eyes. 6-7" - $185.00-225.00.

Children: All bisque: 3½" - $95.00, 5½" - $125.00. Bisque/cloth: 3½" - $95.00; 5½" - $125.00.

Man or Woman with Glass Eyes/Wigs: 6-7" - $325.00-400.00.

Man or Woman with Molded Hair, Glass Eyes: 6-7" - $385.00.

Grandparents, Old People, or Molded-on Hats: 6-7" - $265.00.

Military Men, Original: 6-7" - $585.00 up.

Black Man or Woman: Molded hair, all original. 6-7" - $450.00.

Swivel Neck: Wig or molded hair. 6-7" - $800.00 up.

China Glaze: Early hairdos: 4-5" - $300.00-385.00; **Low brow/common hairdo:** 1900's and after. $100.00-185.00.

DOOR OF HOPE DOLLS

Door of Hope dolls were created at the Door of Hope Mission in China from 1901 into 1910's. They have cloth bodies and head and limbs are carved of wood. The carvers came from Ning-Po Province. They usually are between 8-13" tall, and if marked, it will have label "Made in China."

Manchu: Mandarin man or woman - $775.00 up.

Mother and Baby: $725.00.
Adult: 9" - $625.00; 11" - $750.00.
Child: 6" - $485.00; 8" - $565.00.
Bride: $825.00.
Carved flowers in hair: $800.00 up.
Priest: $900.00.
Widow: $900.00.
Mourner: $850.00.
Groom: $785.00
Bridesmaid: $825.00.
Grandfather: $785.00.
Amah (Governess): $765.00.

11" "Buddhist Priest." Carved hair with attached headpiece, original. 11" - $900.00.
Courtesy Shirley Bertrand.

11" "Widow and Mourner." Both in original sackcloth of starched muslin. Widow - $900.00; Mourner - $850.00. Courtesy Shirley Bertrand.

11" "Bride and Groom." Her headpiece has seed pearls around edges. Both are original. Bride - $825.00; Groom - $785.00. Courtesy Shirley Bertrand.

11" "Bridesmaid." Pink headpiece, pink/blue tassels on hat and skirt. Bridesmaid - $825.00. Courtesy Shirley Bertrand.

11" "Grandfather" or "Philosopher." Gold skirt and lavender top, character carved face. Grandfather/Philosopher - $785.00. Courtesy Shirley Bertrand.

11" "Man and Woman" that are all original. Wood with painted features. Costumes can have variations of colors. Man/Woman - $750.00. Courtesy Shirley Bertrand.

11" and 9" men. Character face carved on larger doll. Both are original. Costumes can have color variations. 9" - $625.00; 11" - $750.00. Courtesy Shirley Bertrand.

6" and 8" children with 11" "Amah." All are original. 6" - $485.00; 8" - $565.00; 11" - $765.00. Courtesy Shirley Bertrand.

Cuno & Otto Dressel operated in Sonneberg, Thuringia, Germany and were sons of the founder. Although the firm was in business in 1700, they are not listed as dollmakers until 1873. They produced dolls with bisque heads, composition over wax, which can be on cloth, kid, or jointed composition body. Some of their heads were made for them by other German firms, such as Simon & Halbig, Heubach, etc. They registered the trademark for "Jutta" in 1906 and by 1911 were also making celluloid dolls. Prices are for undamaged, clean and nicely dressed dolls.

Marks:

C.O.D.

C.O.D 49 D.E.P.
Made in Germany

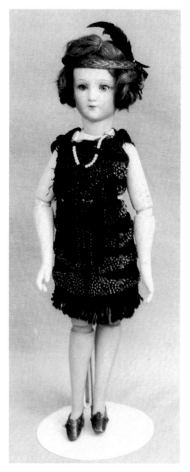

Babies: 1910 on. Marked "C.O.D." but without the word "Jutta." Allow more for toddler body. 12" - $365.00. 14" - $495.00; 19" - $625.00; 23" - $765.00.

Child: 1893 on. Jointed composition body, with open mouth. 16" - $365.00; 19" - $425.00; 23" - $550.00; 28" - $750.00; 33" - $1,000.00; 38" - $1,800.00.

Child: On kid, jointed body, open mouth. 16" - $350.00; 20" - $450.00; 25" - $575.00.

Jutta: 1910–1922. **Baby:** Open mouth and five-piece bent limb body. 12" - $525.00; 16" - $650.00; 19" - $800.00; 23" - $1,350.00; 25" - $1,450.00.

Toddler Body: 8" - $585.00; 16" - $850.00; 19" - $1,200.00; 23" - $1,500.00; 27" - $2,000.00.

Child: Marked with **"Jutta"** or with S&H **#1914, #1348, #1349,** etc.: 13" - $585.00; 15" - $650.00; 19" - $700.00; 23" - $975.00; 25" - $1,050.00; 30" - $1,300.00.

14" Flapper lady marked "C.O.D." Glass eyes, closed mouth, jointed body. Hose painted on entire legs, original. Has trunk and wardrobe. 14" - $3,500.00. With trunk/wardrobe - $4,200.00 up. Courtesy Ellen Dodge.

Lady Doll: 1920's with adult face, closed mouth and on five-piece composition body with thin limbs and high heel feet. Mark **#1469**. 16" - $4,300.00; 18" - $5,200.00.

Character Dolls: 1909 and after. Closed mouth, painted eyes, molded hair or wig. 10" - $1,600.00; 14" - $2,400.00; 18" - $2,900.00.

Character Dolls: Same as above, but with glass eyes. 14" - $2,400.00; 16" - $2,900.00; 18" - $3,200.00; 24" - $3,500.00.

Composition: Shoulder head of 1870's, glass or painted eyes, molded hair or wig and on cloth body with composition limbs with molded-on boots. Will be marked with Holz-Masse:

With wig: Glass eyes. 16" - $375.00; 19" - $465.00; 23" - $550.00. Molded hair: 17" - $400.00; 24" - $565.00.

Portrait Dolls: 1896. Such as Uncle Sam, Farmer, Admiral Dewey, Admiral Byrd, Old Rip, Witch, etc. Portrait bisque head, glass eyes, composition body. Some will be marked with a "D" or "S." Heads made for Dressel by Simon & Halbig. Prices for clean, undamaged and originally dressed. **Military dolls:** (See photo in Series 6, pg. 72) 9" - $900.00; 13" - $1,800.00; 16" - $2,500.00. **Old Rip or Witch:** 9" - $750.00; 13" - $1,600.00; 16" - $1,900.00. **Uncle Sam:** 9" - $825.00; 13" - $1,675.00; 16" - $2,250.00.

Fur covered: Glued on body/limbs. 8-9" – $185.00; 12" - $265.00.

30" marked "Jutta 1348/Simon & Halbig." Sleep eyes with lashes, open mouth. 30" - $1,300.00. Courtesy Turn of Century Antiques.

E. Denamur of Paris made dolls from 1885 to 1898. The E.D. marked dolls seem to be accepted as being made by Denamur, but they could have been made by E. Dumont, Paris. Composition and wood jointed bodies. Prices are for excellent quality bisque, no damage and nicely dressed.

Marks:

E 6 D

Closed Mouth: 14" - $2,850.00; 17" - $3,250.00; 23" - $3,600.00; 27" - $4,200.00, 29" - $4,600.00.

Open Mouth: 15" - $1,650.00; 18" - $1,900.00; 22" - $2,400.00.

Black: Open mouth. 19" - $2,500.00; 25" - $3,200.00.

Left: 25" marked "E. 11 D./Depose." Open mouth with four upper teeth. Lamb's wool wig, jointed body. Right: 14½" closed mouth marked "Depose Tete Jumeau BTE. S.G.D.G. 5." 25" - $2,700.00; 14½" - $3,900.00. Courtesy Frasher Doll Auctions.

EDEN BÉBÉ

Fleischmann & Bloedel of Fürth, Bavaria; Sonneberg, Thuringia; and Paris, France was founded in 1873 and making dolls in Paris by 1890. The company became a part of S.F.B.J. in 1899. Dolls have composition jointed bodies and can have open or closed mouths. Prices are for dolls with excellent color and quality bisque, no damage and nicely dressed.

Marks:

EDEN BÉBÉ PARIS

Closed Mouth: Pale bisque. 16" - $2,650.00; 20" - $3,100.00; 24" - $3,600.00; 27" - $4,000.00.

Closed Mouth: High color bisque. 16" - $1,700.00; 20" - $2,200.00; 24" - $2,400.00; 27" - $2,700.00.

Open Mouth: 16" - $1,500.00; 20" - $2,300.00; 24" - $2,800.00; 27" - $3,100.00.

Walking Kissing Doll: Jointed body with walker mechanism, head turns and one arm throws a kiss. Heads by Simon & Halbig using mold #1039 (and others). Bodies assembled by Fleischmann & Bloedel. Price for perfect, working doll. 23" - $1,500.00 up.

19" marked "Eden Bébé Paris Depose." Open mouth
and on fully jointed French body. 19" - $2,300.00.
Courtesy Frasher Doll Auctions.

EINCO

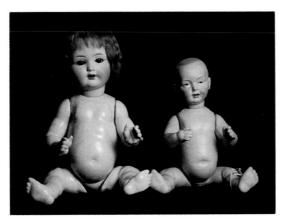

Right: 14½" rare marked Einco baby, ca. 1910–1912. Intaglio eyes and lightly
painted hair. Made by Eisenmann & Co. (1881–1930), Bavaria, Germany. Left:
18" Steinbacker with sleep eyes, marked "EStP." 14½" - $2,100.00-2,800.00; 18" -
$950.00-1,100.00. Courtesy Helen & Bill Moore. Photo by Mike Krambeck.

Joel Ellis made dolls in Springfield, Vermont, in 1873 and 1874 under the name Co-operative Manufacturing Co. All wood jointed body has tenon and mortise joints, arms are jointed in same manner. The hands and feet are made of pewter. Has molded hair and painted features.

Springfield Wooden Doll: It must be noted that dolls similar to the Joel Ellis ones were made in Springfield, Vt. also by Joint Doll Co. and D.M. Smith & Co. They are very much like the Joel Ellis except when standing the knee joint will be flush with the method of jointing not showing. The hips are cut out with the leg tops cut to fit the opening, and the detail of the hands is not as well done.

Doll in fair condition: Does not need to be dressed. 12" - $500.00. Excellent condition: 12" - $900.00 up; 15" - $1,100.00 up; 18" - $1,800.00 up.

16" Joel Ellis 1874 doll. All wood with metal hands and feet. Sausage curls around head. Original maid outfit. 16" - $1,200.00 up. Courtesy Henri & John Startzel.

These "adult" style dolls were made by a number of French firms from about 1860 into 1930's. Many will be marked only with a number or have a stamp on the body, although some of the stamps/labels may be the store where they were sold from and not the maker. The most available fashion doll seems to be marked F.G. dolls. Price are for dolls in perfect condition with no cracks, chips, or repairs and in beautiful old or newer clothes made of appropriate age materials.

Articulated Wood: Marked or unmarked. Or blown kid bodies and limbs. Some have bisque lower arms. 16" - $6,500.00 up; 20" - $8,400.00 up.

Articulated: Marked or unmarked. With bisque lower legs and arms with excellent modeling detail. 15" - $8,500.00 up; 21" - $9,500.00 up.

Marked "Bru": (Also see Smiling Mona Lisa in this section.) 1860's. Round face, swivel neck, glass eyes: (See photo in Series 6, pg. 79.) 14" - $3,000.00; 17" - $4,850.00; 20" - $5,500.00 up. Wood body: 14" - $11,000.00.

Marked "Huret": Bisque or china glazed shoulder head, kid body with bisque lower arms. Painted eyes: 14" - $6,900.00; 17" - $8,900.00. Glass eyes: 14" - $7,500.00; 17" - $9,000.00 up. Wood body: 16" - $8,800.00 up; 20" - $14,000.00 up. Gutta Percha body: 18" - $9,500.00 up.

Huret Child: 18" - $26,000.00; 24" - $32,000.00.

Marked "Rohmer": (See photo in Series 7, pg. 65.) Bisque or china glazed shoulder head (can be jointed). Kid body with bisque lower arms (or china). Glass eyes: 16" - $7,500.00; 19" - $13,500.00; Painted eyes: 16" - $6,500.00; 19" - $12,000.00. Wood body: 16" - $8,000.00; 19" - $14,000.00.

Unmarked Rohmer or Huret Type: Painted eyes, china glaze: 16" - $3,500.00; 20" - $4,600.00; 26" - $6,200.00. Wire controlled sleep eyes: Controled eyes. 27" - $12,000.00.

Marked "Jumeau": (See photo in Series 7, pg. 79.) Will have number on head and stamped body. Portrait-style head: 15" - $3,800.00; 17" - $5,600.00; 23" - $6,200.00; 26" - $7,000.00. 29-30" - $9,800.00 Wood body: 18" - $9,000.00 up; 24" - $12,000.00 up.

Left: 18" early Fashion with round swivel head, bisque shoulderplate, kid body. White ivory-like bisque, almond cut glass eyes. Right: 16" Rohmer Fashion with green oval stamp "Breveté S.G.D.G." China glazed porcelain head and arms and kid body. Wears original gown. 18" - $2,800.00 up; 16" - $7,000.00 up. Courtesy Frasher Doll Auctions.

Left: Jumeau Fashion with red check marks on head and marked Jumeau body. 16" with swivel head, kid body. Right: 18" marked "4" on head. Swivel head, articulated wood body with bisque lower arms and legs, original. 16" - $6,000.00; 18" - $5,600.00. Courtesy Frasher Doll Auctions.

Marked "F.G.": 1860 on. All kid body, one-piece shoulder and head, glass eyes. 12" - $1,000.00; 14" - $1,400.00; 17" - $1,900.00. Painted eyes: 12" - $850.00; 14" - $1,000.00.

Marked "F.G.": 1860 on. All kid body (or bisque lower arms), swivel head on bisque shoulder plate. 10-12" - $1,600.00; 14-15" - $2,500.00; 17-18" - $2,800.00; 21-22" - $3,300.00; 25-26" - $4,000.00. Black: 13" - $2,000.00; 17" - $3,200.00.

Marked "F.G.": Early face, Gesland cloth-covered body with bisque lower arms and legs. 15" - $4,800.00; 18" - $5,500.00; 23" - $6,200.00; 26" - $6,500.00.

25½" smiling "Mona Lisa" accepted Bru fashion. Marked "Depose K" on forehead and "K" on back of head. Bisque shoulder plate, kid body, original wig. 25½" - $6,400.00. Courtesy Frasher Doll Auctions.

Marked "F.G.": Gesland cloth-covered body with composition or papier maché lower arms and legs. 15" - $3,350.00; 18" - $4,200.00; 23" - $4,750.00; 26" - $5,400.00.

Smiling "Mona Lisa": After 1866. Now being referred to as made by Bru. Kid body with leather lower arms, stitched fingers or bisque lower arms. Swivel head on bisque shoulder plate. Marked with letter (example: E, B, D, etc.) 12-13" - $2,750.00; 15" - $3,650.00; 18" - $4,550.00; 22" - $5,750.00; 26" - $6,400.00; 29" - $12,750.00. (Allow more for wood body or arms.)

Unmarked with Numbers Only: With one-piece head and shoulder. Extremely fine quality bisque, undamaged. Glass eyes: 12" - $1,400.00; 14" - $1,650.00; 22" - $2,300.00; 18" - $2,700.00. Painted eyes: 14" - $850.00; 17" - $1,450.00; 22" - $1,600.00.

Unmarked with Numbers Only: Swivel neck with bisque shoulder plate. Extremely fine quality bisque and un-damaged. 14" - $2,200.00; 16" - $2,800.00; 18" - $3,200.00; 20" - $3,800.00. Black: 14" - $3,000.00 up.

Unmarked: Medium to fair quality. One-piece head and shoulder: 12" - $700.00; 15" - $850.00-1,000.00. Swivel head on bisque shoulder plate: 15" - $1,000.00; 19" - $1,700.00 up.

Marked E.B. (E. Barrois): 1854–1877. (See photo in Series 7, pg. 67.) Glass eyes: 16" - $3,400.00; 20" - $4,900.00. Painted eyes: 17" - $3,200.00; 21" - $3,900.00.

Marked Simone: Glass eyes: 20" - $5,500.00; 24" - $6,500.00.

China glazed Fashion with glass eyes and marked "E 2 DEPOSE B." Shoulder head on kid body with kid arms and wired fingers. Very rare marked doll. (Head shown has been removed from body.) 16" - **$3,600.00 up.** Courtesy Ellen Dodge.

24" Fashion incised "9." Most likely an F.G. Made by Gauthier. Swivel head on bisque shoulder plate. All kid body with separate stitched fingers. 24" - **$5,000.00.** Courtesy Frasher Doll Auctions.

17" beautiful unmarked Fashion with swivel head on bisque shoulderplate. Glass eyes and kid body. 17" - **$4,000.00.** Courtesy Turn of Century Antiques.

F. Gaultier (earlier spelled Gauthier) is the accepted maker of the F.G. marked dolls. These dolls are often found on the cloth-covered or all composition bodies that are marked "Gesland." The Gesland firm was operated by two brothers. One of them had the initial "F" (1887–1900).

Marks:

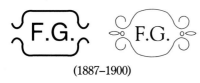

(1887–1900)

F. 8 G.
(1879–1887 Block Letter Mark)

Child with Closed Mouth: Scroll mark. Excellent quality bisque, no damage and nicely dressed. 15" - $2,800.00; 17" - $3,200.00; 20" - $3,600.00; 23" - $3,900.00; 27" - $4,700.00; 30" - $5,100.00.

Child with Closed Mouth: Same as above, but with high face color, no damage and nicely dressed. 15" - $1,900.00; 17" - $2,100.00; 20" - $2,300.00; 23" - $2,700.00; 27" - $3,300.00.

Child with Open Mouth: Scroll mark. Excellent quality bisque, no damage and nicely dressed. 15" - $1,800.00; 17" - $2,100.00; 20" - $2,900.00; 23" - $3,100.00; 27" - $3,700.00.

Child with Open Mouth: Scroll mark. With high face color, very dark lips, no damage and nicely dressed. 15" - $775.00; 17" - $950.00; 20" - $1,200.00; 23" - $1,700.00; 27" - $2,200.00.

Marked "F.G. Fashion": See Fashion section.

Child on Marked Gesland Body: Bisque head on stockinette over wire frame body with composition limbs. Closed mouth: 17" - $4,700.00; 20" - $5,200.00; 24" - $6,000.00. Open mouth: 17" - $3,000.00; 21" - $3,600.00; 26" - $4,500.00.

Block Letter (so called) F.G. Child: 1879–1887. Closed mouth, chunky composition body, excellent quality and condition. 16-17" - $4,600.00; 19-21" - $4,900.00; 23-24" - $5,400.00; 26-27" - $5,850.00.

Block Letter (so called) F.G. Child: Closed mouth, bisque swivel head on bisque shoulder plate with gusseted kid body and bisque lower arms. 17" - $4,600.00; 21" - $4,900.00; 26" - $5,800.00.

Right: 15½" Gesland bodied doll marked "F.G. 5" on head. Gesland marked body. Fully posable stockinette body with composition shoulder plate and lower limbs. Open mouth with two rows of teeth. Left: 15" marked "E. 6 D." on a marked Jumeau body, closed mouth. 15½" - $4,500.00; 15" - $2,850.00.
Courtesy Frasher Doll Auctions.

12" boy marked "F.G." with painted eyes, kid body, molded brown hair. Very unusual. 12" - $1,600.00 up. Courtesy Ellen Dodge.

24" marked "F 10 G" in block letters. Closed mouth and on fully jointed French body. Made by Francois Gauthier. 24" - $5,400.00.

FRENCH BÉBÉ, MAKER UNKNOWN

A variety of French doll makers produced unmarked dolls from the 1880's into the 1920's. These dolls may only have a head size number or be marked "Paris" or "France." Many of the accepted French dolls that have a number are now being attributed to German makers and it will be questionable for some time.

Unmarked French Bébé: Closed or open/closed mouth, paperweight eyes, excellent quality bisque and artist painting on a French body. Prices are for clean, undamaged and nicely dressed dolls.

Early Desirable, Very French-style Face: Marks such as "J.D.," "J.M. Paris," numbers only. 15" - $12,000.00; 19" - $17,000.00; 23" - $22,000.00; 26" - $25,000.00 up.

Jumeau Style Face: 14" - $2,800.00; 17" - $3,200.00; 23" - $4,500.00; 27" - $5,400.00.

Excellent Quality: Unusual face. 14" - $4,100.00; 16" - $4,500.00; 21" - $5,600.00; 27" - $7,800.00.

Medium Quality: May have poor painting and/or blotches to skin tones: 16" - $1,600.00; 21" - $2,100.00; 26" - $2,600.00.

Open Mouth: 1890's and later. Will be on French body. Excellent quality: 15" - $1,800.00; 18" - $2,100.00; 22" - $2,600.00; 25" - $3,200.00.

Open Mouth: 1920's with high face color and may have five-piece papier maché body. 16" - $700.00; 20" - $850.00; 24" - $1,000.00.

13" French child marked "W.D." Large paperweight eyes, closed mouth on jointed French body. 13" - $7,500.00. Courtesy Ellen Dodge.

15" typical Belton-type face with open/closed mouth and white space between lips. She is marked "7" and has a French cut pate. Jointed composition body with straight wrists. 15" - $2,800.00. Courtesy Barbara Earnshaw-Cain.

Right: A wonderful 29" doll marked "137." Maker is unknown. Open/closed mouth with space between lips. Cut pate, jointed body and original mohair wig. 29" - $3,600.00. Courtesy Frasher Doll Auctions.

Right: 23" marked "9" and other faint marks not readable. P.D. type doll with pewter hands. Closed mouth and jointed French body. Left: 19" toddler marked "S.F.B.J. 251 Paris" with sleep eyes and open mouth. 23" - $7,400.00 up; 19" $1,900.00. Courtesy Frasher Doll Auctions.

FREUNDLICH, RALPH

Freundlich Novelty Company operated in New York in 1923. Most of their dolls have a cardboard tag and will be unmarked or may have name on the head, but no maker's name.

Baby Sandy: (See photo in Series 6, pg. 85) 1939–1942. All composition with molded hair, sleep or painted eyes. Marked "Baby Sandy" on head. Excellent condition with no cracks, craze or chips, original or appropriate clothes: 8" - $165.00; 12" - $225.00; 16" - $325.00; 19" - $500.00. With light crazing, but clean and may be redressed: 8" - $85.00; 12" - $100.00; 16" - $125.00; 19" - $200.00.

General Douglas MacArthur: (See photo in Series 6, pg. 85) Ca. 1942. Portrait doll of all composition, painted features and molded hat. Jointed shoulders and hips. Excellent condition and original. 16" - $285.00; 18" - $325.00. Light craze, clothes dirty: 16" - $100.00; 18" - $125.00.

Military Dolls: (See photo in Series 5, pg. 65; Series 6, pg. 85) Ca. 1942 and on. All composition with painted features, molded-on hats and can be a woman or man (W.A.V.E, W.A..A.C., sailor, Marine, etc.) In excellent condition, original and no crazing: 16" - $200.00. Light craze and clothes in fair condition: 16" - $95.00.

Ventriloquist Doll: (See photo in Series 7, pg. 73.) **Dummy Dan:** Looks like Charlie McCarthy. 21" - $300.00 up.

Frozen Charlotte and Charlie figures can be china, partly china (such as hair and boots), stone bisque or fine porcelain bisque. They can have molded hair, have painted bald heads or take wigs. The majority have no joints, with hands extended and legs separate (some are together). They generally come without clothes and they can have painted-on boots, shoes and socks or be barefooted.

It must be noted that in 1976 a large amount of the 15½-16" "Charlie" figures were reproduced in Germany and are excellent quality. It is almost impossible to tell these are reproductions.

Prices are for doll figures without any damage. More must be allowed for any with unusual hairdos, an early face or molded eyelids or molded-on clothes.

All China: Glazed with black or blonde hair, excellent quality of painting and unjointed. 2" - $55.00; 5" - $110.00; 7" - $135.00; 9" - $225.00; 10" - $250.00. Bald head with wig: 6" - $145.00; 8" - $195.00; 10" - $275.00. **Charlie:** Molded black hair, flesh tones to neck and head. 14" - $400.00; 17" - $550.00. Blonde: 14-15" - $500.00.

Untinted Bisque (Parian): Molded hair, unjointed. 4" - $150.00; 7" - $185.00.

Untinted Bisque: 1860's. Molded hair, jointed at shoulders. 4" - $160.00; 7" - $250.00.

Stone Bisque: Unjointed, molded hair, medium to excellent quality of painting. 4" - $55.00; 8" - $75.00.

Black Charlotte or Charlie: Unjointed, no damage. 3" - $200.00; 5" - $365.00; 7" - $400.00. Jointed at shoulders: 4" - $225.00; 7" - $425.00.

Molded Head Band: Excellent quality: 5" - $250.00; 8" - $385.00. Medium quality: 5" - $125.00; 8" - $175.00.

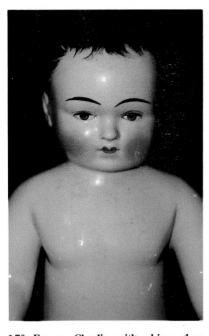

15" Frozen Charlie with china glaze finish. Made all in one piece. Light flesh tones on head and neck. Brush strokes around face. 15" - $465.00. Courtesy Shirley Bertrand.

16½" Frozen Charlie with garter type ribbon holding tiny Frozen Charlottes. Shown with 32" marked "F. 11 G." (block letters). Pale bisque and closed mouth with modeled tongue. Fully jointed body. 16½" - $585.00. 32" - $6,400.00. Courtesy Frasher Doll Auctions.

Molded-on Clothes or Bonnet: Unjointed, no damage and medium to excellent quality. 6" - $450.00; 8" - $550.00.

Dressed: In original clothes. Unjointed Charlotte or Charlie. No damage and in overall excellent condition. 5" - $135.00; 7" - $185.00.

Jointed at Shoulder: Original clothes and no damage. 6" - $175.00; 8" - $285.00.

Molded-on, Painted Boots: Unjointed, no damage. 5" - $185.00; 7" - $265.00. Jointed at shoulders: 5" - $225.00; 7" - $350.00.

FULPER

Fulper Pottery Co. of Flemington, N.J. made dolls from 1918-1921. They made children and babies and used composition and kid bodies.

Marks:

Made in U.S.A.

Child: Fair to medium quality bisque head painting. No damage, nicely dressed. Composition body, open mouth: 15" - $450.00; 17" - $565.00; 21" - $675.00. Kid body, open mouth: 15" - $400.00; 17" - $500.00; 21" - $625.00.

Child: Poor quality (white chalky look, may have crooked mouth and be poorly painted.) Composition body: 16" - $350.00; 21" - $450.00. Kid body: 16" - $200.00; 21" - $365.00.

Baby: Bent limb body. Fair to medium quality bisque, open mouth, no damage and dressed well. Good artist work on features. 14-15" - $525.00; 525.00; 19" - $650.00; 26" - $1,000.00.

Toddler: Same as baby but has toddler jointed or straight leg body. 17" - $700.00; 26" - $1,200.00.

Baby: Poor quality bisque and painting. 17" - $225.00; 26" - $475.00.

Toddler: Poor quality bisque and painting. 17" - $345.00; 26" - $700.00.

Left: 30" marked "Fulper" with open mouth and two upper teeth. On fully jointed body. Right: 30" child marked "DEP 13." Open mouth, on French jointed body. 30" - $1,700.00; DEP - $2,300.00. Courtesy Frasher Doll Auctions.

GANS & SEYFARTH

Dolls with the "G.S." or "G & S" were made by Gans & Seyfarth of Germany who made dolls from 1909 into the 1930's. Some dolls will be marked with the full name.

Child: Open mouth, composition body. Good quality bisque, no damage and nicely dressed. 14" - $295.00; 17" - $365.00; 21" - $485.00; 27" - $850.00.

Baby: Bent limb baby body, in perfect condition and nicely dressed. 16" - $425.00; 19" - $600.00.; 23" - $750.00; 26" - $875.00. (Add more for toddler body.)

GERMAN DOLLS, MAKER UNKNOWN

Some of these unmarked dolls will have a mold number and/or a head size number and some may have the mark "Germany."

Closed Mouth Child: 1880-1890's. Composition jointed body, no damage and nicely dressed. 12" - $1,200.00; 15" - $1,500.00; 20" - $2,100.00; 24" - $2,600.00.

Closed Mouth Child: On kid body (or cloth). May have slight turned head, bisque lower arms. 12" - $600.00; 15" - $800.00; 20" - $1,100.00; 24" - $1,300.00.

Open Mouth Child: Late 1880's to 1900. Excellent pale bisque, jointed composition body. Glass eyes, no damage and nicely dressed. 12" - $385.00; 15" - $465.00; 20" - $600.00; 23" - $700.00; 26" - $850.00; 30" - $1,300.00.

13" marked "3094." Maker unknown. Open mouth, kid body with bisque lower arms. Glass eyes and original costume. 13" - $425.00.

16" unmarked German lady. Solid dome shoulder head with closed mouth. Cloth body with sewn-on boots and leather arms. 16" - $2,400.00. Courtesy Frasher Doll Auctions.

Open Mouth Child: Same as above, but on kid body with bisque lower arms. 12" - $185.00; 15" - $325.00; 20" - $465.00; 23" - $550.00; 26" - $700.00; 30" - $1,000.00.

Open Mouth Child: 1900-1920's. With very "dolly" type face. Overall excellent condition, composition jointed body. 12" - $265.00; 15" - $325.00; 18" - $425.00; 22" - $600.00.

Open Mouth Child: Same as above, but with kid body and bisque lower arms. 12" - $125.00; 15" - $225.00; 18" - $325.00; 22" - $475.00.

Belton Type: 12" - $1,350.00; 15" - $1,650.00; 20" - $2,250.00; 24" - $2,500.00.

Bonnet or Hatted: Bisque head with modeled-on bonnet or hat, molded hair and painted features. Cloth body with bisque limbs. No damage and nicely dressed. Dates from about 1880's into 1920's.

Bisque: 12" - $450.00 up; 16" - $650.00 up.

Stone Bisque: White-ish and more porous than bisque. 11" - $250.00; 15" - $475.00.

Glass Eyes, Closed Mouth: Excellent overall quality. 16" - $2,400.00; 19" - $3,000.00; 23" - $3,800.00.

All Bisque: See "All Bisque – German" section.

Molded Hair: See that section.

Infants: Bisque head, molded/painted hair, cloth body with composition or celluloid hands, glass eyes. No damage. 10-12" - $365.00; 16" - $645.00; 20" - $800.00.

Babies: Solid dome or wigged, glass eyes, five-piece baby body, open mouth, nicely dressed and no damage. (Allow more for closed or open/closed mouth or very unusual face and toddler doll.) 8-9" - $265.00; 14" - $500.00; 17" - $600.00; 22" - $750.00. Toddler: 14" - $600.00; 17" - $700.00.

Babies: Same as above, but with painted eyes. 8-9" - $285.00; 14" - $485.00; 17" - $600.00; 22" - $785.00.

8½" marked "18" on head. On five-piece paper maché body. All original with metal helmet and has crown on belt buckle. 8½" - $485.00. Courtesy Shirley Bertrand.

Tiny Unmarked Doll: Head is bisque of good quality on five-piece papier maché or composition body, glass eyes, open mouth. No damage. 6" - $245.00; 9" - $325.00; 12" - $425.00.

Tiny Doll: Same as above, but on full jointed composition body. 6" - $295.00; 9" - $450.00; 12" - $525.00.

Tiny Doll: Closed mouth, jointed body. 6" - $350.00; 9" - $465.00; 12" - $650.00. Five-piece body: 6" - $275.00; 9" - $375.00; 12" - $445.00.

Character Child: Unidentified, closed mouth, very character face, may have wig or solid dome, glass eyes, closed or open/closed mouth. Excellent quality bisque, no damage and nicely dressed. 16" - $3,600.00; 20" - $4,500.00.

Character: Closed mouth, glass eyes. Mold numbers 128, 134, and others of this quality. 16" - $7,500.00 up; 22" - $10,000.00 up. Painted eyes: 16" - $6,000.00 up; 22" - $8,500.00 up. **Mold #111:** Glass eyes: 20" - $22,000.00 up. Painted eyes: 20" - $14,000.00 up. **Mold #163:** 14-15" - $925.00.

6" party favors with bisque heads, glass eyes, crepe paper clothes. Both have closed mouths and wood handle "bodies." 6" - $400.00 up. Courtesy Shirley Bertrand.

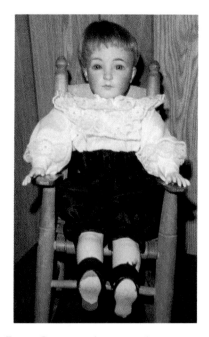

Rare German character from mold number 111. Maker unknown but suspected to be one of the missing Kammer & Reinhardt numbers. Glass eyes, closed mouth and very sweet expression. 20" - $22,000.00. Courtesy Violette Steinke.

This very desirable German character is marked "111" and is thought to be the missing Kammer & Reinhardt "111." Sweet expression, closed mouth and sleep eyes, jointed composition body. 12" - $11,000.00. Courtesy Frasher Doll Auctions.

Gladdie was designed by Helen Jensen in 1929. The German-made doll was distributed by George Borgfeldt. The cloth body has composition limbs, and the head has glass eyes. (See photos in Series 5, pg. 69; Series 6, pg. 92; Series 7, pg. 79.)

Ceramic Style Head: 16-17" - $975.00; 19-20" - $1,150.00 up.

Bisque Head: Mold #1410. 16-17" - $4,200.00; 19-20" - $5,300.00; 25-26" - $6,700.00.

18" "Gladdie" with biscaloid swivel head, molded hair, sleep eyes and open/closed mouth with teeth and tongue. Cloth body with composition limbs. 18" - $1,000.00. Courtesy Frasher Doll Auctions.

GOEBEL

The Goebel factory has been operating since 1879 and is located in Oeslau, Germany. The interwoven W.G. mark has been used since 1879. William Goebel inherited the factory from his father, Franz Detlev Goebel. About 1900, the factory only made dolls, dolls heads and porcelain figures. They worked in both bisque and china glazed items.

Marks:

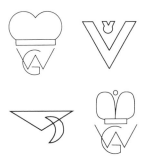

Child: 1895 and later. Open mouth, composition body, sleep or set eyes with head in perfect condition, dressed and ready to display. 16" - $395.00; 20"- $500.00; 24" - $625.00.

Child: Open/closed mouth, wig, molded teeth, shoulder plate, kid body, bisque hands. 17" - $800.00; 20" - $950.00.

Child: Deeply molded hair, intaglio eyes, open/closed mouth, smile, jointed body. (See photo in Series 7, pg. 80.) 12" - $1,800.00; 15" - $3,200.00; 18" - $4,000.00.

Character: After 1910. Molded hair that can be in various styles, with or without molded flowers or ribbons, painted features and on five-piece papier maché body. No damage and nicely dressed. 7" - $365.00; 9" - $465.00; 12" - $575.00.

Character Baby: After 1909. Open mouth, sleep eyes and on five-piece bent limb baby body. No damage and nicely dressed. 13" - $450.00; 16" - $600.00; 20" - $700.00; 25" - $950.00. Toddler:

13" - $585.00; 16" - $750.00; 20" - $850.00.

Molded-on Bonnet: Closed mouth, five-piece papier maché body, painted features and may have various molded-on hats or bonnets and painted hair. 7" - $385.00; 9" - $525.00; 12" - $650.00.

26" marked Goebel baby with sleep eyes and hair lashes, open mouth and on five-piece bent limb baby body. 26" - $1,500.00 up. Courtesy Turn of Century Antiques.

GOOGLY

Bisque head with glass or set eyes to the side, closed smiling mouth, impish or watermelon-style mouth, original composition or papier maché body. Molded hair or wigged. 1911 and after. Not damaged in any way and nicely dressed.

All Bisque: See All Bisque section.

Armand Marseille: #200: 8" - $1,600.00; 12" - $2,600.00. **#210:** 9" - $2,400.00; 11" - $3,000.00. **#223:** 6" - $850.00; 9" - $1,100.00. **#240, 241:** 10-11" - $2,450.00; 13" - $2,900.00. **#248:** 9" - $1,100.00. **#252:** 7" - $900.00. **#253, 353:** 6" - $750.00; 8" - $900.00; 12" - $1,300.00. **#254:** 9" - $975.00. **#255-#310:** (Just Me) 8-9" - $1,200.00; 11" - $1,600.00; 13-13½" - $1,850.00. **#310** with painted bisque: 8" - $775.00; 12"- $1,000.00. **#320:** 9" - $1,300.00. Glass eyes: $1,100.00. Painted eyes: 6" - $750.00; 8" - $900.00. **#323:** Fired-in color: 6" - $675.00; 9" - $1,050.00; 12" - $1,550.00. On baby body: 13" - $1,300.00.

Painted bisque: 8" - $500.00; 12" - $775.00. **#325:** 8" - $750.00; 11" - $950.00.

B.P. (Bahr & Proschild) #686: 12" - $2,500.00; 14" - $2,900.00 Baby: 12" - $1,500.00.

Demalcol: (See photo in Series 7, pg. 82) 10" - $650.00; 14" - $850.00.

Hertel Schwab: See that section.

Heubach Einco: 9-10" - $4,800.00; 15" - $7,500.00; 17" - $8,200.00.

Heubach (marked in square): 8" - $975.00; 12" - $1,800.00. **#8676:** 6½" - $725.00; 10" - $1,100.00. **#9573:** 9" - $1,800.00; 12" - $2,200.00. **#9578, 11173:** Called "Tiss Me." 8" - $1,200.00 up.

Heubach Koppelsdorf: (See photo in Series 6, pg. 96) **#260, 261, 263, 264:** 6" - $365.00; 8-9" - $475.00. **#318:** 8" - $1,200.00; 13" - $2,000.00. **#319:** 7" - $675.00; 11" - $1,200.00. **#417:** 8" - $550.00; 12" - $1,200.00.

Kestner: #163, 165: (This number now attributed to Hertel & Schwab): 14" - $4,700.00; 16" - $5,600.00. **#172-173** (Attributed to Hertel & Schwab): 14" - $5,600.00; 16" - $6,400.00. **#217, 221:** 6" - $1,300.00; 10" - $3,500.00; 12-13" - $4,600.00; 14" - $5,100.00; 16" - $5,700.00; 17" - $5,850.00.

Kammer & Reinhardt (K star R): 9" on five-piece body: $2,700.00. **#131:** 10" - $5,400.00; 14" - $7,300.00.

Kley & Hahn (K&H): Mold #180. 15" - $2,900.00; 17" - $3,400.00.

Oscar Hitt: 13" - $6,000.00; 16" - $8,000.00.

P.M. (Otto Reinecke): #950: 7" - $1,150.00; 9" - $1,400.00; 14" - $2,600.00.

S.F.B.J.: #245: (See photo in Series 6, pg. 96) 9" on five-piece body: $1,600.00. 12" on fully jointed body: 12" - $2,800.00; 15" - $5,800.00.

Steiner, Herm: 9" - $900.00; 12" - $1,000.00.

Composition Face: Very round composition face mask or all composition head with wig, glass eyes to side and closed impish watermelon-style mouth. Body is stuffed felt. In original clothes and all in excellent condition. 7" - $450.00; 11" - $675.00; 13" - $900.00; 15" - $1,100.00; 19" - $1,600.00. Fair condition, cracks or crazing, nicely redressed: 7" - $175.00; 11" - $325.00; 13" - $450.00; 15" - $525.00; 19" - $750.00.

Left to right: 16" Hertel Schwab mold #165 with jointed body and glass eyes. 12" marked "D.R.G.M. 9546-49" with disc googly eyes, cloth body, flange neck, molded hair. 12" Kestner 221 on fully jointed body, large glass eyes. 10" Gebruder Heubach winker with molded hair and on five-piece body. 16" - $5,600.00; 12" "D.R.G.M." - $2,200.00; 12" Kestner - $4,600.00; 10" - $1,800.00. Courtesy Ellen Dodge.

Painted Eyes: Composition or papier maché body with painted-on shoes and socks. Bisque head with eyes painted to side, closed smile mouth and molded hair. Not damaged and nicely dressed (such as A.M. 320, Goebel, R.A., Heubach, etc.): 6" - $365.00; 8" - $525.00; 10" - $645.00; 12" - $725.00.

Disc Eyes: Bisque socket head or shoulder head with molded hair (can have molded hat-cap), closed mouth and inset celluloid disc in large googly eyes. 10" - $1,100.00; 14" - $1,400.00; 17" - $1,700.00; 21" - $2,100.00.

Molded-on Military Hat: (See photo in Series 5, pg. 71; Series 7, pg. 82) Marked "Elite." 12" - $2,800.00; 16" - $4,400.00. Japanese Soldier: 12" - $3,400.00.

Left: 12" very rare two-face Googly marked "DEP Elite." Faces have inset glass eyes. One side has red cap and represents a Turk; the other side represents Austria. Right: 12" marked "DEP Elite" with German uniform and helmet. Both dolls have jointed bodies. Two-faced - $4,000.00; German - $2,700.00. Courtesy Frasher Doll Auctions.

Left to right: 6" marked "Nobbikid 1-B A.M. 253 Reg. U.S. Pat. Off. Germany 11/0." Cute 7" A.M. 253 with pale bisque. Same mold as other, but lips differ. 12" "Baby Bright Eyes" marked "A.M. 252 G.B." Intaglio eyes, baby body. 8" A.M. "Just Me," mold #310. Five-piece body, tagged "Vogue" clothes. 8" original Gebruder Heubach with molded hair, five-piece body. 6" - $750.00; 7" - $800.00; 12" - $1,100.00; 8" "Just Me" - $900.00; 8" Heubach - $975.00. Courtesy Ellen Dodge.

Large 13" "Just Me," mold number 310 by Armand Marseille. Googly glass eyes to the side, closed mouth, original wig and most likely original clothes. Fired-in face color. Shown with two 10" German bisque head candy containers, ca. 1900. Smiling open/closed mouth and painted eyes. Girl has bisque legs. 13" "Just Me" - $1,400.00; Containers - $550.00 pair. Courtesy Frasher Doll Auctions.

Right: 8" impish "Gretel" designed by Hansi. Molded and painted hair and features. Jointed body with modeled-on shoes and socks. Original clothes. Made of composition celluloid-type material called "prialytine." Left: 12" Kammer & Reinhardt, mold #114. Jointed body, original clothes. 8" - $350.00; 12" - $3,400.00. Courtesy Frasher Doll Auctions.

GREINER

Ludwig Greiner of Philadelphia, PA, made dolls from 1858 into the late 1800's. The heads are made of papier maché, and they can be found on various bodies. Some can be all cloth; many homemade. Many have leather arms or can be found on Lacmann bodies that have stitched joints at the hips and the knees and are very wide at the hip line. The Lacmann bodies will be marked "J. Lacmann's Patent March 24th, 1874" in an oval. The Greiner heads will be marked "Greiner's Patent Doll Heads/

Pat. Mar. 30, '58." Also "Greiner's/Improved/Patent Heads/Pat. Mar. 30, '58." The later heads are marked "Greiner's Patent Doll Heads/Pat. Mar. 30, '58. Ext. '72."

Greiner Doll: Can have black or blonde molded hair, blue or brown painted eyes and be on a nice homemade cloth body with cloth arms or a commerical cloth body with leather arms. Dressed for the period and clean, with head in near perfect condition with no paint chips and not repainted.

With '58 Label: 17" - $900.00; 23" - $1,200.00; 26" - $1,400.00; 29" - $1,650.00; 34" - $1,900.00; 37" - $2,300.00. With chips and flakes or repainted: 17" - $550.00; 23" - $750.00; 26" - $875.00; 29" - $950.00; 34" - $1,100.00; 37" - $1,500.00.

With '72 Label: 18" - $650.00; 24" - $1,000.00; 29" - $1,300.00; 35" - $1,500.00. With chips and flakes or repainted: 18" - $400.00; 25" - $525.00; 29" - $700.00; 35" - $900.00.

Glass Eyes: 22" - $2,200.00; 27" - $2,700.00. With chips and flakes or repainted: 22" - $975.00; 27" - $1,200.00.

Unmarked: So called "Pre-Greiner," ca. 1850. Papier maché shoulder head, cloth body can be home-made. Leather, wood or cloth limbs. Painted hair, black eyes with no pupils. Glass eyes, old or original clothes. Good condition: 19" - $1,100.00; 27" - $1,600.00; 32" - $2,150.00. Fair condition: 19" - $700.00; 27" - $875.00; 32" - $1,000.00.

30" Greiner in beautiful condition. Has Mar. 30th, '58 patent date. Papier maché with cloth body and cloth/leather limbs. Eyes painted, blonde hair with comb marks. 30" - **$1,750.00.** Courtesy Turn of Century Antiques.

HALF DOLLS (PINCUSHIONS)

Half dolls can be made of any material including bisque, papier maché and composition. Not all half dolls were used as pin cushions. They were also used for powder box tops, brushes, tea cozies, etc. Most date from 1900 into the 1930's. The majority were made in Germany, but many were made in Japan. Generally, they will be marked with "Germany" or "Japan." Some have numbers; others may have the marks of companies such as William Goebel or Dressel, Kister & Co.

The most desirable are the large figures, or any size for that matter, that have both arms molded away from the body or are jointed at the shoulder.

(Allow more if marked by maker.)

Arms and hands extended: Prices can be higher depending on detail and rarity of figure. China or bisque: 3" - $125.00 up; 5" - $265.00 up; 8" - $575.00 up; 12" - $1,000.00 up.

Arms extended: But hands attached to figure. China or bisque: 3" - $65.00; 5" - $95.00; 8" - $125.00. Papier maché or composition: 5" - $35.00; 7" - $95.00.

Bald Head: Arms away: 4" - $145.00 up. Arms attached: 4" - $85.00 up.

Common Figures: Arms and hands attached. China: 3" - $30.00; 5" - $40.00; 8" - $55.00. Papier maché or composition: 3" - $20.00; 5" - $30.00; 8" - $40.00.

Jointed Shoulders: China or bisque: 5" - $100.00; 8" - $125.00; 10" - $165.00. Papier maché: 4" - $35.00; 7" - $75.00. Wax over papier maché: 4" - $40.00; 7" - $100.00.

Children or Men: 3" - $50.00; 5" - $75.00; 7" - $100.00. Jointed shoulders: 3" - $65.00; 5" - $95.00; 7" - $165.00.

Japan marked: 3" - $20.00; 5" - $30.00; 7" - $50.00.

Top: Marked with Goebel crown "45.4." 5½" tall with molded eyelids, original wig. Both arms are away from body. Lower left: Beautiful Dressel & Kister with modeled-on hat and both arms away. Right: 5½" Dressel & Kister with molded scarf that is fanned out in the back. Jointed arms, molded eyelids. 5½" - $450.00 up. Courtesy Ellen Dodge.

All three are 5-5½" tall and have arms molded away from body. Lower right figure has modeled on bracelet. 5-5½" - $450.00 up. Courtesy Ellen Dodge.

6½" beautiful half doll marked with crown. Serene face and both arms molded away from body. 6½" - $300.00 up.

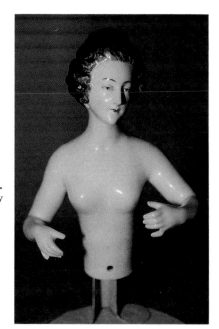

HALF DOLLS (PINCUSHIONS)

5½" wonderful half doll by Goebel. Detailed "Woman from upper Bavaria with rose in hand." Fine adult features and excellent overall modelling. Shown with 27" Kestner child. Closed mouth and fully jointed body. 5½" - $450.00; 27" - $4,000.00. Courtesy Frasher Doll Auctions.

Left: 2" with legs attached to base. Right: 3" attached to base. 2", not on base - $45.00; 3", not on base - $65.00. Courtesy Frasher Doll Auctions.

HANDWERCK, HEINRICH

Heinrich Handwerck began making dolls and doll bodies in 1876 at Gotha, Germany. Majority of their heads were made by Simon & Halbig. In 1897 they patented, in Germany, a ball jointed body #100297 and some of their bodies will be marked with this number.

Mold numbers include: **12x, 19, 23, 69, 79, 89, 99, 100, 109, 118, 119, 124, 125, 139, 152, 189, 199, 1001, 1200, 1290.**

Child: No mold number. After 1885. Open mouth, sleep or set eyes, on ball jointed body. Bisque head with no cracks, chips or hairlines, good wig and nicely dressed. 14" - $400.00; 17" - $485.00; 21" - $575.00; 24" - $695.00; 28" - $1,000.00; 32" - $1,400.00; 37" - $1,900.00; 41" - $2,500.00.

Sample mold marks:

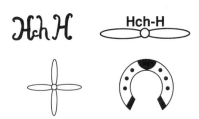

Child: Same as above but with mold marks. 12" - $525.00; 14" - $575.00; 17" - $625.00; 21" - $700.00; 24" - $825.00; 28" - $1,100.00; 32" - $1,600.00; 35-36" - $2,000.00; 42" - $3,500.00.

Kid Body: Bisque shoulder head, open mouth. All in good condition and nicely dressed. 15" - $350.00; 20" - $475.00; 24" - $600.00; 26" - $875.00.

Closed Mouth: Mold #79, 89, 99, etc. Marked with company name and sometimes with Simon & Halbig. 12" - $1,400.00; 16" - $1,800.00; 20" - $2,200.00; 24" - $2,600.00.

Life-size 45" marked "79/19 Handwerck/ Germany 9." Original wig and boxed nude in original shipping case with padded silk lining. Because of the size, this doll may have been designed as a mannequin. Doll was purchased at the King Farouk Estate Sale in 1977. 45" - $4,500.00. Courtesy Frasher Doll Auctions.

32" marked "Heinrich/S&H." Has almond-shaped eyes with hair lashes, open mouth and on fully jointed body. 32" - $1,400.00. Courtesy Turn of Century Antiques.

Max Handwerck started making dolls in 1900 and his factory was located at Waltershausen, Germany. In 1901, he registered "Bébé Elite" with the heads made by William Goebel. The dolls from this firm are marked with the full name, but a few are marked with "M.H."

Child: Bisque head, open mouth, sleep or set eyes, on fully jointed composition body, no damage and nicely dressed. **Mold #287, 291, etc.:** 15" - $400.00; 19" - $500.00; 23" - $625.00; 27" - $775.00; 34" - $1,400.00; 39" - $2,100.00.

Bébé Elite: (See photo in Series 7, pg. 88) Bisque heads with no cracks or chips, sleep or set eyes, open mouth. Can have a flange neck on cloth body with composition limbs or be on a bent leg composition baby body. Upper teeth and smile: 16" - $465.00; 20" - $665.00. Toddler: 16" - $600.00; 20" - $800.00; 25" - $1,200.00. Socket head on fully jointed body: 16" - $585.00; 20" - $800.00.

HERTEL, SCHWAB & CO.

Hertel, Schwab & Co. has been recognized as the maker of many dolls that were attributed to other companies all these years (by the German authors Jurgen and Marianne Cieslik.) There does not seem to be a "common denominator" to the Hertel, Schwab line of dolls and it can include any style.

Babies: Bisque head, molded hair or wig, open or open/closed mouth, sleep or painted eyes, bent limb baby body. No damage and all in good condition.

Mold #125, 127 ("Patsy"): 12-13" - $925.00; 16" - $1,050.00.

Mold #126: "Skippy" 11" - $975.00; 14-15" - $1,200.00.

Mold numbers: 130, 136, 142, 150, 151, 152, 153, 154: 9" - $300.00; 11" - $425.00; 14" - $550.00; 18" - $625.00; 23" - $825.00.

Child: Bisque head, painted or sleep eyes, closed mouth, jointed composition body, no damage and nicely dressed. **#119, 134, 141, 149:** 15" - $5,000.00; 19" - $7,200.00. **#154 with Closed Mouth:** 17" - $2,500.00; 23" - $2,800.00. Open Mouth: 18" - $1,200.00; 22" - $1,600.00. **#169:** Closed mouth. 21" - $3,700.00; 24" - $4,200.00. **Toddler:** 21" - $3,900.00; 24" - $4,500.00. Open mouth: 21", $1,200.00; 24" - $1,600.00.

18½" turned head with closed mouth, excellent quality bisque, and glass eyes. Kid body with bisque lower arms. 18½" - $2,500.00. Courtesy Frasher Doll Auctions.

All Bisque: One-piece body and head, glass eyes, closed or open mouth. All in perfect condition. **Prize Baby (mold #208):** 6" - $350.00; 8" - $550.00. Swivel Neck: 6" - $485.00; 8" - $750.00; 10" - $875.00. (See #222 below.)

Googly: Wig or molded hair. Large, side glance sleep or set eyes. Closed mouth, no damage and nicely dressed. **#163:** 11" - $3,000.00; 15" - $5,400.00. **#165:** 11" - $3,000.00; 15" - $5,600.00; **#172, 173:** 11" - $4,000.00; 15" - $6,600.00 **#222 (Our Fairy):** Painted eyes, molded hair. 9" - $1,600.00; 11" - $2,250.00. Wig and glass eyes. 9" - $1,900.00; 11" - $2,500.00.

10" Hertel, Schwab & Co. baby marked "151." Sleep eyes and open/closed mouth. 10" - $400.00. Courtesy Frasher Doll Auctions.

HEUBACH, GEBRUDER

The Heubach Brothers (Gebruder) made dolls from 1863 into the 1930's at Lichte, Thuringia, Germany. They started producing character dolls in 1910. Heubach dolls can reflect almost every mood and are often found on rather crude, poor quality bodies, and many are small dolls.

Marks:

Character Dolls: Bisque head, open/closed or closed mouth, painted eyes (allow more for glass eyes), on kid, papier maché or jointed composition bodies. Molded hair or wig. No damage and nicely dressed.

#1017: Baby faced toddler with open mouth. 20" - $1,600.00; 24" - $1,950.00; 30" - $2,500.00.

#2850: Open/closed mouth, two rows teeth. Molded braided hair, blue ribbon bow. 16" - $9,500.00 up; 20" - $12,000.00 up.

#5636: Laughing child, intaglio painted eyes. 9" - $900.00; 12" - $1,200.00. Glass eyes: 12" - $1,600.00; 15" - $2,100.00.

#5689: Open mouth, smiling. 15" - $1,800.00; 19" - $2,500.00; 26" - $4,200.00.

#5730 (Santa): 15" - $2,500.00; 19" - $3,000.00; 28" - $3,500.00.

30" marked **"1017 14 Heubach"** in square. 18" head circumference. Open mouth with two upper teeth. Toddler body with composition arms and legs and stuffed cloth torso, flange type neck on bisque head. 30" - $2,500.00. Courtesy Frasher Doll Auctions.

#5777, 7307, 9355 (Dolly Dimples): Ball jointed body. 15" - $1,700.00; 21" - $3,000.00; 25" - $3,500.00.

#6692: Shoulder head, smiling, intaglio eyes. 16" - $975.00.

#6736, 6894: Laughing, wide open/closed mouth, molded lower teeth. 9" - $850.00; 15" - $1,800.00.

#6896: Pouty, jointed body. 16" - $875.00; 20" - $1,200.00.

#6969, 6970, 7246, 7347, 8017, 8420: Pouty boy or girl, jointed body, painted eyes. 10" - $975.00; 12" -

$1,250.00; 15" - $1,900.00; 19" - $2,300.00. Toddler: 20" - $2,600.00; 24" - $3,200.00. Glass eyes: 15" - $2,900.00; 19" - $3,500.00; 23" - $4,100.00. Toddler, glass eyes: 19" - $3,700.00; 24" - $4,500.00.

#7172, 7550: 15" - $1,600.00.

#7448: Open/closed mouth, eyes half shut. 15" - $2,900.00.

#7602: Painted eyes and hair, long face pouty, closed mouth. 15" - $2,700.00; 21" - $3,100.00 up. Glass eyes: 15" - $3,500.00; 21" - $3,700.00 up.

#7604: Laughing, jointed body, intaglio eyes. 10" - $525.00; 13" - $775.00. Baby: 15" - $875.00.

#7616: Open/closed mouth with molded tongue. Socket or shoulder head. Glass eyes: 13" - $1,600.00; 16" - $2,100.00.

#7622, 76262: Molded hair, intaglio eyes, closed mouth and light cheek dimples. 14" - $1,900.00; 17" - $2,800.00.

#7623: Molded hair, intaglio eyes, open/closed mouth, molded tongue, on bent limb baby body. 11" - $800.00; 15" - $1,250.00. Jointed body: 16" - $1,600.00; 20" - $1,900.00.

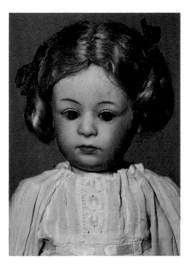

14" Heubach mold **#6969** with glass eyes, pouty closed mouth, original wig. 14" - **$2,900.00.** Courtesy Barbara Earnshaw-Cain.

#7634: Crying, squinting eyes. 13" - $975.00; 16" - $1,350.00.

#7636: 12" - $975.00.

#7644: Laughing, socket or shoulder head, intaglio eyes. 14" - $800.00; 17" - $1,100.00.

#7665: Smile. 16" - $1,850.00

#7661, 7686: Black, wide open/closed mouth, deeply molded hair. 10" - $1,200.00; 13" - $2,600.00; 16" - $3,800.00. White: 13" - $2,200.00; 16" - $3,600.00.

#7669, 7679: Open/closed mouth, laughing, glass eyes. Walker: 13" - $1,800.00; 16" - $2,200.00.

7668, 7671: Black, intaglio eyes. Open/closed mouth. 9" - $1,400.00; 11" - $2,000.00; 13" - $2,400.00.

#7679: Whistler, socket head. 15" - $1,300.00; 17" - $1,600.00.

Mold #7679 character Gebruder Heubach with open/closed mouth, glass eyes. (Some marked #7669 also.) Key wound walker with composition body, wire upper arms and bisque lower arms. Original clothes and wig. 12" - $1,800.00; 16" - $2,200.00 up. Courtesy Barbara Earnshaw-Cain.

11½" Gebruder Heubach mold #7246 with very pouty expression. Closed mouth and glass sleep eyes. Fully jointed body. Shown with 4" all bisque in sitting position with modeled bottle in one hand and kitten in other. Made in Germany. 11½" - $975.00; 4" - $200.00. Courtesy Frasher Doll Auctions.

#7684: Screamer. 13" - $975.00; 15" - $1,250.00

#7701: Pouty, intaglio eyes. 16" - $1,600.00; 19" - $2,000.00.

#7711: Open mouth, jointed body. 12" - $465.00; 15" - $875.00; 21" - $900.00; 23" - $1,100.00.

#7745: Wide open/closed mouth, two painted lower teeth, molded hair. Baby or toddler: 16" - $1,975.00.

#7764: Open/closed mouth, intaglio eyes to side, deeply sculptured hair, large bow. 5-piece body or toddler body. 14" - $1,100.00 up; 17" - $1,800.00 up.

#7768, #7788: "Coquette," tilted head, molded hair and can have ribbon modeled into hairdo. 10" - $725.00; 12" -

$975.00; 14" - $1,100.00; 17" - $1,800.00. Swivel neck: 8" - $550.00; 10" - $875.00.

#7849: Closed mouth, intaglio eyes. 12" - $750.00.

#7852, 7862, 119: Braids coiled around ear (molded), intaglio eyes. 16" - $2,800.00 up; 18" - $3,300.00 up.

#7911: Grin. 14-15" - $1,250.00.

#7925, 7926: Adult, painted eyes: 16" - $3,600.00 up. Glass eyes: 18" - $4,600.00.

#7958: Deeply modeled hair and bangs. Dimples, open/closed mouth, intaglio eyes. 17" - $4,000.00.

#7959: Intaglio eyes, molded on bonnet and deeply molded hair, open/closed mouth. 16" - $3,500.00; 20" - $4,600.00 up.

#7977, #7877: "Stuart Baby," molded baby bonnet. Painted eyes: 10" - $1,100.00; 13" - $1,450.00; 15" - $1,800.00; 17" - $2,200.00. Glass eyes: 12" - $2,150.00, 14" - $2,400.00; 16" - $2,650.00.

17" Heubach, mold #7862. Has bisque shoulderplate, open/closed mouth, modeled teeth, and molded coiled hair braids. Kid body with bisque lower arms. Shown with 3½" Kewpie seated in wicker chair. 17" - $3,200.00; Kewpie - $500.00. Courtesy Frasher Doll Auctions.

#8050: Lightly modeled hair, intaglio eyes, open/closed laugh mouth with two rows of teeth. 17" - $2,800.00.

#8053: Round cheeks, closed mouth, painted eyes to side, large ears. 20" - $3,400.00.

#8145: Closed smile mouth, painted eyes to side, painted hair. Toddler: 15" - $1,500.00 up; 18" - $1,800.00 up.

#8191: Smiling openly, jointed body. 13" - $1,100.00; 15" - $1,300.00; 18" - $1,600.00.

#8192: Open/closed smiling mouth with tongue molded between teeth. 9" - $525.00; 12" - $800.00; 16" - $1,400.00; 23" - $2,500.00. Open mouth: 15" - $725.00; 18" - $1,000.00.

#8316: Open/closed mouth, molded teeth, smile, glass eyes, wig. 16" - $3,500.00 up; 19" - $4,700.00 up. Painted eyes: 14" - $1,200.00 up.

#8381: Closed mouth, pensive expression, painted eyes, molded hair, ribbon around head with bow, exposed ears. 17-18" - $3,400.00 up.

#8420: Pouty, painted eyes. 15" - $800.00; 18" - $975.00. Glass eyes: 13" - $1,500.00; 16" - $1,850.00; 20" - $3,000.00.

#8459, 8469: Wide open/closed laughing mouth, glass eyes. 12" - $2,700.00; 15" - $3,300.00.

#8555: Shoulder head, painted bulging eyes. 14" - $4,800.00.

#8556: Open/closed mouth, two teeth rows, intaglio eyes, molded hair, ribbon. 18" - $8,500.00; 21" - $9,800.00.

#8590: Closed mouth, puckered lips: 14" - $1,300.00; 17" - $1,900.00. Baby: 14" - $1,300.00; 16" - $1,600.00.

#8596: Smile, intaglio eyes. 15" - $800.00; 17" - $1,000.00.

#8648: Extremely pouty closed mouth, intaglio eyes to side. 19" - $2,600.00; 22" - $3,400.00.

#8774: "Whistling Jim," eyes to side and mouth modeled as if whistling. 14" - $1,000.00; 17" - $1,500.00.

#8868: Molded hair, glass eyes, closed mouth, very short chin. 16" - $1,800.00; 20" - $2,400.00.

#9141: Winking. Glass eyes: 9" - $1,500.00. Painted eyes: 7-8" - $950.00.

#9355: Shoulder head. 17" - $1,000.00; 23" - $1,800.00.

#9457: Indian. 16-17" - $4,600.00.

#9891: Molded-on cap, intaglio eyes. 12-13" - $1,800.00 up.

#10532: Open mouth, jointed body. 10" - $425.00; 14" - $675.00; 17" - $900.00; 20" - $1,300.00.

#10586, #10633: Child with open mouth, jointed body. 17" - $700.00; 22" - $950.00; 26" - $1,300.00.

#11173: Glass eyes, five-piece body, pursed closed mouth with large indented cheeks. Called "Tiss-Me." 8" - $1,500.00 up.

Child with Dolly-type Face (non-character): Open mouth, glass sleep or set eyes, jointed body, bisque head with no damage and nicely dressed. 14" - $475.00; 17" - $600.00; 21" - $850.00; 25" - $1,000.00.

Googly: Marked with a Heubach mark. Glass eyes: 8" - $975.00; 12" - $1,800.00; 14" - $2,600.00.

Indian Portrait: Man or woman. 14" - $3,500.00 up.

Babies or Infants: Bisque head, wig or molded hair, sleep or intaglio eyes, open/closed pouty-type mouths.

Mold #6894, #6898, #7602: 6" - $275.00; 9" - $400.00; 13" - $525.00; 16" - $650.00; 19" - $850.00; 24" - $1,200.00; 28" - $1,800.00.

Mold #7604: Laughing. 12-13" - $650.00.

Mold #7745, 7746: Laughing. 15-16" - $4,200.00.

Molded Bonnet: Deep modeling to bonnet. Molded hair to front and sides of face. 10-11" - $1,800.00.

16½" "Coquette" marked "Germany 4" and "Heubach" in square. Open/closed mouth and modeled ribbon and molded hair. Intaglio eyes to side. This style has painted teeth and others will not. This one has a bisque shoulder head and others will be a socket head. 16½" - $1,600.00. Courtesy Frasher Doll Auctions.

This 14" Heubach, mold #8555, is an extremely rare doll. Bisque shoulder-head with molded hair. Large, bulging, googly eyes that are looking downward. Open/closed mouth, kid body with bisque lower arms and composition lower straight legs. 14" - $4,800.00. Courtesy Frasher Doll Auctions.

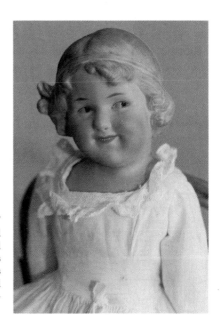

Ernst Heubach began making dolls in 1887 in Koppelsdorf, Germany and the marks of this firm can be the initials "E.H." or the dolls can be found marked with the full name, Heubach Koppelsdorf, or:

Some mold numbers from this company: **27X, 87, 99, 230, 235, 236, 237, 238, 242, 250, 251, 262, 271, 273, 275, 277, 283, 300, 302, 312, 317, 320, 321, 330, 338, 339, 340, 342, 349, 350, 367, 399, 407, 410, 417, 438, 444, 450, 452, 458, 616, 1310, 1342, 1900, 1901, 1906, 1909, 2504, 2671, 2757, 3027, 3412, 3423, 3427, 7118, 32144.**

Child: #250, 275, 302 etc.: After 1888. Jointed body, open mouth, sleep or set eyes. No damage and nicely dressed. 8" - $200.00; 10" - $225.00; 14" - $325.00; 18" - $425.00; 22" - $525.00; 26" - $700.00; 30" - $950.00; 35" - $1,200.00.

Child: On kid body with bisque lower arms, bisque shoulder head, some turned head, open mouth. No damage and nicely dressed. 15" - $225.00; 19" - $365.00; 23" - $425.00; 28" - $750.00.

Child: Painted bisque. 8" - $145.00; 12" - $200.00.

Babies: #300, 320, 342, etc. 1910 and after. On five-piece bent limb baby body, open mouth with some having wobbly tongue and pierced nostrils. Sleep eyes. No damage and nicely dressed. 6" - $265.00; 10" - $365.00; 14" - $450.00; 19" - $550.00; 25" - $900.00.

Baby on Toddler Body: Same as above, but on a toddler body. 9-10" - $365.00; 15" - $575.00; 18" - $650.00; 22" - $875.00; 25" - $975.00.

Baby, Painted Bisque: Baby, 12" - $245.00; 15" - $325.00. Toddler, 16" - $500.00.

Infant: 1925 and after. Molded or painted hair, sleep eyes, closed mouth, flange neck bisque head on cloth body with composition or celluloid hands. No damage and nicely dressed. **#338, #340:** 12" - $600.00; 14" - $850.00. **#339, #349, #350:** 12" - $585.00; 14" - $785.00. **#399** (White only): 12" - $345.00.

18" marked "Heubach 275 4/0 Koppelsdorf" with open mouth, kid body with bisque lower arms and sleep eyes. 11" A.M. 390 in all original Scottish outfit with painted-on leggings and shoes. 6¾" all bisque with molded-on clothes. 18" - $425.00; 11" - no price available; 6¾" - $400.00. Courtesy Frasher Doll Auctions.

Infant: #339, 349, 350. Same as above but with fired-in tan or brown color. 12" - $585.00; 14" - $650.00.

#335, 340: Fired-in brown color. 14" - $750.00; 16" - $850.00.

#452: Tan/brown fired-in color bisque head with same color toddler body, open mouth, painted hair. Earings. No damage and originally dressed or redressed nicely. 12" - $525.00; 14" - $650.00.

Black or Dark Brown: #320, #339, #399: Painted bisque head, on five-piece baby body or toddler cut body. Sleep eyes, painted hair or wig. No damage and very minimum amount of paint pulls (chips) on back of head and none on face. 12" - $525.00; 14" - $585.00; 17" - $700.00; 21" - $950.00.

Character Child: 1910 on. Molded hair, painted eyes and open/closed mouth. No damage. **#262, #330 and others:** 12" - $500.00; 15" - $950.00.

24" Heubach Koppelsdorf baby with sleep eyes, open mouth and on five-piece bent limb baby body. 24" - $800.00. Courtesy Frasher Doll Auctions.

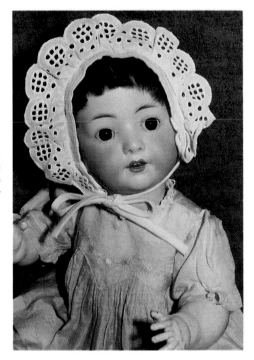

Large Heubach Koppelsdorf baby, mold #320. Open mouth, sleep eyes, and on five-piece bent limb baby body. 25" - $900.00. Courtesy Frasher Doll Auctions.

12" loveable character child marked "DEP. T.H./German 09." Made by Theodor Hornlein. Molded eyelids, intaglio eyes, open/closed mouth with teeth resting on molded tongue. On fully jointed body. 12" - $7,800.00; 16" - $10,000.00.
Courtesy Frasher Doll Auctions.

JULLIEN

Jullien marked dolls were made in Paris, France from 1875 to 1904. The heads will be marked Jullien and a size number. In 1892, Jullien advertised "L'Universal" and the label can be found on some of his doll bodies. (See photo in Series 7, pg. 96.)

Child: Closed mouth, paperweight eyes, French jointed body of composition, papier maché with some having wooden parts. Undamaged bisque head and all in excellent condition. 16" - $3,750.00; 19" - $4,300.00; 21" - $4,800.00; 23" - $5,000.00; 27" - $5,400.00.

Child: Same as above, but with open mouth. 16" - $1,700.00; 19" - $2,100.00; 21" - $2,400.00; 23" - $2,600.00; 27" - $3,000.00. Poor quality, high color: 16" - $1,200.00; 19" - $1,700.00; 21" - $2,000.00; 23" - $2,200.00.

JUMEAU

Known Jumeau Sizes: 0 – 8-9"; 1 – 10"; 2 – 11"; 3 – 12"; 4 – 13"; 5 – 14-15"; 6 – 16"; 7 – 17"; 8 – 19"; 9" – 20"; 10 – 21-22"; 11 – 24-25"; 12 – 26-27"; 13 – 29-30".

Tete Jumeau: 1879–1899 and later. Marked with red stamp on head and oval sticker on body. Closed mouth, paperweight eyes, jointed body with full joints or jointed with straight wrists. Pierced ears with larger sizes having applied ears. No damage at all to bisque head, undamaged French body, dressed and ready to place into collection. 9-10" - $4,900.00 up; 12" - $3,500.00; 14" - $3,800.00; 16" - $4,300.00; 18" - $4,600.00; 20" - $4,800.00; 22" - $5,300.00; 24" - $5,700.00; 28" - $6,600.00; 30" - $7,400.00.

Tete Jumeau on Adult Body:
19-20" - $6,400.00. (See photo in Series 5, pg. 87.)

Tete Jumeau: Same as above, but with open mouth. 14" - $2,200.00; 16" - $2,500.00; 19" - $2,650.00; 20" - $2,750.00; 22" - $3,100.00; 24" - $3,400.00; 28" - $3,900.00; 30" - $4,100.00.

1907 Jumeau: Incised 1907, sometimes has the Tete Jumeau stamp. Sleep or set eyes, open mouth, jointed French body. No damage, nicely dressed. 14" - $1,700.00; 16" - $2,200.00; 19" - $2,600.00; 22" - $2,800.00; 25" - $3,300.00; 29" - $3,700.00.

E.J. Child: Ca. early 1880's. Head incised "Depose/E. 6 J." Paperweight eyes, closed mouth, jointed body with straight wrist (unjointed at wrist). Larger dolls will have applied ears. No damage to head or body and nicely dressed in excellent quality clothes. 10" - $5,500.00 up; 14" - $5,800.00; 16" - $6,400.00; 18" - $6,600.00; 22" - $7,500.00; 24" - $9,500.00.

E.J. Child: Mark with number over the E.J. (Example: E.^{6}J.) 17-18" - $10,000.00; 22-23" - $16,000.00.

E.J./A Child: 19" - $1,450.00; 22" - $19,000.00; 26" - $25,000.00 up.

Depose Jumeau: (Incised) 1880. Head will be incised "Depose Jumeau" and body should have Jumeau sticker. Closed mouth, paperweight eyes and on jointed body with straight wrists, although a few may have jointed wrists. No damage at all and nicely dressed. 16" - $5,700.00; 19" - $6,600.00; 23" - $7,400.00; 26" - $8,500.00.

Long Face (Triste Jumeau): 1870's. Closed mouth, applied ears, paperweight eyes and straight wrists on Jumeau marked body. Head is generally marked with a size number. No damage to head or body, nicely dressed. 20-21" - $24,000.00 up; 25-26"- $26,000.00 up; 29-30" - $29,000.00 up; 33-34" - $34,000.00.

16½" Tete Jumeau with closed mouth and on marked Jumeau body with straight wrists. 16½" - **$4,300.00 up.**
Courtesy Frasher Doll Auctions.

21" marked "E. 10 A." has almond shaped eyes, open/closed mouth with space between, applied ears and on body with straight wrists. 21" - **$7,200.00.** Courtesy Barbara Earnshaw-Cain.

Stunning 26" "Long Face Triste" Jumeau with closed mouth and Jumeau body with straight wrists. Shown with doll is French parlour game. 26" - $26,000.00; Game - $325.00. Courtesy Frasher Doll Auctions.

14½" early portrait face Jumeau. Closed mouth, marked body with straight wrists, factory original dress. 15½" closed mouth Jumeau on Jumeau fully jointed body. 14½" - $5,800.00; 15½" - $4,100.00. Courtesy Frasher Doll Auctions.

19" portrait Jumeau with closed mouth, applied ears and on Jumeau marked body with straight wrists. Marked "E.^{9}J." and is earliest mark with number above the E.J. Courtesy Barbara Earnshaw-Cain.

An exceptional quality 20" Jumeau doll incised "1907." Has pull strings to "mama/papa" cryer. 20" - $2,700.00. Courtesy Turn of Century Antiques.

Portrait Jumeau: 1870's. Closed mouth, usually large almond-shaped eyes and jointed Jumeau body. Head marked with size number only and body has the Jumeau sticker or stamp. 10" - $5,800.00; 12" - $5,400.00; 15" - $6,200.00; 21" - $8,400.00; 25" - $10,000.00; 28" - $12,000.00. Very almond-shaped eyes: 12" - $6,200.00; 15-16" - $8,200.00; 18-19" - $9,400.00; 24" - $14,500.00.

Phonograph Jumeau: Bisque head with open mouth. Phonograph in body. No damage, working and nicely dressed. 20" - $8,500.00; 25" - $13,000.00 up.

Wire Eye (Flirty) Jumeau: Lever in back of head operates eyes. Open mouth, jointed body, straight wrists: 18" - $6,600.00; 21" - $7,900.00; 26" - $9,300.00.

Walker: Open mouth: 20" - $2,100.00; 24" - $2,500.00. Throws kisses: 20" - $2,300.00; 24" - $2,800.00.

Celluloid Head: Incised Jumeau. 14" - $675.00 up.

Mold Number 200 Series: Examples: **201, 203, 205, 208, 211, 214, 223.** (See photo in Series 7, pg. 100.) *Very character faces* and marked Jumeau. Closed mouth. No damage to bisque or body. 22" - $72,000.00 up.

Mold Number 230 Series: Ca. 1906. Open mouth. 14" - $1,200.00; 16-17" - $1,500.00; 20" - $1,700.00 up.

S.F.B.J. or Unis: Marked along with Jumeau. Open mouth, no damage to head and on French body. 16" - $1,400.00; 20" - $1,800.00. Closed mouth: 16" - $2,400.00; 20" - $3,000.00.

Two-Faced Jumeau: Has two different faces on same head, one crying and one smiling. Open/closed mouths, jointed body. No damage and nicely dressed. 14" - $13,000.00 up.

Fashion: See Fashion section.

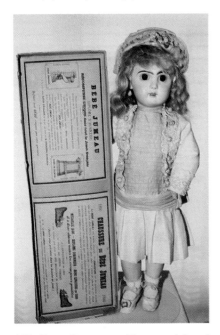

18" Tete Jumeau with open/closed mouth and is all original. Also shown is the inside of the original box lid. 18" - $4,400.00; 18" in box - $4,800.00. Courtesy Barbara Earnshaw-Cain.

28" Jumeau incised "13" and red artist marks. Open mouth with six teeth, pierced ears and on Jumeau fully jointed body. 28" - $4,000.00.

Mold 221: Ca. 1930's. Small dolls (10") will have a paper label "Jumeau." Adult style bisque head on five-piece body with painted-on shoes. Closed mouth and set glass eyes. Dressed in original ornate gown. No damage and clean. 10" - $1,000.00.

Mold 306: Jumeau made after formation of Unis and mark will be "Unis/France" in oval and "71" on one side and "149" on other, followed by "306/Jumeau/1939/Paris." Called "Princess Elizabeth." Closed mouth, flirty or paperweight eyes. Jointed French body. No damage and nicely dressed. 20" - $2,400.00; 30" - $3,800.00.

Marked Shoes: $300.00 up.

29" Tete Jumeau with fully marked head and body. Open mouth, applied ears. 29" - $4,100.00. Courtesy Turn of Century Antiques.

Kammer and Reinhardt dolls generally have the Simon and Halbig name or initials incised along with their own name or mark, as Simon & Halbig made most of their heads. They were located in Thuringia, Germany at Waltershausen and began in 1895, although their first models were not on the market until 1896. The trademark for this company was registered in 1895. In 1909, a character line of fourteen molds (#100-#114) were exhibited at the Leipzig Toy Fair.

Marks:

Character Boy or Girl: Closed or open/closed mouth, on jointed body or five-piece body. No damage and nicely dressed.

#101: Boy "Peter"; girl "Marie" on five-piece body. 8" - $1,300.00; 11" - $1,900.00. 8" on fully jointed body - $1,600.00; 11" - $2,000.00. 14" - $2,600.00; 16" - $3,600.00; 18" - $4,200.00; 22" - $5,300.00. Glass eyes: 14" - $6,400.00; 17" - $7,500.00; 21" - $10,000.00.

#102: Boy "Karl," extremely rare. 12" - $24,000.00 up; 15" - $30,000.00. Glass eyes: 17" - $34,000.00; 22" - $37,000.00 up.

#103: Closed mouth, sweet expression, painted eyes **or #104:** Open/closed mouth, dimples, mischievous expression, painted eyes, extremely rare. 18" - $55,000.00 up.

#105: Extremely rare. Open/closed mouth and much modeling around intaglio eyes. 21" - $85,000.00 up.

#106: Extremely rare. Full round face, pursed closed full lips, intaglio eyes to side and much chin modeling. 21" - $58,000.00.

#107: Pursed, pouty mouth, intaglio eyes. 15" - $20,000.00 up; 22" - $38,000.00 up. Glass eyes: 18" - $38,000.00.

#109: "Elise." Very rare. 14" - $16,000.00; 20" - $25,000.00. Glass eyes: 20" - $30,000.00.

#112, #112X, #112A: (See photo in Series 5, pg. 91.) Very rare. 15" - $9,800.00; 18" - $19,000.00; 23" - $26,000.00. Glass eyes: 18" - $22,000.00; 24" - $30,000.00.

#114: Girl "Gretchen"; boy "Hans." 8" - $1,850.00; 10" - $3,000.00; 15" - $4,300.00; 19" - $5,600.00; 23" - $8,400.00. Glass eyes: 18" - $8,800.00; 24" - $14,500.00.

#117: Closed mouth. 15" - $4,200.00; 18" - $5,000.00; 22" - $6,200.00; 25" - $7,200.00; 28" - $8,000.00.

#117A: Closed mouth. 15" - $4,500.00; 18" - $5,400.00; 22" - $6,700.00; 25" - $7,700.00; 28" - $8,450.00.

18" "Elise" is an extremely rare model, marked "K*R 109/46." Modelled eyelids, painted features, closed mouth and on fully jointed body. 18" - $20,000.00; with trunk/wardrobe - $28,500.00. Courtesy Frasher Doll Auctions.

15" "Marie," mold #101 by Kammer &
Reinhardt. Painted downcast eyes,
closed pouty mouth, wears original wig
and sailor dress. 15" - $2,800.00.
Courtesy Frasher Doll Auctions.

27" "Hans," marked "K*R 114," has
fully jointed body, painted eyes, and
closed mouth. His expression is sweeter
and not as pouty as most #114 dolls.
He holds an old German papier maché
dog with string operated mouth and
"barker" noise box. 27" - $9,000.00.
Courtesy Shirley Bertrand.

Beautiful 23½" example of a #114
"Gretchen." Closed, pouty mouth, painted
eyes, and on fully jointed body. 23½" -
$8,400.00. Courtesy Frasher Doll Auctions.

#117n: Open mouth, flirty eyes (Take off $200.00 for just sleep eyes): 17" - $1,700.00; 21" - $2,300.00; 24" - $2,500.00; 27" - $2,900.00.

#123, #124 (Max & Moritz): 17" - $25,000.00 up each.

#127: Molded hair, open/closed mouth. Toddler or jointed body: 17" - $2,000.00; 21" - $2,600.00; 25" - $3,300.00.

Character Babies: Open/closed mouth or closed mouth on five-piece bent limb baby body, solid dome or wigged. No damage and nicely dressed.

#100: Called "Kaiser Baby." Intaglio eyes, open/closed mouth. 10" - $550.00; 14" - $850.00; 17" - $1,000.00; 20" - $1,600.00. Glass eyes: 16" - $2,200.00; 18" - $2,800.00. Black: 16" - $5,300.00; 18" - $5,800.00.

#115, #115a "Phillip": 15" - $4,550.00; 18" - $4,900.00; 24" - $5,500.00; 26" - $5,900.00. Toddler: 16" - $4,750.00; 18" - $5,200.00; 24" - $5,800.00.

#116, #116a: 16" - $2,600.00; 19" - $3,400.00; 23" - $4,900.00. Toddler: 16" - $3,000.00; 20" - $3,900.00; 25" - $5,300.00. Open Mouth: 16" - $1,300.00; 18" - $1,950.00.

#119: 18" - $4,000.00 up; 26" - $4,800.00.

#127: 13" - $1,200.00; 17" - $1,700.00; 21" - $2,100.00; 24" - $2,500.00. Toddler: 16" - $1,900.00; 20" - $2,400.00; 25" - $2,900.00. Child: 14" - $1,450.00; 17" - $1,600.00; 22" - $1,950.00; 25" - $2,400.00.

Babies with Open Mouth: Sleep eyes on five-piece bent limb baby body. Wigs, may have tremble tongues or "mama" cryer in body. No damage and nicely dressed. Allow more for flirty eyes.

#118a: 14" - $1,600.00; 17" - $1,900.00. 21" - $2,500.00.

#119: 16" - $4,000.00; 20" - $4,900.00.

#121: 14" - $775.00; 18" - $1,050.00; 23" - $1,500.00. Toddler: 16"- $1,200.00; 19" - $1,600.00; 24" - $1,900.00.

Very rare 17" K*R dolls called "Max" and "Moritz." On left is mold #124; on right, #123. The glass sleep eyes are also flirty. Very character faces with closed mouths. All original. Heads were made by Simon & Halbig for Kammer and Reinhardt so they will bear S&H mark as well as the K*R. 17" - $25,000.00 up each. Courtesy Frasher Doll Auctions.

#122, #128: 14" - $800.00; 17" - $1,100.00; 21" - $1,500.00; 24" - $1,800.00. Toddler: 16" - $1,400.00; 19" - $1,900.00.

#126: 12" - $550.00; 16" - $775.00; 20"- $950.00; 24" - $1,400.00; 28" - $2,000.00. Toddler: 9" - $650.00; 16" - $925.00; 21" - $1,400.00; 24" - $1,800.00; 29" - $2,200.00.

#135: 15" - $1,400.00; 21" - $2,300.00.

Child Dolls: 1895–1930's. Open mouth, sleep or set eyes and on fully jointed body. No damage and nicely dressed. Most often found mold numbers are: **#400, #403, #109.** Add more for flirty eyes. Add 50% for all original clothes. 8" - $485.00; 12" - $565.00; 15" - $695.00; 18" - $825.00; 21" - $900.00; 24" - $1,150.00; 29" - $1,500.00; 34" - $1,900.00; 39" - $2,400.00; 42" - $3,600.00.

#192: Closed mouth, sleep eyes, fully jointed body. No damage. 7-8"- $585.00; 16" - $2,300.00; 22"- $2,650.00; 25" - $3,100.00. Open mouth: 7-8" - $325.00; 15" - $825.00; 21" - $1,150.00; 24" - $1,400.00.

Small Child Dolls: Open mouth, sleep eyes (some set) and on five-piece bodies. No damage. 5" - $385.00; 8" - $525.00. Jointed body: 8" - $550.00; 10" - $650.00.

Small Child Doll: Open mouth, flapper style, painted bisque. 8" - $425.00.

Small Child Doll: Closed mouth: 7" - $565.00; 10" - $785.00.

Googly: See Googly section.

Celluloid: See Celluloid section.

Infant: 1924 on. Molded hair and glass eyes, open mouth and cloth body with composition hands. 14" - $1,850.00; 17" - $2,450.00.

30" marked "K*R" Simon & Halbig child with open mouth, sleep eyes, and on fully jointed body. 30" - $1,500.00. Courtesy Frasher Doll Auctions.

28" and 18" #117 and #117A "Mein Liebling." Both have sleep eyes and closed mouths. 28" - $8,000.00; 18" - $5,400.00. Courtesy Frasher Doll Auctions.

24" marked "K*R 116A" with wonderful face modeling, dimples, open/closed mouth, sleep eyes. Shown with a smaller version of the #116A. The dimples show but facial modeling is not as pronounced as on larger doll. 24" - $5,000.00; 14" - $2,300.00. Courtesy Turn of Century Antiques.

15" K*R mold #122 character on jointed toddler body. Sleep eyes, open mouth. 15" - $800.00. Courtesy Turn of Century Antiques.

Left: 8" painted bisque Flapper marked "K*R/21." Sleep eyes with blue eyeshadow, open mouth with two teeth, slender five-piece body with painted on high heel shoes. Right: 5" bisque head marked "K*R." Sleep eyes, open mouth with two teeth and on five-piece body with painted-on shoes and socks. Both costumed by owner. 8" - $425.00; 5" - $385.00. Courtesy Glorya Woods.

5½" bisque head on five-piece body, original. Set glass eyes, closed mouth. Molded dark blue ribbed socks, two-strapped tan shoes with heels. Marked "192/9/0." 5½" - $550.00. Courtesy Joanne Brunken.

KESTNER, J.D.

Johannes Daniel Kestner's firm was founded in 1802, and his name was carried through the 1920's. The Kestner Company was one of the few that made entire dolls, both body and heads. In 1895, Kestner started using the trademark of the crown and streams. (Also see German - All Bisque.)

Sample marks:

B MADE IN 6
GERMANY
J.D.K.
126

F GERMANY 11

J.D.K.
208
GERMANY

Child Doll: Ca. 1880. Closed mouth, some appear to be pouties, sleep or set eyes, jointed body with straight wrist. No damage and nicely dressed.

#X, XII, XV: 15" - $2,700.00; 18" - $2,950.00; 22" - $3,450.00; 27" - $4,000.00.

#XI, 103: Very pouty. (See photo in Series 7, pg. 106.) 11-12" - $2,950.00; 15" - $3,350.00; 19" - $3,985.00; 23" - $4,200.00; 26" - $4,350.00.

#128 Pouty or 169: 7" - $1,000.00; 10" - $2,000.00; 12" - $2,200.00; 14" - $2,400.00; 18" - $2,700.00; 22" - $3,100.00; 26" - $3,600.00; 29" - $4,000.00.

Turned Shoulder Head: Ca. 1880's. Closed mouth. Set or sleep eyes, on kid body with bisque lower arms. No damage and nicely dressed. (Allow more for swivel neck.) 18" - $1,000.00; 22" - $1,400.00; 26" - $1,800.00. Open mouth: 18" - $600.00; 22" - $750.00; 26" - $900.00.

Early Child: Square cut porcelain teeth, jointed body and marked with number and letter. 12" - $765.00; 14" - $900.00; 18" - $1,300.00; 22" - $1,700.00 up; 26-27" - $2,800.00.

A.T. Type: Composition jointed body with straight wrists. Closed mouth: 11" - $12,000.00; 13" - $15,000.00; 15" - $18,000.00; 17" - $21,000.00. Open Mouth: 13" - $2,100.00; 15" - $2,900.00; 17" - $3,300.00.

Bru Type: (See photo in Series 7, pg. 107.) Open/closed mouth, modeled teeth. Composition lower arms, kid body: 18" - $2,800.00; 24" - $3,200.00. Bisque lower arms: 18" - $5,900.00; 24" - $6,400.00. On jointed composition body, straight wrists: 20" - $5,800.00; 26" - $6,800.00.

Character Child: 1910 and after. Closed mouth or open/closed unless noted. Glass or painted eyes, jointed body and no damage and nicely dressed.

#175, 176, 177, 178, 179, 180, 181, 182, 183, 184, 185, 187, 188, 189, 190: These mold numbers can be found on the boxed set doll that has one body and interchangable four heads. (See photos

The Kestner dolls that are marked with an "X" or "XI" have become highly sought after. This example is an "XI" with much detail around mouth which is fully closed, set eyes and on fully jointed body. 19" - $3,985.00. Courtesy Turn of Century Antiques.

11" A.T.-type Kestner marked "5." Sleep eyes, closed mouth and on jointed body with straight wrists. 11" - $12,000.00. Courtesy Frasher Doll Auctions.

in Series 5, pg. 96; Series 6, pg. 124.) Boxed set with four heads: 11-12" - $9,000.00 up. Larger size with painted eyes, closed or open/closed mouth: 12" - $2,200.00; 16" - $3,400.00; 18" - $4,500.00. Same as above but has glass eyes: 12" - $2,900.00; 16" - $4,100.00; 18" - $5,200.00. Glass eyes, molded-on bonnet: 16" - $4,600.00; 18" - $5,600.00.

#151: 16" -$2,600.00; 20" - $3,400.00.

#155: Five-piece body: 8-9" - $500.00. Jointed body: 8-9" - $785.00.

#206: Fat cheeks, closed mouth. Child or toddler: 15" - $16,000.00; 19" - $21,000.00; 24" - $25,000.00.

#208: Painted eyes: 18" - $8,200.00; 24" - $12,000.00. Glass eyes: 18" - $9,400.00; 24" - $13,000.00.

16½" extremely rare Kestner marked "F Made in Germany 10/206." Closed mouth, plaster pate and on fully jointed body. 16½" - $19,000.00. Courtesy Frasher Doll Auctions.

26" Bru-type Kestner with Bru Brevette style face. Marked "16" on head. Bisque shoulderplate, sleep eyes, open/closed mouth with molded teeth, kid body and bisque lower arms. 7" A.M. #323 googly on five-piece body. 10" mask-face googly with composition head on kid and cloth body, original. Shown with French puzzles, ca. 1900. 26" - $3,400.00; 7" - $675.00; 10" - $600.00; Puzzles - $275.00 each. Courtesy Frasher Doll Auctions.

#212: 12" - $2,300.00; 16" - $3,500.00.

#239: Child or toddler. (Also see "Babies."): 17" - $3,600.00; 21" - $4,600.00; 26" - $6,000.00.

#241: (See photo in Series 7, pg. 108.) Open mouth, glass eyes: 15" - $4,250.00; 21"- $5,600.00.

#249: 22" - $2,000.00.

#260: Jointed or toddler body: 8" - $650.00; 12" - $850.00; 16" - $1,300.00; 22" - $1,800.00.

Child Doll: Late 1880's to 1930's. Open mouth on fully jointed body, sleep eyes, some set, with no damage and nicely dressed.

#128, 129, 134, 136, 141, 142, 144, 146, 152, 156, 159, 160, 161, 162, 164, 168, 174, 196, 211, 214, 215: 10" - $450.00; 15" - $725.00; 18" - $785.00; 21" - $885.00; 24" - $925.00; 27" - $1,100.00; 32" - $1,500.00; 36" - $2,200.00; 40" - $3,400.00.

#143, 189: (See photo in Series 6, pg. 126.) Character face, open mouth. 9" - $765.00; 12" - $885.00; 18" - $1,300.00; 21" - $1,500.00.

#192: 15" - $675.00; 18" - $800.00; 21" - $975.00.

Child: Open mouth, square cut teeth part of head (not separate). 10-11" - $750.00; 14" - $900.00; 16-17" - $1,200.00; 20-21" - $1,600.00; 25" - $2,600.00; 28" - $2,800.00.

Child Doll: "Dolly" face with open mouth, sleep or set eyes, bisque shoulder head on kid body with bisque lower arms. No damage and nicely dressed.

#145, 147, 148, 149, 155, 166, 167, 170, 195, etc. (Add more for fur eyebrows): 12" - $365.00; 16" - $475.00; 19" - $550.00; 22" - $650.00; 25" - $900.00; 29" - $1,200.00.

#154, #171: Most often found mold numbers. "Daisy," jointed body, open mouth. 16" - $625.00; 19" - $865.00; 23" - $975.00; 26" - $1,300.00; 30" - $1,600.00; 39" - $2,400.00. Same mold numbers, but with swivel bisque head on bisque shoulder head. Open mouth: 17" - $750.00; 21" - $950.00; 26" - $1,400.00. Same mold, numbers on kid body: 17" - $575.00; 21" - $700.00; 26" - $1,000.000.

Character Babies: 1910 and later. On bent limb baby bodies, sleep or set eyes, open mouth, can be wigged or have solid dome with painted hair. No damage and nicely dressed.

#121, 142, 150, 151, 152, 153, 154: 10" - $385.00; 14" - $550.00; 17" - $600.00; 20" - $725.00; 24" - $975.00.

#211, 226, 236, 260: 9" - $465.00; 14"- $525.00; 17" - $700.00; 21" - $1,000.00; 25" - $1,500.00.

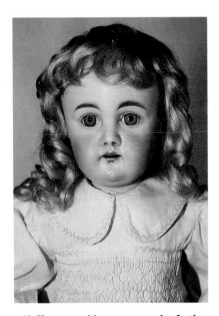

14" Kestner with open mouth, feather eyebrows, and a character look to her face. 14" - $2,300.00. Courtesy Barbara Earnshaw-Cain.

13" Kestner #143 character child with large set eyes, open mouth, and jointed body. 13" - $950.00 up. Courtesy Barbara Earnshaw-Cain.

#220: (Add more for toddler body) 15" - $5,800.00; 19" - $6,400.00.

#234, 235, 238: 14" - $675.00; 17" - $800.00; 21" - $1,000.00; 25" - $1,400.00.

#237, 245, 1070 (Hilda): Wigged or solid dome. 12" - $2,800.00; 15" - $3,500.00; 21" - $5,100.00; 25" - $6,800.00. Kestner Toddler: 16" - $5,300.00; 21" - $5,400.00; 24" - $6,600.00.

#239: 15" - $2,600.00; 17" - $3,000.00; 23" - $3,500.00.

#247: 12" - $1,300.00; 15" - $1,900.00; 17" - $2,400.00; 22" - $5,100.00; 26" - $5,500.00.

#249: 17" - $1,800.00; 23" - $2,300.00.

#257: 9" - $485.00; 14" - $650.00; 18" - $875.00; 21" - $1,000.00; 25" - $1,600.00.

#262: 12" - $525.00; 16" - $700.00; 21" - $965.00.

#257, 262: Toddler. 22" - $1,500.00; 27" - $2,000.00;

#279, 200 (Century Doll): Molded hair with part, bangs, cloth body, composition hands. 16" - $1,000.00; 20" - $1,600.00.

#281 (Century Doll): Open mouth: 22" - $950.00.

J.D.K. Marked Baby: Called "Sally" or "Sammy." Solid dome, painted eyes and open mouth. 12" - $965.00; 16" - $1,300.00; 21" - $2,000.00.

Adult Doll, #162: Sleep eyes, open mouth, adult jointed body (thin waist and molded breasts) with slender limbs. No damage and very nicely dressed. 15" - $1,400.00; 18" - $1,800.00; 23" - $2,400.00.

26" large Kestner solid dome baby with brush painted hair, sleep eyes and open mouth. 26" - $5,500.00.
Courtesy Frasher Doll Auctions.

13" beautiful small Kestner #247 baby with open mouth, sleep eyes and original fur wig. 13" - $1,300.00.
Courtesy Shirley Betrand.

Adult #172: 1910, "Gibson Girl." Bisque shoulder head with closed mouth, kid body with bisque lower arms, glass eyes. No damage and beautifully dressed. 12" - $1,400.00; 18" - $2,900.00; 23" - $4,200.00.

Oriental #243: Olive fired-in color to bisque. Matching color five-piece bent limb baby body (or jointed toddler-style body), wig, sleep or set eyes. No damage and dressed in oriental style. 15" - $5,200.00; 19" - $7,400.00. Child: Same as above, but on jointed Kestner olive-toned body. 15" - $5,500.00; 19" - $8,000.00. Molded hair baby: 15" - $6,000.00.

Small Dolls: Open mouth, five-piece bodies or jointed bodies, wigs, sleep or set eyes. No damage and nicely dressed. 7" - $485.00; 9" - $645.00.

#133: 8" - $675.00.

#155: Five-piece body: 8-9" - $500.00. Jointed body: 8-9" - $785.00.

This small 7½" doll is marked "K★R Halbig 10." Open mouth, very nice five-piece body with painted-on shoes and socks. Detailed hands to the sides. 7½" - $550.00. Courtesy Frasher Doll Auctions.

22" Gibson Girl with tilted up chin shoulder head, glass eyes, closed smile mouth. Original kid body with bisque lower arms. 22" - $4,200.00. Courtesy Turn of Century Antiques.

All prices are for dolls that have no chips, hairlines or breaks. Designed by Rose O'Neill and marketed from 1913. (See Modern section for composition and vinyl Kewpies.)

Labels:

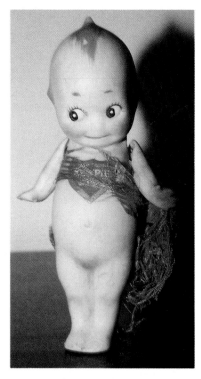

4½" Kewpie that is all bisque, jointed at shoulders only. Paper label on front and also marked on back. 4½" - $185.00. Courtesy Gloria Anderson.

All Bisque: One-piece body and head, jointed shoulders only. Blue wings, painted features with eyes to one side. 1½" - $125.00; 2½" - $165.00; 4½" - $185.00; 6" - $200.00; 7" - $250.00; 9" - $450.00; 12" - $1,400.00.

All Bisque: Jointed at hips and shoulders. 4" - $465.00; 9" - $875.00; 12" - $1,500.00. Painted shoes and socks: 4-5" - $545.00.

Shoulder Head: Cloth body. 6-7" - $600.00.

Action Kewpie: Arms folded: 4½" - $600.00. Confederate Soldier: 4½" - $700.00. Cowboy: Big hat, gun. Made as lamp. (See photo in Series 7, pg. 11.) 10½" - $850.00. Farmer: 4" - $495.00. Gardener: 4" - $495.00. Governor: 4" - $450.00. Groom with Bride: 4" - $485.00. Guitar Player: 3½" - $400.00. Holding Pen: 3" - $385.00. Holding cat: 4" - $500.00; Holding butterfly: 4" - $525.00. Hugging: 3½" - $300.00. On stomach, called "Blunderboo": 4" - $465.00. Soldier: 4½" - $625.00. Thinker: 4" - $425.00; 6" - $550.00. Traveler (tan or black suitcase): 3½" - $325.00. With broom: 4" - $450.00. With dog, Doodle: 3½" - $2,200.00. With helmet: 6" - $700.00. With outhouse: 2½" - $1,200.00. With Rabbit: 2½" - $400.00. With rose: 2" - $375.00. With Teddy Bear: 4" - $750.00. With turkey: 2" - $365.00. With umbrella and dog: 3½" - $2,300.00.

Kewpie Soldier & Nurse: 6" - $2,000.00 up.

Kewpie Tree: (Or mountain) 17 figures. $20,000.00 up.

Kewpie Driving Chariot: $2,800.00 up.

Kewpie on Inkwell: Bisque: 3½" - $650.00. Cast metal: 3½" - $400.00.

Kewpie In Basket With Flowers: 3½" - $650.00.

Kewpie With Drawstring Bag: 4½" - $600.00.

Blunderboo: On stomach, head to side: 4" - $465.00.

Buttonhole Kewpie: $165.00.

Kewpie Doodle Dog: 1½" - $700.00; 3" - $1,600.00.

Hottentot Black Kewpie: 3½" - $400.00; 5" - $500.00; 9" - $900.00.

Kewpie Perfume Bottle: 3½" - $475.00 up.

Pincushion Kewpie: 2½" - $350.00.

Celluloid Kewpies: 2" - $45.00; 5" - $90.00; 9" - $165.00. Black: 5" - $145.00. Jointed shoulders: 3" - $60.00; 5" - $110.00; 9" - $175.00; 12" - $250.00; 16" - $600.00 up; 22" - $900.00 up.

Cloth Body Kewpie: With bisque head, painted eyes. 10" - $2,400.00. Glass eyes: 12" - $2,700.00 up; 16" - $5,000.00 up. Composition head and half arms: 13" - $450.00.

Glass Eye Kewpie: On chubby toddler, jointed. Bisque head. Marks: "Ges. Gesch./O'Neill J.D.K." 10" - $4,200.00; 12" - $4,600.00; 16" - $6,500.00; 20" - $8,400.00.

All Cloth: (Made by Kreuger) All one-piece with body forming clothes, mask face. Mint condition: 7-8" - $165.00; 12" - $185.00; 15" - $325.00; 21" - $500.00; 26" - $1,000.00. Fair condition: 12" - $90.00; 15" - $150.00; 21" - $250.00; 26" - $450.00.

All Cloth: Same as above, but with original dress and bonnet. Mint condition: 12" - $265.00; 15" - $400.00; 21"- $650.00; 26" - $1,200.00.

Tiny 7" all cloth "Cuddles Kewpie" in perfect condition. Tag marked "Pat. #1785800 copyright/Richard G. Kreuger Inc. Rose O'Neill/New York/ Sole mfrs. & distributors." 7" - $165.00 up. Courtesy Shirley Bertrand.

Kewpie Tin or Celluloid Talcum Container: Excellent condition: 7-8" - $225.00. See Modern Section for composition.

Kewpie Soaps: 4" - $85.00 each. Boxed set of five: $500.00.

Japan: Bisque: 2" - $45.00; 3" - $80.00; 4" - $95.00; 5" - $110.00; 6" - $135.00.

Left to right: 4" Kewpie with dog, Doodle; 5" jointed at hips and shoulders, sitting; Sitting Kewpie with one-piece body, holding cat. Front: Blunderboo. 4" with dog - $500.00; 5" - $525.00; 4" with cat - $500.00; Blunderboo - $465.00. Courtesy Ellen Dodge.

Kley & Hahn operated in Ohrdruf, Germany from 1895 to 1929. They made general dolls as well as babies and fine character dolls.

Marks:

K & H   ⟩ KᴐH ⟨

Character Child: Boy or girl. Painted eyes (some with glass eyes), closed or open/closed mouth; on jointed body. No damage and nicely dressed.

#320, 520, 523, 525, 526, 531, 536, 546, 549, 552: 17" - $3,500.00; 21" - $4,800.00; 23" - $5,200.00; 25" - $5,500.00.

Same Mold Numbers on Toddler Bodies: 15" - $1,700.00; 21" - $2,400.00; 23" - $2,800.00.

Same Mold Numbers on Bent Limb Baby Body: 14" - $1,000.00; 17" - $1,500.00; 21" - $2,300.00; 25" - $2,700.00.

Same Mold Numbers with Glass Eyes: 14" - $3,000.00; 17" - $3,800.00; 21" - $5,200.00; 25" - $5,900.00.

Character Baby: Molded hair or wig, glass sleep eyes or painted eyes. Can have open or open/closed mouth. On bent limb baby body, no damage and nicely dressed.

#130, 132, 138, 142, 150, 151, 158, 160, 162, 167, 176, 199, 458, 522, 531, 538, 585, 680: 12" - $485.00; 15" - $675.00; 21" - $1,000.00; 25" - $1,500.00; 28" - $1,900.00.

Same Mold Numbers on Toddler Bodies: 14" - $625.00; 17" - $825.00; 20" - $1,100.00; 25" - $1,650.00; 28" - $1,950.00.

#547: Closed mouth, glass eyes. 18" - $6,200.00.

#548, #568: 15" - $725.00; 19" - $975.00; 22" - $1,250.00. Toddler: 19" - $1,400.00; 26" - $1,900.00.

#162 with Talker Mechanism in Head: 18" - $1,600.00; 24" - $2,600.00; 26" - $3,000.00.

26" Kley & Hahn 169-13 with sleep eyes, closed mouth, and on jointed toddler body. Shown with three-sided wooden grocery store that is 20" x 9". 26" - $4,200.00; Store - $500.00 up. Courtesy Frasher Doll Auctions.

26" Kley & Hahn 538-15 with open/ closed mouth, modeled tongue and teeth. Toddler body. Shown with 14" rattler that whistles when twirled. 26" - $1,700.00; Marotte - $600.00. Courtesy Turn of Century Antiques.

#162 with Flirty Eyes and Clockworks in Head: 19" - $1,900.00; 26" - $3,500.00.

#680: 17" - $900.00. Toddler: 18" - $1,300.00.

#153, 154, 157, 166, 169: (See photo in Series 7, pg. 114.) Child, closed mouth: 15" - $3,000.00; 20" - $3,900.00. Open mouth: 15" - $1,300.00; 20" - $1,700.00.

#159 Two-faced Doll: 12" - $2,400.00; 15" - $3,000.00.

#166: With molded hair and open mouth. 18-19" - $1,700.00. Closed mouth: 17" - $2,800.00.

#169: Closed mouth. Toddler: 14" - $2,300.00; 18" - $3,400.00. Open mouth: 20" - $1,400.00.

#119: Child, glass eyes, closed mouth. 21" - $4,800.00. Painted eyes: 21" - $3,300.00. Toddler: Glass eyes. 21" - $4,900.00.

Child Dolls: Walküre and/or **#250**. Sleep or set eyes, open mouth, jointed body. No damage and nicely dressed. 17" - $525.00; 21" - $700.00; 25" - $800.00; 29" - $1,000.00; 34" - $1,700.00.

26" and 24" Kley & Hahn "Walkure" marked girls. Each doll is original and has a mohair wig, open mouth, sleep eyes, and on fully jointed body. 26" - $900.00; 24" - $750.00. Courtesy Turn of Century Antiques.

KONIG & WERNICKE

Konig & Wernicke made dolls from 1912 on. (See photo in Series 7, pg. 115; Series 6, pg. 132.)

Mark:

K & W
100

Baby: Bisque head. (Allow more for toddler body or flirty eyes.)

Mold #98, 99, 100, 1070: 10" - $435.00; 15" - $565.00; 17" - $675.00; 21" - $825.00; 24" - $965.00; 26" - $1,150.00.

Käthe Kruse began making dolls in 1910. In 1916, she obtained a patent for a wire coil doll and in 1923, she registered a trademark of a double "K" with the first one reversed, along with the name Käthe Kruse. The first heads were designed after her own children and copies of babies from the Renaissance period. The dolls have a molded muslin head that are handpainted in oils and a jointed cloth body. These early dolls will be marked "Käthe Kruse" on the foot and sometimes with a "Germany" and number.

Early Marked Dolls, Model I: 1910. In excellent condition and with original clothes. (See photo in Series 7, pg. 116.) 16" - $3,500.00; 19" - $3,950.00. In fair condition, not original: 16" - $1,800.00; 19" - $2,200.00. Ball jointed knees: 16" - $4,200.00; 19" - $4,700.00.

Model II: 1922 on. Smile, baby. 14" - $2,200.00.

Model III, IV: 1923 on. Serious child. 16" - $1,800.00 up.

Model V, VI: 1925 on. Typical Kruse. 20" - $3,400.00; 24" - $3,800.00.

Model VII: 1927 on. (See photo in Series 7, pg. 116.) 15-16" - $1,400.00; 19" - $1,850.00.

Model VIII, IX: 1929 on. 15" - $1,400.00; 20" - $2,250.00. Good condition: 20" - $1,450.00.

Model X: 1935 on. 14-15" - $1,200.00.

1920's Dolls: Model IH and others. (See photo in Series 7, pg. 116.) Molded hair, hips are wide. In excellent condition and original: 16" - $2,250.00; 21" - $3,000.00. In fair condition, not original: 16" - $1,400.00; 21" - $2,000.00.

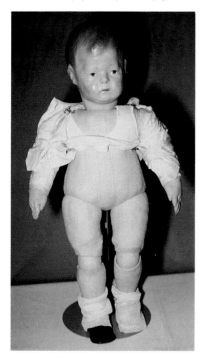

19" #1 made for Kammer & Reinhardt. Wide hips, double sewn seams and jointed at knees. 19" - $4,700.00. Courtesy Shirley Bertrand.

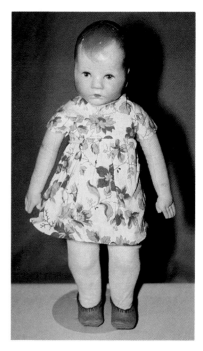

14" Kruse model #VII with "Du Mein" head. Possibly original dress. 14" - $1,800.00. Courtesy Shirley Bertrand.

U.S. Zone: Germany 1945–1951 (Turtle mark.) 17" - $1,000.00.

Plastic Dolls: 1950's–1975. With glued-on wigs, sleep or painted eyes. Marked with turtle mark and number on head and on back "Modell/Käthe Kruse/" and number. 15" - $500.00; 18" - $585.00.

Baby: Painted closed or open eyes. 1925. 19" - $3,400.00.

Celluloid: 15" - $600.00; 18" - $900.00.

1975 to date: 9" - $225.00; 13" - $375.00; 17" - $475.00.

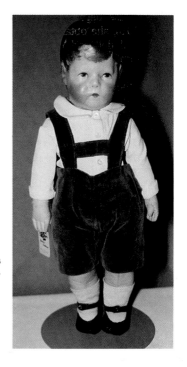

This 18" Kruse boy is a Model V and has free-standing sewn thumbs. Original. 18" - $3,000.00. Courtesy Shirley Bertrand.

19" girl, Model #1H, and boy, Model #VII. Both are all original. 19" Girl - $2,800.00; 19" Boy - $1,850.00. Courtesy Shirley Bertrand.

Kuhnlenz made dolls from 1884 to 1930 and was located in Kronach, Bavaria. Marks from this company include the "G.K." plus numbers such as 56-38, 44-26, 41-28, 56-18, 44-15, 38-27, 44-26, etc. Other marks now attributed to this firm are:

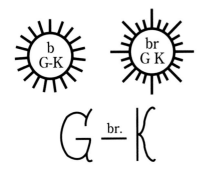

Child with Closed Mouth: Mold #31, 32. Bisque head in perfect condition, jointed body and nicely dressed. 10" - $665.00; 15" - $1,000.00; 19" - $1,600.00; 23" - $1,950.00.

Mold #34: Bru type. 17" - $2,850.00.

Mold #38: Kid body, bisque shoulder head. 15" - $685.00; 22" - $1,000.00.

Child with Open Mouth: Mold #41, 44, 56. Bisque head in perfect condition, jointed body and nicely dressed. 15" - $600.00; 19" - $850.00; 23" - $1,050.00.

Mold #61: Shoulder head, kid body. 20" - $725.00.

Mold #165: Bisque head in perfect condition, jointed body and nicely dressed. 17" - $475.00; 23" - $685.00.

Tiny Dolls, Mold #44, 46 and others: Bisque head in perfect condition, five-piece body with painted-on shoes and socks, open mouth. 8" - $225.00. Closed mouth: 8" - $685.00.

LANTERNIER (LIMOGES)

A. Lanternier & Cie of Limoges, France made dolls from about the 1890's on into the 1930's. Before making dolls, they produced porcelain pieces as early as 1855. Their doll heads will be fully marked and some carry a name such as "LaGeorgienne Favorite, Lorraine, Cherie," etc. They generally are found on papier maché bodies but can be on fully jointed composition bodies. Dolls from this firm may have nearly excellent quality bisque to very poor quality.

Child: 1915. Open mouth, set eyes on jointed body. No damage and nicely dressed. Good quality bisque with pretty face. 15" - $775.00; 21" - $985.00; 24" - $1,100.00; 27" - $1,600.00. Poor quality bisque with very high coloring or blotchy color bisque. 15" - $475.00; 21" - $595.00; 24" - $700.00; 27" - $800.00.

Marks:

FABRICATION
FRANCAISE

**AL & CIE
LIMOGES**

"Jumeau" Style Face: Has a striking Jumeau look. Good quality bisque: 19" - $1,200.00; 23" - $1,500.00. Poor quality bisque: 19" - $650.00; 23" - $800.00.

Character: 1915. Open/closed mouth with teeth, smiling fat face, glass eyes, on jointed body. No damage and nicely dressed. Marked "Toto." 17" - $900.00; 21" - $1,500.00.

Lady: 1915. Adult-looking face, set eyes, open/closed or closed mouth. Jointed adult body. No damage and nicely dressed. 15" - $975.00; 18" - $1,400.00.

21" marked "France G Dor 6D Lianne Verlingue." Open mouth and set eyes. On jointed French body. 21" - $985.00.
Courtesy Sylvia Bryant.

LENCI

Lenci dolls are all felt with a few having cloth torsos. They are jointed at neck, shoulder and hips. The original clothes will be felt or organdy or a combination of both. Features are oil painted and generally eyes are painted to the side. Size can range from 5" to 45". (Mint or rare dolls will bring higher prices.)

Marks: On cloth or paper label: "Lenci Torino Made in Italy." "Lenci" may be written on bottom of foot or underneath one arm.

Children: No moth holes, very little dirt, doll as near mint as possible and all in excellent condition. 14" - $950.00 up; 16" - $1,200.00 up; 18" - $1,400.00 up; 20" - $1,800.00 up. Dirty, original clothes in poor condition or redressed: 14" - $300.00; 16" - $500.00; 18" - $650.00; 20" - $850.00.

Baby: (See photos in Series 5, pg. 108.) 16" - $1,500.00; 20" - $2,000.00.

Fair condition: $600.00-950.00.

Tiny Dolls (Called Mascottes): (See photos in Series 7, pg. 120.) In excellent condition: 5" - $285.00; 9-10" - $365.00. Dirty, redressed or original clothes in poor condition: 5" - $85.00; 9-10" - $145.00.

Ladies with Adult Faces: "Flapper" or "Boudoir" style with long limbs. (See photos in Series 5, pg. 107, Series 6, pg. 136.) In excellent condition: 24" - $1,900.00 up; 27" - $2,200.00 up. Dirty or in poor condition: 24" - $700.00; 28" - $950.00.

Clowns: Excellent condition: 18" - $1,600.00; 27" - $2,000.00. Poor condition: 18" - $600.00; 27" - $950.00.

Indians or Orientals: Excellent condition: 17" - $3,700.00. Dirty and poor condition: 17" - $1,100.00.

Golfer: Excellent, perfect condition: 16" - $2,200.00. Poor condition: 16" - $700.00.

Shirley Temple Type: Excellent condition: 28" - $2,500.00. Dirty and poor condition: 28" - $1,000.00.

Bali Dancer: Excellent condition: 21" - $2,200.00. Poor condition: 22" - $650.00.

Smoking Doll: In excellent condition, painted eyes: 25" - $2,000.00 up. Poor condition: 25" - $950.00.

Glass Eyes: Excellent condition: 17" - $2,600.00; 22" - $3,300.00. Poor condition: 17" - $950.00; 22" - $1,200.00.

"Surprise Eyes" Doll: Very round painted eyes and "O"-shaped mouth. 15" - $1,900.00; 19" - $2,500.00. With glass eyes that are flirty: 15" - $2,500.00; 19" - $3,200.00.

Boys: Side part hairdo. Excellent condition: 18" - $2,000.00 up; 23" - $2,600.00. Poor condition: 18" - $750.00; 23" - $975.00.

Babies: Excellent condition: 15" - $1,400.00; 21" - $2,000.00. Poor condition: 16" - $600.00; 20" - $950.00.

Lenci Type: Can be made in Italy, Germany, France, Spain, or England. 1920's through 1940's. Felt and cloth.

Child: Felt or cloth, mohair wig, cloth body. Original clothes. 16" - $775.00; 18" - $850.00.

Small Dolls: 7-8" - $65.00; 12" - $125.00.

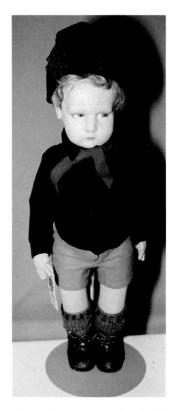 

Left: 17" Lenci pouty boy that is dressed in Italy's Youth uniform. All original. 17" - $1,800.00. Right: 19" sad-looking early Lenci girl, all original. 19" - $1,750.00. Both dolls courtesy Shirley Bertrand.

Wonderful 15" Pinocchio. All wood, including apple and books. Felt clothes and shoes. Marked with paper "Lenci" label on back. No price available. Courtesy Shirley Bertrand.

Left: 18" brown Lenci type. Felt body, jointed shoulders and hips. Swivel head, felt clothes. Right: 19" glass eye Lenci type with felt head and limbs, pink cloth body. Stitched joints at shoulders and hips. Replaced wig. 18" - $775.00; 19" - $950.00. Courtesy Frasher Doll Auctions.

5" grasshopper that is all felt and tagged "Lenci/Torino/Made in Italy." Has hat sewn onto one leg. Ca. 1950. 5" - $450.00. Courtesy Shirley Bertrand.

LENCI

Left photo: Lenci 17½" "Black Pregnant Girl" from 1925. Exotic International Series. All felt with swivel head, painted features. Pregnant-shaped torso, grass skirt, and six wood carvings around waist and neck. 17½" - $3,200.00. Courtesy Frasher Doll Auctions. Right photo: 12" Lenci "Piemonte" boy and girl "Mascotte." Both are original, ca. 1950. 12" boy and girl, each - $145.00 up. Courtesy Shirley Bertrand.

LIMBACH

These dolls were made mostly from 1893 into the 1920's by Limbach Porzellanfabrik, Limbach, Germany.

Mark:

MADE IN GERMANY

Child: 1893–1899. Incised with clover mark. Bisque head, open mouth, glass eyes. Jointed body. No damage and nicely dressed. 15" - $450.00; 17" - $585.00; 20" - $650.00; 23" - $775.00.

Same as above, with closed mouth: 15" - $1,500.00; 17" - $1,800.00; 20" - $2,200.00; 23" - $2,800.00.

Same as above, with incised name: Ca. 1919. Incised names such as "Norma," "Rita," "Wally," etc. 17" - $525.00; 20" - $600.00; 23" - $700.00.

22½" rare closed mouth character made by Limbach and incised with the clover mark. Jointed body with straight wrists. Shown with all original German pull toy. Wood and wire body attached to wooden platform. Has open mouth. When pulled, arms move from side to side. 22½" - $2,850.00. Pull toy - $850.00. Courtesy Frasher Doll Auctions.

LORI

The "Lori Baby" is marked "D Lori 4" with green stamp "Geschuz S & Co." and was made by Swaine & Co. It has lightly painted hair, sleep eyes, open/closed mouth, and on five-piece bent limb baby body.

Glass Eyes: (See photo in Series 7, pg. 122.) 14" - $1,600.00; 20" - $2,600.00; 23" - $3,200.00; 26" - $3,700.00.

Intaglio Eyes: (See photo in Series 6, pg. 138.) 20" - $2,000.00; 24" - $2,500.00.

Flocked Hair: 20" - $2,700.00; 25" - $3,400.00.

Right: 15" "Lori Baby" marked "Germany 232 5." Ca. 1910. Sleep eyes, open mouth with two upper teeth, and on five-piece bent limb body. Shown with 30" marked head and body Tete Jumeau. Closed mouth, jointed body, straight wrists. 15" - $1,650.00; 30" - $7,400.00. Courtesy Frasher Doll Auctions.

Mascotte Dolls were made by May Freres Cie. They operated from 1890 to 1897, then became part of Jules Steiner in 1898. This means the dolls were made from 1890 to about 1902, so the quality of the bisque can vary greatly, as well as the artist painting. Dolls will be marked "BÉBÉ MASCOTTE PARIS" and some incised with "M" and a number.

Child: Closed mouth and marked "Mascotte." Excellent condition and no damage. 14" - $3,450.00; 17" - $4,200.00; 19" - $4,800.00; 23" - $5,700.00; 27" - $6,200.00.

Child: Same as above, but marked with "M" and a number. 14" - $3,000.00; 17" - $3,800.00; 19" - $4,200.00; 23" - $5,200.00; 27" - $5,800.00.

30" beautiful closed mouth doll marked "Mascotte M." Shown with 6" and 7½" doll house dolls and 3¾" German all bisque boy and girl. 30" - **$6,700.00;** 6" women, each - **$150.00;** 7½" man - **$685.00;** 3¾" all bisque, each - **$195.00.** Courtesy Frasher Doll Auctions.

MECHANICALS

A. Theroude mechanical walker patented in 1840 with papier maché head, bamboo teeth in open mouth and stands on three wheels (two large and one small), tin cart with mechanism attached to legs. 16" - $3,600.00.

Autoperipatetikos: Base is like clockworks and has tin feet and when key wound, the doll walks. Heads can be china, untinted bisque or papier maché. Early China Head: 11" - $1,800.00. Untinted Bisque: 11" - $1,200.00. Papier maché: 11" - $900.00.

Hawkins, George: Walker with pewter hands and feet, wood torso. Hands modeled to push a carriage, which should be a Goodwin, patented in 1867–1868. Carriage has two large wheels and one small one in front. Molded hair and dolls head will be marked "X.L.C.R./Doll head/Pat. Sept. 8, 1868." (China heads may not be marked.) 11" - $2,200.00.

Jumeau: Raises and lowers both arms and head moves. Holds items such as a hankie and bottle, book and fan, etc. - one in each hand. Key wound music box in base. Closed mouth and marked "Jumeau." 15" - $3,800.00 up; 20" - $4,700.00 up. Same with open mouth: 15" - $2,500.00 up; 20" - $3,600.00 up.

Jumeau: Marked "Jumeau." Standing or sitting on key wound music box and doll plays an instrument. 14" - $4,0000.00 up; 18" - $5,500.00 up.

Jumeau: Marked "Jumeau" walker with one-piece legs, arms jointed at elbows. She raises her arm to an open mouth to throw kisses as head turns. 15" - $2,000.00 up; 21" - $2,900.00 up.

Jumeau: Marked "Jumeau" and stands on three-wheel cart and when cart is pulled, doll's head turns from side to side and arms go up and down. 15" - $3,600.00 up; 18" - $4,200.00 up.

Automaton by Leopold Lambert labeled "Valencia ... Oh! Mademoiselle." Key marked "L.B." 26" tall overall, original. Heavy eyeshadow, real upper lashes, open mouth, and beautiful modeled hands. Head turns, one hand raises lorgnette, one arm raises and lowers baton. $15,000.00. Courtesy Frasher Doll Auctions.

Paris Bébé, R.D., E.D., Eden Bébé: Marked doll standing on key wound music box. Has closed mouth. Holds items in hands and arms move and head nods or moves from side to side. 21" - $5,200.00 up.

Jumeau: 18-20" doll stands at piano built to scale and hands attached to keyboard with rods. Key wound piano. $20,000.00 up.

Steiner, Jules: Bisque head, open mouth with two rows of teeth. Key wound, waltzes in circles, original clothes. Glass eyes, arms move as it dances. 17" - $9,600.00.

Steiner, Jules: Bisque head on composition upper and lower torso-chest, also lower legs and all the arms. Twill-

Right: Beautiful ballerina automaton that is 20" tall overall. Has red check marks on head and face of a Jumeau. Open mouth and all original. She turns completely around, bends at waist and tilts head as music plays. Shown with a 30" A-19 Jules Steiner with closed mouth and original jointed Steiner body with straight wrists. Ballerina - $9,500.00; 30" - $8,800.00. Courtesy Frasher Doll Auctions.

covered sections between parts of body. Key wound, cries, moves head and kicks legs. Open mouth with two rows of teeth. 18" - $2,500.00; 23" - $3,100.00. Same as above, but Bisque Torso Sections: 18" - $8,000.00 up.

German Makers: One or two figures on music box, key wound, or pulling cart. Dolls have open mouths. Marked with name of maker: $1,600.00 up. 1960's, 1970's German-made reproductions of this style dolls: $300.00.

METAL HEADS

Metal heads made in Germany, 1888-on; United States, 1917-on.

Marks:

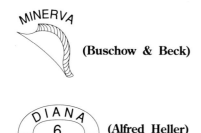

(Buschow & Beck)

(Alfred Heller)

JUNO **(Karl Standfuss)**

Metal Shoulder Head: Cloth or kid body. Molded hair, painted eyes. 14" - $145.00; 17" - $185.00. Molded hair, glass eyes: 14" - $185.00; 17" - $250.00. Wig, glass eyes: 14" - $250.00; 17" - $300.00; 21" - $385.00.

All Metal Child: Wig or molded hair, fully jointed. Some are also jointed at wrist, elbow, knee, and ankle. Open/closed mouth with painted teeth. Some have metal hands and feet with composition body. 15-16" - $350.00; 19-20" - $475.00.

Metal Baby: All metal bent baby body. Some are spring jointed. Painted features, wig or molded hair. 13-14" - $100.00. Glass eyes: 13-14" - $165.00.

MOLDED HAIR BISQUE

The molded hair bisque dolls are just like any other flesh-toned dolls, but instead of having a wig, they have molded hair, glass set eyes or finely painted and detailed eyes, and generally they will have a closed mouth. They almost always are a shoulder head with one-piece shoulder and head. They can be on a kid body or cloth with bisque lower arms, with some having compostion lower legs. These dolls are generally very pretty. Many molded hair dolls are being attributed to A.B.G. (Alt, Beck & Gottschalck) mold numbers 890, 1000, 1008, 1028, 1064, 1142, 1256, 1288, etc.

Child: 6½" - $140.00; 10" - $185.00; 15" - $485.00; 20" - $775.00; 23" - $1,300.00; 26" - $1,500.00.

Boy: 17" - $650.00; 20" - $850.00; 23" - $1,200.00.

Decorated Shoulder Plate: With elaborate hairdo. 20" - $2,300.00 up.

Japan: Marked 𝒯𝒴 or (✱). Bows on sides of head. Cloth body, long legs, black silk feet, oilcloth arms. 17" - $225.00; 20" - $350.00.

Charles Motschmann has always been credited as the manufacturer of a certain style doll, but now his work is only being attributed to the making of the voice boxes in the dolls. Various German makers such as Heinrich Stier and others are being given the credit for making the dolls. They date from 1851 into the 1880's.

The early dolls were babies, children and Orientals. They have glass eyes, closed mouths, heads of papier maché, wax over papier maché or wax over composition. They can have lightly brush stroked painted hair or come with a wig. If the mouth is open, the doll will have bamboo teeth. The larger dolls will have arms and legs jointed at wrists and ankles. The torso (lower) body is composition or wooden, as are the arms and legs, except for the upper parts which will be twill-style cloth. The mid-section will also be cloth. If the doll is marked, it can be found on the upper cloth of the leg and will be stamped:

Baby: Motschmann marked or type. In extremely fine condition: 13" - $650.00; 16" - $750.00; 20" - $975.00; 25" - $1,500.00. In fair condition: 13" - $425.00; 16" - $525.00; 20" - $625.00; 25" - $750.00.

Child: In extremely fine condition: 15" - $800.00; 18" - $975.00; 23" - $1,400.00. In fair condition: 15" - $425.00; 18" - $625.00; 23" - $750.00.

MUNICH ART DOLL

Munich Art character dolls were designed by Marion Kaulitz, 1908–1912. Composition, painted features, on fully jointed body. 18-19" - $3,600.00 up.

19" Munich Art boy. Beautiful character face, all original. Composition with handpainted features. 19" - $3,600.00 up. Courtesy Shirley Bertrand.

Bisque dolls with fired-in Oriental color and on jointed yellowish tinted bodies were made in Germany by various firms. They could be a child or baby and most were made after 1900. All must be in excellent condition in Oriental clothes and no damage to head.

Amusco, Mold #1006: Bisque head. 13" - $965.00.

Armand Marseille: Girl or boy marked only "A.M." 7" - $700.00; 11" - $900.00. Painted Bisque: 8" - $250.00; 12" - $475.00.

#353 Baby: 12" - $1,150.00; 15" - $1,400.00; 19" - $2,200.00. Painted bisque: 15" - $650.00.

Bruno Schmidt (BSW) #220: Closed mouth. 16" - $3,850.00.

#500: 14" - $2,200.00; 18" - $3,200.00. All bisque: 6" - $750.00.

Kestner (J.D.K.) #243: Baby: 15" - $5,200.00; 19" - $7,400.00. Molded hair baby: 15" - $6,000.00. Child: 15" - $5,500.00; 19" - $8,000.00. All bisque: 6" - $1,250.00.

Schoenau & Hoffmeister, #4900: (S, PB in star H) See photo in Series 5, pg. 116.) 15" - $1,700.00; 19" - $2,000.00.

Simon & Halbig (S & H) #164: 15" - $2,400.00; 19" - $2,900.00.

#220: (See photo in Series 6, pg. 145.) Solid dome or "Belton" type. Closed mouth. 18" - $3,400.00.

#1099, 1129, 1159, 1199: (See photo in Series 7, pg. 129.) 15" - $2,750.00; 19" - $3,400.00.

#1329: (See photo in Series 7, pg. 129.) 15" - $2,400.00; 19" - $2,900.00.

All Bisque: Unmarked. 7-8" - $800.00.

13" baby marked "J.D.K. 243." Sleep eyes, open mouth, two upper teeth and tongue. 17" marked "S & H 1199/DEP." Slant sleep eyes, open mouth with four upper teeth. Fully jointed body. 13" - $4,600.00; 17" - $3,250.00. Courtesy Frasher Doll Auctions.

17" Japanese baby marked "2 ⊛ Japan 11." Open mouth, four upper teeth, dimples, and on five-piece baby body. 15" marked "2 ⊛ Japan 11." Open mouth with four teeth and on five-piece baby body. 17" - $425.00; 15" - $365.00. Courtesy Frasher Doll Auctions.

Unmarked: Open mouth: 15" - $1,300.00; 19" - $2,000.00. Closed mouth: 15" - $2,000.00; 19" - $3,000.00. All bisque: Glass eyes: 6" - $485.00; 10-11" - $885.00.

Nippon – Caucasian Dolls Made in Japan: 1918–1922. Most made during World War I. These dolls can be near excellent quality to very poor quality. Morimura Brothers mark is ⊕. Dolls marked 𝒯𝒴 were made by Yamato. Others will just be marked with NIPPON along with other marks such as "J.W.", etc.

Nippon Marked Baby: Good to excellent bisque, well painted, nice body and no damage. 10" - $165.00; 12" - $285.00; 16" - $375.00; 20" - $600.00; 25" - $825.00. Poor quality: 12" - $125.00;

16" - $175.00; 20" - $265.00; 25" - $365.00. "Hilda" look-alike: 18" - $725.00.

Nippon Child: Good to excellent quality bisque, no damage and nicely dressed. 15" - $325.00; 19" - $550.00; 23" - $700.00. Poor quality: 15" - $135.00; 19" - $225.00; 23" - $325.00.

Molded Hair: Molded bows on side, cloth body, oilcloth lower arms, silk feet. Marked 𝒯𝒴 or ⊕. 1920–1930's. 15" - $300.00; 18" - $450.00.

Traditional Doll: Made in Japan. Papier maché swivel head on shoulder plate, cloth mid-section and upper arms and legs. Limbs and torso are papier maché, glass eyes, pierced nostrils. The early dolls will have jointed wrists and ankles and will be slightly sexed.

22½" marked "𝒯𝒴 Nippon." Uses a German mold. Open mouth, set eyes, and high color bisque. 22½" - **$700.00.**
Courtesy Frasher Doll Auctions.

17" marked 𝒯𝒴. **Molded hair bisque with bows on the sides. Original cloth body with long legs and black silk feet. Oil cloth lower arms, painted features. 17" - $245.00.**

Early fine quality: Original dress, 1890's. 14" - $350.00; 19" - $575.00; 26" - $1,000.00.

Early Boy: With painted hair. 16" - $500.00; 21" - $850.00; 28" - $1,400.00. 1930's or later: 14" - $125.00; 17" - $200.00.

Lady: All original and excellent quality. 1920's: 12" - $200.00; 16" - $325.00. Later Lady: 1940's–1950's. 12" - $125.00; 14" - $145.00.

Emperor or Empress in Sitting Position: 1920's–1930's. 8" - $200.00 up; 12" - $400.00 up.

Warrior: 1880's–1890's: 16-18" - $650.00 up. On horse: 16" - $1,200.00 up. Early 1920's: 12" - $300.00 up. On horse: 12" - $800.00 up.

Japanese Baby: With bisque head. Sleep eyes, closed mouth and all white bisque. Papier maché body: Original and in excellent condition. Late 1920's. 8" - $75.00; 12" - $185.00. Glass Eyes: 8" - $90.00; 12" - $195.00.

Japanese Baby: Head made of crushed oyster shells painted flesh color, papier maché body, glass eyes and original. 8" - $85.00; 12" - $145.00; 16" - $200.00; 19" - $300.00.

Oriental Dolls: All composition, jointed at shoulder and hips. Painted features, painted hair or can have bald head with braid of yarn down back with rest covered by cap, such as "Ling Ling" or "Ming Ming" made by Quan Quan Co. in 1930's. Painted-on shoes. 10" - $165.00.

Chinese Traditional Dolls: Man or woman. Composition-type material with cloth-wound bodies or can have wooden carved arms and feet. In traditional costume and in excellent condition. 9" - $350.00; 12" - $575.00.

Door of Hope Dolls: Wooden head, cloth bodies and most have carved hands. Chinese costume. Adult: 11" - $465.00. Child: 7" - $525.00. Mother and Baby: 11" - $685.00. Man: 11" - $500.00. Carved flowers in hair: 12" - $585.00. Brides: 12" - $825.00.

10" **Oriental baby on stomach, holding toy. All original. Flesh-colored crushed oyster shell paste over papier maché, glass eyes. 10" - $165.00 up.** Courtesy Shirley Bertrand.

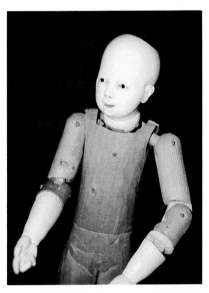

13" Oriental. Wood segmented into ivory. Pupilless glass eyes, open/closed mouth with carved tongue, delicate fingers. Apparently adjustable as to how tall head will go. Ivory hinged door in back of head. Price unknown. Courtesy Shirley Bertrand.

ORSINI

Jeanne I. Orsini of New York designed dolls from 1916 to the 1920's. It is not known who made the heads for her, but it is likely that all bisque dolls designed by her were made by J.D. Kestner in Germany. The initials of the designer are "J.I.O." and the dolls will be marked with those initials along with a year such as 1919, 1920, etc. Since the middle initial is "I," it may appear as a number 1. Dolls can also be marked "Copy. by J.I. Orsini/Germany."

Painted Bisque Character: Can be on a cloth body with cloth limbs or a bent limb baby body, a toddler body, have flirty eyes and an open smiling mouth. Can be wigged or have molded hair and be a boy or a girl. Head is painted or painted clay-like material. Prices are for excellent condition, no damage and nicely dressed. **#1429:** 15" - $2,200.00; 19" - $2,700.00.

Bisque Head Baby: Cloth body with bisque head with wide open screaming mouth, eye squinted and marked "JIO." 12" - $1,200.00; 14" - $1,500.00.

Bisque Head Baby: Fired-in color bisque head with sleep eyes (some may be set), open mouth and has cloth body and painted hair. Marked "KIDDIE JOY JIO. 1926." 15" - $1,900.00; 17" - $2,450.00.

All Bisque: See All Bisque section for Didi, Fifi, Dodo, Zizi, etc.

135

P.D.

P.D. marked dolls were made in Paris, France by Petit & DuMontier, 1878–1890.

Child: Closed mouth, jointed body, metal hands. No damage, nicely dressed. 16" - $16,000.00; 19" - $18,000.00; 22" - $22,000.00; 24" - $26,000.00.

Right: 20½" marked "P. 3 D." with closed mouth and on fully jointed body. Left: 22" "Long Face/Triste" Jumeau with closed mouth, jointed body with straight wrists. 20½" - $21,000.00; 22" - $24,000.00. Courtesy Frasher Doll Auctions.

P.G.

Pintel & Godchaux of Montreuil, France made dolls from 1890 to 1899. They held one trademark—"Bébé Charmant." The heads will be marked "P.G."

Child: 17" - $3,000.00; 22" - $3,600.00; 24" - $4,500.00.

Child, Open Mouth: 15" - $1,600.00; 20" - $2,100.00; 23" - $2,700.00.

18" marked "P 9 G" with open mouth and on French jointed body. 18" - $3,200.00. Courtesy Turn of Century Antiques.

Papier maché dolls were made in U.S., Germany, England, France and other countries. Paper pulp, wood and rag fibers containing paste, oil or glue are formed into a composition-like moldable material. Flour, clay and/or sand is added for stiffness. The hardness of papier maché depends on the amount of glue that is added.

Many so called papier maché parts were actually laminated paper with several thicknesses of molded paper bonded (glued) together or pressed after being glued.

"Papier maché" means "chewed paper" in French, and as early as 1810, dolls of papier maché were being mass produced by using molds.

Marked "M&S Superior": (Muller & Strassburger) Papier maché shoulder head with blonde or black molded hair, painted blue or brown eyes, old cloth body with kid or leather arms and boots. Nicely dressed and head not repainted, chipped or cracked. 15" - $385.00; 17"- $565.00; 23" - $725.00. Glass eyes: 21" - $800.00. With wig: 19" - $725.00. Repainted nicely: 17" - $300.00; 23" - $500.00. Chips, scuffs or not repainted well: 17" - $100.00; 23" - $135.00.

French or French Type: (See photos in Series 5, pg. 151; Series 7, pg. 133.) Painted black hair, some with brush marks, on solid dome. Some have nailed-on wigs. Open mouths have bamboo teeth. Inset glass eyes. In very good condition, nice old clothes. All leather/kid body. 16" - $1,400.00; 18" - $1,800.00; 21" - $2,000.00; 25" - $2,500.00; 29" - $3,500.00.

10" French type papier maché that has unusual face and hairdo. Wooden limbs and holds baby with wooden limbs. All original. 10" - $1,950.00. Courtesy Ellen Dodge.

Large 37" papier maché of the 1830's. Elaborate hairstyle, papier maché shoulder head, leather body with wooden lower limbs, painted features. 37" - $2,700.00 up. 37", restored - $950.00. Courtesy Frasher Doll Auctions.

Early Papier Maché: (See photo in Series 6, pg. 153.) With cloth body and wooden limbs. Early hairdo with top knots, buns, puff curls or braiding. Not restored and in original or very well made clothes. In very good condition and may show a little wear. 10" - $525.00; 14" - $675.00; 18" - $875.00; 21" - $1,100.00; 25" - $1,500.00.

Long Curls: 9" - $625.00; 13" - $725.00.

Covered Wagon/Flat Top Hairdo: 7" - $345.00; 11" - $525.00; 14-15" - $685.00.

1820's – 1860's (Milliners Models): Side curls, braided bun. 9-10" - $785.00; 13-14" - $1,250.00. Side curls with high top knot: 12" - $1,000.00; 17" - $1,900.00. Coiled braids over ears, braided bun: 19-20" - $2,200.00 up.

6" lady with crossed hands, closed eyes and molded hair. Papier maché head on bisque shoulder plate and has cylinder base of porcelain. Use unknown. 6" - $400.00. Courtesy Shirley Bertrand.

Marked "Greiner": Dolls of 1858 on: Blonde or black molded hair, brown or blue painted eyes, cloth body with leather arms, nicely dressed and with very little minor scuffs. See Greiner section.

Motschmann Types: With wood and twill bodies. Separate hip section, glass eyes, closed mouth and brush stroke hair on solid domes. Nicely dressed and ready to display. 15" - $725.00; 21" - $975.00; 25" - $1,500.00.

German Papier Maché: 1870–1900's. Molded various hairdos, painted eyes and closed mouth. May be blonde or black hair. Nicely dressed and not repainted: 17" - $525.00; 21" - $675.00; 25" - $1,400.00; 30" - $1,800.00. Glass eyes: 17" - $650.00; 21" - $800.00; 25" - $1,500.00; 30" - $1,900.00. Showing wear and scuffs, but not touched up: 17" - $250.00; 21" - $300.00; 25" - $400.00; 30" - $600.00.

Turned Shoulder Head: Solid dome, glass eyes and closed mouth. Twill cloth body with composition lower arms. In very good condition and nicely dressed. 16" - $650.00; 21" - $900.00.

German Character Heads: (See photo in Series 6, pg. 152.) These heads are molded just like the bisque ones. Glass eyes, closed mouth and on fully jointed body. In excellent condition and nicely dressed. 15" - $1,000.00; 21" - $1,500.00.

1920's on - Papier Maché: Head usually has bright coloring. Wigged, usually dressed as a child, or in provincial costumes. Stuffed cloth body and limbs or have papier maché arms. In excellent overall condition. 9" - $90.00; 13" - $150.00; 15" - $225.00.

Clowns: Papier maché head with painted clown features. Open or closed mouth, molded hair or wigged and on cloth body with some having composition or papier maché lower arms. In excellent condition. 12" - $385.00; 16" - $650.00.

17" papier maché character heads with swivel necks, removable bonnet and hat. Both are original. Molded hair, painted features, molded-on Dutch-style shoes. He carries in his hand a metal pail with hole molded through it. She carries a broom. Bodies are papier covered over stuffed cloth. Lower arms and legs are plastic-like material that is painted. She has paper underclothes and upper legs are wrapped in paper. 17", each - $1,000.00 up. Courtesy Jeanette and Robert Woodall.

11" hair molded around ear and tucked into coil braid in back. Cloth body with wooden lower limbs, painted features. 11" - $1,000.00 up. Courtesy Shirley Bertrand.

"Parian-type" dolls were made from the 1850's to the 1880's, with the majority being made during the 1870's and 1880's. There are hundreds of different heads, and all seem to have been made in Germany. If marked, it will be found on the inside of the shoulder plate. It must be noted that the very rare and unique unglazed porcelain dolls are difficult to find and their prices will be high.

"Parian-type" dolls can be found with every imaginable thing applied to the head and shirt tops – flowers, snoods, ruffles, feathers, plumes, etc. Many have inset glass eyes, pierced ears and most are blonde, although some will have from light to medium brown hair, and a few will have glazed black hair.

Various Fancy Hairstyles: (See photo in Series 5, pg. 121.) With molded combs, ribbons, flowers, head bands, or snoods. Cloth body with cloth/"parian" limbs. Perfect condition and very nicely dressed. 18" - $1,700.00 up; 22" - $2,200.00 up. Painted eyes, unpierced ears: 18" - $1,000.00; 22" - $1,400.00.

Swivel Neck: 18" - $3,000.00; 22" - $3,600.00.

Molded Necklaces: Jewels or standing ruffles (undamaged). Glass eyes, pierced ears: 18" - $1,800.00 up; 22" - $2,400.00 up. Painted eyes, unpierced ears: 18" - $1,100.00; 22" - $1,500.00.

Bald Head: Solid dome, takes wigs, full ear detail. 1850's. Perfect condition and nicely dressed. 13" - $775.00; 17" - $995.00; 21" - $1,600.00.

Molded Head Band: (See photo in Series 5, pg. 121; Series 7, pg. 137.) Called "Alice." 13" - $350.00; 16" - $585.00; 19" - $850.00.

Very Plain Style: With no decoration in hair or on shoulders. No damage and nicely dressed. 15" - $350.00; 18" - $600.00.

4½" Parian head marked "1042 #4." Painted downcast eyes, modeled-on hat and fully exposed ears. 18" - $2,700.00 up. Courtesy Shirley Bertrand.

3½" tall Parian head with glass eyes, modeled-on hat and swirled hair on brim. 16" - $2,950.00 up. Courtesy Shirley Bertrand.

Men or Boys: Hairdos with center or side part, cloth body with cloth/ "parian" limbs. Decorated shirt and tie. 16" - $850.00; 19" - $1,200.00.

Undecorated Shirt Top: 16" - $375.00; 19" - $550.00; 25" - $875.00.

Molded Hat: 10" - $1,800.00; 15" - $2,700.00.

Right: Glass eye Parian boy that is 15" tall and has modeled curls and hair combed forward. Kid body with bisque lower arms. Left: 14" unmarked, cute sweet-faced child. Closed mouth and jointed body with straight wrists. 15" - $1,850.00; 14" - $1,200.00. Courtesy Frasher Doll Auctions.

PARIS BÉBÉ

These dolls were made by Danel & Cie in France from 1889 to 1895. The heads will be marked "Paris Bébé" and the body's paper label is marked with a drawing of the Eiffel Tower and "Paris Bébé/Brevete."

Paris Bébé Child: Closed mouth, no damage and nicely dressed. 17" - $4,600.00; 21" - $5,000.00; 25" - $5,650.00; 27" - $5,800.00. High color to bisque, closed mouth. 17" - $3,700.00; 21" - $4,000.00; 25" - $4,400.00; 27" - $4,900.00.

16" marked "Paris Bébé." Closed mouth and on chunky jointed French body. All original clothes. 16" - $4,500.00. Courtesy Barbara Earnshaw-Cain.

PARIS BÉBÉ

27" Danel & Cie "Paris Bébé" with closed mouth. French jointed body. 27" - $5,800.00. Courtesy Turn of Century Antiques.

PHÉNIX

Phénix Bébé dolls were made by Henri Alexandre of Paris who made dolls from 1889 to 1900.

Mark:

Child - Closed Mouth: 17" - $4,350.00; 19" - $4,600.00; 23" - $5,350.00; 25" - $5,500.00.
Child - Open Mouth: 17" - $2,200.00; 19" - $2,550.00; 23" - $2,900.00; 25" - $3,150.00.

21" Phénix Bébé marked "Phénix" with star in red, "93" incised. Closed mouth, French body with straight wrists. Original clothes and shoes. 21" - $4,850.00. Courtesy Shirlie Glass.

Piano babies were made in Germany from the 1880's into the 1930's and one of the finest quality makers was Gebruder Heubach. They were also made by Kestner, Dressel, Limbach, etc.

Piano Babies: All bisque, unjointed, molded hair and painted features. The clothes are molded on and they come in a great variety of positions.

Excellent Quality: Extremely good artist workmanship and excellent detail to modeling. 4" - $190.00; 8" - $450.00 up; 12" - $750.00 up; 16" - $900.00 up.

Medium Quality: May not have painting finished on back side of figure. 4" - $125.00; 8" - $265.00; 12" - $400.00; 16" - $550.00.

With Animal, Pot, On Chair, With Flowers or Other Items: (See photos in Series 6, pg. 158; Series 7, pg. 141.) Excellent quality. 4" - $250.00; 8" - $450.00; 12" - $825.00 up; 16" - $1,200.00 up.

Black: Excellent quality: 4" - $365.00; 8" - $475.00; 12" - $625.00; 16" - $1,000.00 up. Medium quality: 4" - $165.00; 8" - $250.00; 12" - $400.00; 16" - $800.00.

Beautiful 10" piano baby marked "743-9." Excellent quality. Has woven basket in one hand. Shown with a fully marked 16" "Hilda" by Kestner. In doll's lap are three all original doll house dolls. 3" and 4" with jointed shoulders and hips. 10" - $500.00; 16" - $3,000.00. Doll house dolls, set: $475.00. Courtesy Frasher Doll Auctions.

RABERY & DELPHIEU

Rabery & Delphieu began making dolls in 1856. The very first dolls have kid bodies and are extremely rare. The majority of their dolls are on French jointed bodies and are marked "R.D." A few may be marked "Bébé de Paris."

Child: With closed mouth, in excellent condition with no chips, breaks or hairlines in bisque. Body in overall good condition and nicely dressed. Pretty face. 12-13" - $2,650.00; 15" -

$3,000.00; 18" - $3,500.00; 21" - $3,800.00; 23" - $4,200.00; 26" - $5,100.00.

Child: With open mouth and same condition as above: 14" - $1,100.00; 18" - $1,700.00; 21" - $2,300.00; 23" - $2,800.00; 26" - $3,200.00.

Child: Lesser quality, high color, poor artist workmanship. Closed mouth: 15" - $2,000.00; 18" - $2,500.00; 21" - $2,800.00. Same, open mouth: 14" - $650.00; 18" - $875.00; 21" - $1,000.00.

18" marked "R.D." Made by Rabery & Delphieu. Closed mouth and on French fully jointed body. 18" - $3,500.00. Courtesy Frasher Doll Auctions.

Marked "R.D." with closed mouth and on French body with early straight wrists. Closed mouth and all original factory clothes. 18" original - $4,400.00. Courtesy Barbara Earnshaw-Cain.

Very early white bisque marked "R.D." with closed mouth and French jointed body with straight wrists. 15" - $3,000.00. Courtesy Barbara Earnshaw-Cain.

Dolls marked with "R.A." were made by Recknagel of Alexandrinenthal, Thuringia, Germany. The R.A. dolls date from 1886 to after World War I and can range from very poor workmanship to excellent quality bisque and artist work. Prices are for dolls with good artist workmanship, such as the lips and eyebrows painted straight, feathered or at least not off-center. Original or nicely dressed and no damage.

Child: 1890's–1914. Set or sleep eyes, open mouth with small dolls having painted-on shoes and socks. 8" - $165.00; 12" - $225.00; 16" - $325.00; 20" - $425.00; 23" - $625.00.

#1907, 1909, 1914, etc.: 8" - $185.00; 12" - $275.00; 16" - $365.00; 20" - $475.00; 23" - $700.00.

Baby: Ca. 1909–1910 on. Five-piece bent limb baby body or straight leg, curved arm toddler body and with sleep or set eyes. No damage and nicely dressed. 7" - $285.00; 9" - $285.00; 12" - $350.00; 16" - $475.00; 20" - $600.00.

Character: With painted eyes, modeled bonnet and open/closed mouth, some smiling, some with painted-in teeth. No damage and nicely dressed. 8" - $685.00; 12" - $950.00.

Character: Glass eyes, closed mouth, and composition bent limb baby body. 7" - $685.00; 10" - $865.00; 14" - $1,000.00.

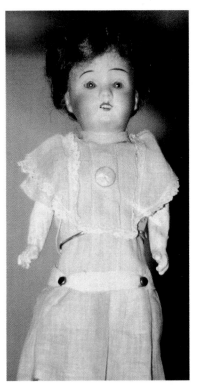

10" bisque head with open mouth and four teeth. Marked "21/Germany/R 10/0 A." Papier maché limbs and cardboard body. Sleep eyes and original. 10" - $285.00. Courtesy Sandra Cummins.

REINECKE

Dolls marked with "P.M." were made by Otto Reinecke of Hof-Moschendorf, Bavaria, Germany from 1909 into the 1930's. The mold number found most often is the #914 baby or toddler. (See photo in Series 7, pg. 144.)

Child: Bisque head with open mouth and on five-piece papier maché body or fully jointed body. Can have sleep or set eyes. No damage and nicely dressed. 10" - $185.00; 14" - $300.00; 17" - $550.00; 21" - $675.00.

Baby: Open mouth, sleep eyes or set eyes. Bisque head on five-piece bent limb baby body. No damage and nicely dressed. 10" - $250.00; 12" - $365.00; 15" - $565.00; 21" - $650.00; 26" - $875.00.

REVALO

The Revalo marked dolls were made by Gebruder Ohlhaver of Thuringia, Germany from 1921 to the 1930's. Bisque heads with jointed bodies, sleep or set eyes. No damage and nicely dressed.

Child: Open mouth. 15" - $425.00; 18" - $575.00; 21" - $675.00; 25" - $750.00.

Molded Hair Child: (See photo in Series 7, pg. 146.) With or without molded ribbon and/or flower. Painted eyes and open/closed mouth. 12" - $685.00; 15" - $875.00.

Baby: Open mouth, sleep or set eyes on five-piece baby body. 14" - $475.00; 17" - $675.00.

Toddler: 16" - $750.00; 18" - $900.00.

SCHMIDT, BRUNO

Bruno Schmidt's doll factory was located in Waltershausen, Germany and many of the heads used by this firm were made by Bahr & Proschild, Ohrdruf, Germany. They made dolls from 1898 on into the 1930's.

Mark:

2033-6

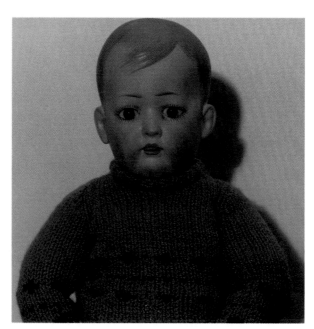

16" "Tommy Tucker" with molded, painted hair, glass eyes, and open/closed mouth with molded tongue. Some have full closed mouths. Jointed composition body. 16" - $1,300.00. Courtesy Turn of Century Antiques.

Child: Bisque head on jointed body, sleep eyes, open mouth, no damage and nicely dressed. 15" - $465.00; 21" - $725.00; 27" - $950.00. Flirty eyes: 21" - $875.00; 29" - $1,500.00.

Character Baby, Toddler or Child: Bisque head, glass eyes or painted eyes, jointed body, no damage and nicely dressed.

#2025, 2026: Closed mouth, glass eyes. 18" - $4,200.00; 23" - $5,100.00.

#2069: Closed mouth, glass eyes, sweet face, jointed body. 14" - $4,000.00; 18" - $6,500.00.

#2048, 2094, 2096 (called "Tommy Tucker"): (See photo in Series 6, pg. 163.) Molded, painted hair, open mouth. 14" - $1,300.00; 18" - $1,600.00; 23" - $2,000.00.

#2048, 2094, 2096: "Tommy Tucker" with closed mouth. Otherwise, same as above. 14" - $2,000.00; 18" - $2,600.00; 23" - $3,000.00.

#2072: Closed mouth, wig. 19" - $3,800.00; 22" - $4,350.00.

#2097: Toddler. 15" - $700.00; 21" - $1,000.00. Baby: 14" - $550.00; 18" - $850.00.

Character Child: Closed mouth, painted eyes or glass eyes, jointed child body, no damage and nicely dressed.

Marked "BSW" in heart: No mold number. (See photo in Series 6, pg. 164.) 17" - $2,700.00; 21" - $3,200.00.

#2033 "Wendy": (See photo in Series 6, pg. 163.) 14" - $17,000.00; 17" - $22,000.00 up; 21" - $25,000.00 up.

Franz Schmidt & Co. began in 1890 at Georgenthal, near Waltershausen, Germany. In 1902, they registered the cross hammers with a doll between and also the F.S.&C. mark.

Mark:

1310

F.S. & Co.

Made in
Germany

10

Baby: Bisque head on bent limb baby body, sleep or set eyes, open mouth and some may have pierced nostrils. No damage and nicely dressed. (Add more for toddler body.)

#1271, 1272, 1295, 1296, 1297, 1310: 10" - $375.00; 16" - $650.00; 21" - $800.00; 25" - $1,200.00. Toddler: 8-9" - $675.00; 16" - $765.00; 21" - $1,100.00; 25" - $1,300.00.

#1267: (See photo in Series 5, pg. 126.) Open/closed mouth, painted eyes. 15" - $2,000.00; 20" - $2,900.00. Glass eyes: 15" - $2,400.00; 20" - $3,400.00.

#1285: 15" - $700.00; 21" - $950.00.

Child: Papier maché and composition body with walker mechanism with metal rollers on feet. Open mouth, sleep eyes. Working and no damage to head, nicely dressed.

#1250: 15" - $800.00; 21" - $1,000.00.

#1262: Closed mouth, almost smiling child. Painted eyes, wig, jointed body. 20" - $4,200.00; 24" - $5,000.00.

#1266, 1267: Child with open mouth and sleep eyes. 21" - $2,500.00.

#1286: Molded hair, ribbon, open mouth smile, glass eyes. 16-17" - $4,200.00.

Child: Marked "S & C." 1890-on. 6-7" - $345.00; 15" - $525.00; 18" - $600.00; 23" - $725.00; 26" - $825.00; 30" - $1,100.00; 36" - $1,800.00; 40" - $2,800.00.

Left: 16" marked "2/F.S. & C./1250/ 30." Walker doll which operates by key. Open mouth and sleep eyes. All original. Has metal rollers on bottom of feet. Below: Detail of metal rollers on feet. 16" - $800.00. Courtesy Jay Minter.

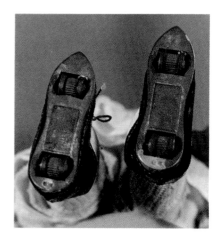

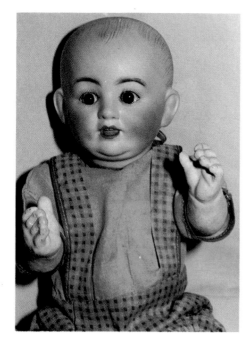

16" marked "F.S. & C./1271/402." Sleep eyes and open mouth with tremble tongue. Five-piece bent limb baby body. 16" - $575.00. Courtesy Frasher Doll Auctions.

Schmitt & Fils produced dolls from 1870's to 1891 in Paris, France. The dolls have French jointed bodies and came with closed mouths or open/closed ones.

Mark:

Child: 1880 – on. Bisque head with long, thin face. Jointed body with closed mouth or open/closed mouth. No damage and nicely dressed. Marked on head and body. 16" - $12,000.00 up; 19" - $17,000.00 up; 23" - $22,000.00 up; 26" - $27,000.00 up; 29" - $32,000.00.

Child: (See photo in Series 6, pg. 166.) Round face. 11-12" - $9,600.00; 16-17" - $17,000.00; 21-22" - $19,000.00 up.

Left: 14" marked "Bte SGDG 0." Body: "Sch" in shield. Early white bisque, closed mouth and French Steiner body with straight wrists. Middle: 14" Gebruder Heubach #7307 with open/closed mouth and two modeled teeth and cheek dimples. Jointed body with straight wrists. Right: 14" Simon & Halbig lady type marked "939." Open/closed mouth with space between, cotton twill body, bisque lower arms. 14" - $9,800.00; #7307: $1,600.00; #939 - $1,650.00. Courtesy Frasher Doll Auctions.

14½" Schmitt & Fils marked with the "SCH" in shield plus crossed hammers on body. Closed mouth, original Schmitt body with straight wrists. Many early Kestner dolls will have this style body but they are not marked. 14½" - $12,000.00. Courtesy Frasher Doll Auctions.

SCHOENAU & HOFFMEISTER

Schoenau & Hoffmeister began making dolls in 1901 and were located in Bavaria. The factory was called "Porzellanfabrik Burggrub" and this mark will be found on many of their doll heads. Some of their mold numbers are **21, 169, 170, 769, 900, 914, 1271, 1800, 1906, 1909, 1923, 4000, 4900, 5000, 5300, 5500, 5700, 5800, 5900** and also Hanna.

Mark:

Princess Elizabeth: Smiling open mouth, set eyes, bisque head on jointed five-piece body and marked with name on head or body. 15" - $2,000.00; 21" - $2,600.00; 24" - $3,200.00.

Hanna: Child with black or brown fired-in color to bisque head. Sleep or set eyes, five-piece body or jointed body. Marked with name on head. 8" - $385.00; 14" - $725.00.

Hanna Baby: Bisque head, open mouth, sleep eyes and on five-piece bent limb baby body. 10" - $400.00; 13" - $700.00; 16" - $800.00; 23" - $1,200.00; 25" - $1,400.00. Toddler: 14" - $900.00; 20" - $1,100.00.

Character Baby: #169, 769, 1271, etc. 1910–on. Bisque head on five-piece bent limb baby body. 12" - $365.00; 16" - $575.00; 19" - $700.00; 23" - $800.00. Toddler body: 18" - $850.00; 21" - $1,000.00.

34" marked "S", "PB" in star, "H." 1906. Open mouth, sleep eyes and on fully jointed body. 34" - $1,400.00.
Courtesy Frasher Doll Auctions.

42" marked "S", "PB" in star, "H." Sleep eyes, open mouth and on fully jointed chunky body. 12½" Gussie P. Decker all leather doll of 1903. Twirling doll on stick that plays music and has a Simon & Halbig marked "950" head with closed mouth. 42" - $3,700.00 up; 12½" - $700.00; "950" - $995.00.
Courtesy Turn of Century Antiques.

Child: #1800, 1906, 1909, 5500, 5900, 5800, etc. Bisque head with open mouth, sleep or set eyes, jointed body. No damage and nicely dressed. 10" - $185.00; 16" - $400.00; 19" - $500.00; 22" - $625.00; 27" - $875.00; 30" - $1,100.00; 34" - $1,400.00.

Painted Bisque: Painted head on five-piece body or jointed body. 10" - $165.00; 13" - $250.00.

Das Lachende Baby (The Laughing Baby): 20" - $2,000.00; 25" - $2,500.00.

Beautiful 41" marked "PB" in star, along with S.H. Set eyes, open mouth and chunky ball-jointed body. 41" - $3,700.00 up. Courtesy Turn of Century Antiques.

SCHOENHUT

The Albert Schoenhut & Co. was located in Philadephia, PA, from 1872 until the 1930's. The dolls are all wood with spring joints, have holes in bottom of feet to fit in a metal stand.

Marks:

(1911–1913)   **(1913–1930)**

SCHOENHUT DOLL
PAT. JAN. 17, '11, USA
& FOREIGN COUNTRIES
(Incised 1911–on)

Child With Carved Hair: May have comb marks, molded ribbon, comb or bow. Closed mouth. Original or nice clothes. Excellent condition: 14" - $2,450.00; 21" - $2,750.00. Very good condition with some wear: 14" - $1,500.00; 21" - $2,000.00. Poor condition with chips and dents: 14" - $550.00; 21" - $675.00.

Man With Carved Hair: 19", mint - $3,000.00; some wear - $1,800.00; chips, dirty - $800.00.

Baby Head: Can be on regular body or bent limb baby body. Bald spray painted hair or wig, painted decal eyes. Nicely dressed or original. Excellent condition: 12" - $550.00; 16" - $700.00; 18" - $775.00. Good condition: 16" - $450.00; 18" - $550.00. Poor condition: 16" - $200.00; 18" - $250.00.

Toddler: Excellent condition. 15" - $850.00; 17" - $900.00.

Child, character face: 1911–1930. Wig, intaglio eyes. Open/closed mouth with painted teeth. Suitably redressed or original. Excellent condition: 14" - $1,700.00; 21" - $2,200.00. Good condition: 14" - $975.00; 21" - $1,350.00. Poor condition: 14" - $350.00; 21" - $650.00.

Cap Molded To Head: 14" - $3,200.00 up.

Tootsie Wootsie: (See photo in Series 6, pg. 170.) Molded, painted hair, open/closed mouth with molded tongue and two upper teeth. Toddler or regular body: 12" - $2,200.00; 17" - $3,000.00.

"Dolly" Face: 1915–1930. Common doll, wigged, open/closed mouth with painted teeth, decal painted eyes. Original or nicely dressed. Excellent condition: 14" - $775.00; 21" - $975.00. Good condition: 14" - $550.00; 21" - $800.00. Poor condition: 14" - $150.00; 16" - $200.00.

15" girl with modeled-on bonnet cap. Intaglio painted eyes and open/closed mouth. 1912. 15" - $3,200.00. Courtesy Ellen Dodge.

Sleep Eyes: Has lids that lower down over the eyes and has an open mouth with teeth or just slightly cut open mouth with carved teeth. Original or nicely dressed. Excellent condition: 13-14" - $1,350.00; 22" - $1,500.00. Good condition: 16" - $700.00; 21" - $850.00. Poor condition: 17" - $200.00; 22" - $275.00.

Walker: 1919–1930. One-piece legs with "walker" joints in center of legs and torso. Painted eyes, open/closed or closed mouth. Original or nicely dressed. Excellent condition: 15" - $900.00; 18" - $1,100.00; 21" - $1,400.00. Good condition: 15" - $550.00; 18" - $650.00;

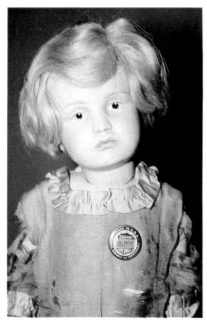

Rare Schoenhut girl patterned after Kammer & Reinhardt's model #101 "Maria" pouty. K*R sued and Schoenhut stopped making this doll. All original, 1911. 21" - $4,000.00. Courtesy Shirley Bertrand.

21" - $850.00. Poor condition: 15" - $125.00; 18" - $185.00; 21" - $250.00.

All Composition: Molded curly hair, "Patsy"-style body, paper label on back, 1924. 14" - $600.00.

Circus Animals: $95.00 - 500.00.

Clowns: $150.00 - 300.00.

Ringmaster: $200.00 - 350.00.

Two carved hair girls with both hairdos pulled back in braids and with bow in back. Decal painted eyes. Doll on right is 17" and dated 1911; on left, 19" and dated 1912. 17" - $2,500.00; 19" - $3,200.00.
Courtesy Shirley Bertrand.

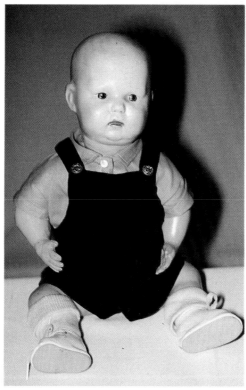

16" Schoenhut bent limb baby. Decal painted eyes, open/closed mouth and lightly spray painted hair. 1912. 16" - $700.00 up.
Courtesy Shirley Bertrand.

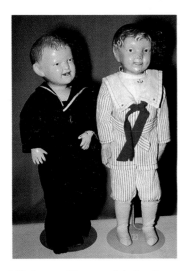 

Left: 15" boys with carved hair. One on left has an open/closed mouth and two lower teeth. One on right has dimples, open/closed mouth and painted upper teeth. Both are original, dated 1911. 15", each - $2,100.00. Right: Two girls with carved hair. The one on the left is a 17" pouty with a headband, dated 1912. The 21" doll on the right, dated 1911, has open/closed laughing mouth with painted teeth and original chemise. 17" - $2,650.00; 21" - $2,900.00. Courtesy Shirley Bertrand.

22" with sleep eyes, open/closed mouth with painted teeth. 15" with open mouth, two upper teeth, and glass eyes. 1913. 22" - $950.00; 15" - $775.00. Courtesy Shirley Bertrand.

9" Schoenhut cow with leather eyes. Wooden box with wood milk bottles made by Schoenhut. Box marked "Alderney Dairy Co. 26 Bridge St. Newark, N.J." The metal cream separator is marked "McCormick-Deering." 9" cow - $300.00; Bottles/case - $225.00. Courtesy Shirley Bertrand.

Two roly-poly figures made of papier maché and marked "Schoenhut/Pat. Dec. 14, 1914." Each - $300.00. Courtesy Shirley Bertrand.

SCHUETZMEISTER & QUENDT

Schuetzmeister & Quendt made dolls from 1893 to 1898. This short term factory was located in Boilstadt, Germany.

Marks:

Child: Mold #251, 252, etc. Can have cut pate or be a bald head with two string holes. No damage and nicely dressed, open mouth. 15" - $500.00; 21" - $685.00; 25" - $800.00.

Baby: Includes mold #201 & 301. Five-piece bent limb baby body. Not damaged and nicely dressed. Open mouth. 12" - $365.00; 15" - $525.00; 18" - $665.00; 23" - $825.00. Toddler: 15" - $1,000.00; 19" - $1,500.00; 23" - $1,900.00.

Right: 16" S&Q baby with sleep eyes and open mouth. Left: 18" Fran Schmidt character baby. Both are on bent limb baby bodies. 16" - $525.00; 18" - $700.00. Courtesy Frasher Doll Auctions.

SIMON & HALBIG

Simon & Halbig began making dolls in the late 1860's or early 1870's and continued until the 1930's. Simon & Halbig made many heads for other companies and they also supplied some doll heads from the French makers. They made entire dolls, all bisque, flange neck dolls, turned shoulder heads and socket heads.

All prices are for dolls with no damage to the bisque and only minor scuffs to the bodies, well dressed, wigged and have shoes. Dolls should be ready to place into a collection.

Marks:

S // H
729

1279-3
DEP

SH

GERMANY

Child: 1889 to 1930's. Open mouth and jointed body. **#600, 719, 720 (kid body), 739, 749, 939, 979, 1019, etc.:** 17" - $1,800.00; 21" - $2,400.00; 26" - $2,850.00; 29" - $3,100.00.

#949: Open mouth. 19" - $1,650.00; 21" - $1,950.00; 25" - $2,400.00.

#130, 530, 540, 550, 570, 600, 1039, 1040, etc: Open mouth. (More for flirty eyes.) 12" - $475.00; 16" - $565.00; 19" - $725.00; 23" - $800.00; 27" - $1,100.00; 32" - $1,800.00; 35" - $2,000.00; 40" - $2,800.00.

#1009, 1049, 1078, 1079, 1099: Open mouth. 11-12" - $565.00; 15" - $650.00; 17" - $700.00; 21" - $785.00; 24" - $850.00; 26" - $1,000.00; 32" - $1,500.00; 35" - $1,900.00; 42" - $3,600.00.

#1009: With fashion kid body. 19" - $950.00; 24" - $1,100.00; 26" - $1,400.00. Jointed body: 16" - $950.00; 19" - $1,300.00; 21" - $1,600.00.

#1019: Open mouth, smiling. Jointed body. 17" - $6,500.00. Composition shoulder plate, ball jointed arms, cloth body and upper legs. Ball jointed lower legs. 16½" - $7,350.00.

#1010, 1029, 1040, 1080, 1170, etc: Open mouth and kid body. 10-11" - $345.00; 15" - $500.00; 22" - $675.00; 26" - $875.00; 29" - $1,200.00.

#1109: 15" - $700.00; 22" - $950.00.

#1250, 1260: Open mouth, kid body. 16" - $575.00; 19" - $700.00; 25" - $975.00.

Characters: 1910 and after. Wig or molded hair, glass or painted eyes, with open/closed, closed, or open mouth. On jointed child bodies.

#IV: 20" - $22,000.00 up.

#IV: Open mouth. 23" - $2,500.00.

#120: 15" - $1,800.00; 23" - $2,900.00.

#150: (See photo in Series 7, pg. 155.) 16" - $14,000.00; 19" - $18,000.00 up; 23" - $21,000.00 up.

#151, 1388: (See photo in Series 7, pg. 155.) 15" - $5,500.00; 23" - $13,000.00.

#153 "Little Duke": 15" - $32,000.00; 17" - $42,000.00; 21" - $50,000.00.

16½" marked "979/8" Made by Simon & Halbig. Sleep eyes, closed mouth, and on jointed body with straight wrists. 16½" - $3,600.00. Courtesy Frasher Doll Auctions.

Extremely rare Simon & Halbig mold #153. 17" tall with deeply modeled hair, closed mouth, and painted eyes. Excellent face modeling. 17" - $42,000.00. Courtesy Frasher Doll Auctions.

Right: 15" marked "S 9 H 949." Set eyes, open mouth and square cut teeth. On fully jointed body. Left: 15" Kestner toddler, mold #257, with sleep eyes and open mouth. #949 - $785.00; #257 - $800.00. Courtesy Frasher Doll Auctions.

36" marked "1079 17 S&H DEP." Sleep eyes and open mouth on fully jointed body. 36" - $2,400.00. Courtesy Frasher Doll Auctions.

14" marked "S 4 H 1009 DEP." Swivel head on bisque shoulder plate, open mouth, kid body with bisque lower arms. 14" - $650.00. Courtesy Frasher Doll Auctions.

#540, 550, 570, Baby Blanche: 16" - $565.00; 22" - $750.00

#600: 15" - $850.00; 19" - $1,200.00; 23" - $1,700.00.

#603: 10-12" - $5,500.00.

#718, 719, 720: 15" - $2,200.00; 21" - $3,300.00.

#729: Slight open mouth, smiling. 16" - $2,800.00 up; 19" - $4,000.00.

#729: 16" - $2,400.00; 20" - $3,000.00.

#739: 17" - $2,750.00.

#740: Kid body, closed mouth. 10" - $600.00; 16" - $1,400.00; 18" - $1,600.00.

#740: Jointed body. 10" - $675.00; 17" - $1,600.00; 21" - $2,200.00.

#749: Closed mouth, jointed body. 17" - $2,600.00; 21" - $3,200.00.

#759: Open mouth, deep cheek dimples, rare. 24" - $18,000.00.

#905, 908: (See photo in Series 6, pg. 173.) Closed mouth. 15" - $2,700.00; 18" - $3,200.00. Open mouth. 15" - $1,800.00; 21" - $2,200.00; 29" - $3,200.00.

#919: Open/closed mouth. 16" - $5,000.00; 20" - $7,000.00.

#929: Closed mouth. 18" - $3,600.00; 21" - $4,600.00. Open mouth: 18" - $2,700.00; 21" - $3,700.00.

#939: Closed mouth: 15" - $2,200.00; 18" - $2,600.00; 21" - $3,300.00; 26" - $4,200.00. Kid body. 18" - $2,000.00; 21" - $2,700.00; 26" - $3,200.00.

#939, Black, closed mouth: 18"- $3,200.00; 21" - $4,300.00; 26" - $5,000.00. Open mouth: (See photo in Series 5, pg. 132.) 18" - $1,800.00; 21" - $2,300.00; 26" - $2,900.00.

#940, 950: (See photo in Series 7, pg. 156.) 21" - $2,000.00.

#949: Closed mouth. 18" - $2,500.00; 21" - $2,900.00; 26" - $3,300.00. Open mouth. 18" - $1,400.00; 21" - $1,700.00; 26" - $2,300.00.

#949, Black, closed mouth: 18" - $2,700.00; 21" - $3,200.00. Open mouth: 18" - $1,500.00; 21" - $2,000.00. Kid body: 18" - $1,600.00; 21" - $2,100.00; 26" - $2,600.00.

#969, 970: Open mouth grin, puffed cheeks. 16" - $9,500.00.

#979: Open mouth, square teeth, slight smile. 16" - $3,750.00.

#1248, 1249, 1250, 1260, Santa: 14-15" - $925.00; 17" - $1,000.00; 21" - $1,300.00; 25" - $1,700.00.

#1279: (See photo in Series 5, pg. 134.) 10" - $1,000.00; 14" - $1,650.00; 17" - $2,500.00; 20" - $3,000.00; 26" - $4,700.00; 30" - $6,400.00.

#1299: 18" - $1,200.00; 22" - $1,600.00.

#1302: See Black Dolls.

#1303: Closed mouth, thin lips. 17" - $7,400.00 up.

#1304: 15" - $6,800.00; 18" - $8,200.00.

#1305: Open/closed mouth, long nose. 16" - $10,000.00.

#1308: 18" - $6,200.00.

23½" marked "Halbig S & H Germany 10." Sleep eyes/lashes, open mouth and fully jointed body. 23½" - $800.00. Courtesy Frasher Doll Auctions.

#1309: Character with open mouth. 10" - $1,400.00; 16" - $1,950.00; 20" - $3,000.00.

#1310: Open/closed mouth, modeled mustache. 19½" - $18,000.00.

#1338: Open mouth, jointed body. 19" - $1,600.00; 25" - $2,800.00; 29" - $3,600.00.

#1339: (See photos in Series 5, pg. 135; Series 7, pg. 157.) Character face, open mouth. 19" - $1,700.00; 25" - $3,000.00.

#1345: 16" - $3,000.00; 18" - $4,800.00.

#1358: Black. 18" - $5,700.00; 21" - $6,400.00; 25" - $7,000.00.

#1388, 1398: Lady Doll. 22" - $17,500.00 up.

#1428: 21" - $2,450.00.

#1448: Full closed mouth. 20" - $21,000.00 up.

20" marked "1294 Simon & Halbig" Sleep eyes with lashes, open mouth, two upper teeth, and on five-piece bent limb baby body. 20" - $850.00. Courtesy Frasher Doll Auctions.

#1448: Open/closed mouth, laughing, modeled teeth. 20" - $26,000.00 up.

#1478: 17" - $9,500.00 up.

#1488: 17" - $3,750.00; 21" - $4,200.00.

Character Babies: 1909 to 1930's. Wigs or molded hair, painted or sleep eyes, open or open/closed mouth and on five-piece bent limb baby bodies. (Allow more for toddler body.)

#1294: 16" - $675.00; 19" - $825.00; 23" - $1,200.00; 26" - $1,800.00. With clockwork in head to move eyes. 25-26" - $3,000.00.

#1299: With open mouth. 10" - $385.00; 16" - $975.00. Toddler: 16" - $1,100.00; 18" - $1,300.00.

#1428 Toddler: (See photo in Series 7, pg. 158.) 12" - $1,550.00; 16" - $1,800.00; 20" - $2,200.00; 26" - $2,800.00.

#1428 Baby: 12" - $1,050.00; 16" - $1,600.00; 20" - $2,000.00.

#1488 Toddler: (See photo in Series 6, pg. 175.) 18" - $3,500.00; 22" - $4,000.00. Baby: 18" - $2,300.00; 22" - $2,600.00; 26" - $3,200.00.

#1489: Erika Baby. (See photos in Series 6, pg. 176; Series 7, pg. 159.) 20" - $3,300.00; 22" - $4,000.00; 26" - $4,700.00.

#1498 Toddler: (See photo in Series 6, pg. 175.) 17" - $7,000.00; 21" - $8,000.00. Baby: 17" - $6,400.00; 21" - $7,400.00.

#1039 Walker: Key wound. 17" - $2,400.00; 19" - $2,850.00; 21" - $3,600.00. Walking/Kissing: 19" - $1,000.00; 23" - $1,300.00.

Miniature Dolls: Tiny dolls with open mouth on jointed body or five-piece body with some having painted-on shoes and socks.

#1078, 1079, etc.: Fully jointed: 8" - $585.00; 10-12" - $685.00. Five-piece Body: 8" - $425.00; 10-12" - $545.00.

#1160: "Little Women" type. Closed mouth and fancy wig. 6" - $400.00; 10" - $550.00.

Ladies: Ca. 1910. Open mouth, molded lady-style slim body with slim arms and legs.

#1159, 1179: 12-13" - $925.00; 15" - $1,350.00; 19" - $1,900.00; 26" - $2,900.00.

Ladies: Closed mouth. Ca. 1910. Adult slim limb body.

#1303: 16" - $11,000.00; 19" - $14,500.00.

#1305: Lady. Open/closed mouth, long nose. 18" - $9,000.00 up; 22" - $12,000.00 up.

#1307: Lady, long face. 18" - $15,500.00 up; 24" - $22,500.00 up.

#1308: Man. 12-13" - $5,700.00; 16" - $6,850.00.

#1398: 18" - $10,000.00 up.

#1468, 1469: 16" - $3,000.00; 19" - $4,400.00.

#1527: 20" - $9,500.00 up; 24" - $11,500.00 up.

#152 Lady: 17" - $16,000.00 up.

14" "Flapper" marked "S & H 1159/6." Sleep eyes, mohair wig, open mouth, slender body with legs jointed above the knees. Has original hat, silk hose, high heels and chemise. Dress by owner. Shown with 10" Cissette "Flapper" made by Madame Alexander, 1988-1989. 14" - $1,350.00; 10" - available. Courtesy Glorya Woods.

Simon & Halbig mold #1303 man with slim adult jointed body, glass eyes and character face. Original wig and clothes. 16" - $11,000.00. Courtesy Etta Anderson.

17" Simon and Halbig lady with mold #1469. Sleep eyes, closed mouth. Adult body with narrow waist, slim limbs, and high-heeled feet. 17" - $3,950.00. Courtesy Frasher Doll Auctions.

S.F.B.J.

The Société Française de Fabrication de Bébés et Jouets (S.F.B.J.) was formed in 1899 and known members were Jumeau, Bru, Fleischmann & Blodel, Rabery & Delphieu, Pintel & Godchaux, P.H. Schmitz, A. Bouchet, Jullien, and Danel & Cie. By 1922, S.F.B.J. employed 2,800 people. The Society was dissolved in the mid-1950's. There are a vast amount of "dolly-faced" S.F.B.J. dolls, but some are extremely rare and are character molds. Most of the characters are in the 200 mold number series.

Marks:

S.F.B.J.
239
PARIS

DEPOSE
S.F.B.J.
301

Child: 1899. Sleep or set eyes, open mouth and on jointed French body. No damage and nicely dressed.

#60: 15" - $650.00; 21" - $975.00; 25" - $1,100.00.

#301: 8" - $425.00; 14" - $775.00; 18" - $900.00; 21" - $1,100.00; 29" - $1,800.00.

Bluette: 1930's–1960's. Made exclusively for Gautier-Languereau and their newspaper for children, *La Semaine de Suzette.* (Just as "Betsy McCall" was used by *McCall's* magazine.) Marked "SFBJ" or "71 Unis France 149 301" with "1½" at base of neck socket. Body marked "2" and feet marked "1." Sleep eyes, open mouth. (See photo in Series 7, pg. 36.) 11½-12" - $1,100.00.

Jumeau Type: (See photo in Series 7, pg. 163.) Open mouth: 17" - $1,400.00; 21" - $1,800.00; 25" - $2,300.00. Closed mouth: 17" - $2,500.00; 21" - $3,100.00; 25" - $3,500.00.

Lady #1159: Open mouth, adult body. 22" - $2,500.00.

Character: Sleep or set eyes, wigged, molded hair, jointed body. (Allow more for flocked hair.) No damage and nicely dressed.

#211: 17" - $5,800.00.

#226: 15" - $1,800.00; 20" - $2,500.00. Painted eyes: 15" - $1,500.00.

#227: (See photo in Series 5, pg. 136.) 17" - $2,600.00; 22" - $3,000.00.

#229: 17" - $4,000.00.

#230: 15" - $1,550.00; 21" - $1,950.00; 24" - $2,300.00.

#233: Screamer. 15" - $3,400.00; 18" - $4,500.00.

#234: 17" - $3,200.00; 22" - $3,700.00.

#235: 15" - $2,300.00; 22" - $3,000.00. Painted eyes: 15" - $1,600.00; 19" - $2,000.00.

#236, 262 Toddler: 12" - $1,200.00; 17" - $2,000.00; 21" - $2,400.00; 26" - $2,800.00; 28" - $3,200.00. **Baby:** 15" - $1,500.00; 20" - $1,900.00; 24" - $2,400.00.

#237: (See photo in Series 7, pg. 161.) 17" - $2,400.00; 22" - $2,900.00.

18" "Laughing Jumeau" boy and girl marked "S.F.B.J. 236 Paris 8." Each doll has a toddler body, an open/closed mouth and two upper teeth. 18" - $2,200.00.
Courtesy Frasher Doll Auctions.

#238: 15" - $3,700.00; 22" - $4,200.00. **Lady:** 21" - $4,400.00.

#239 Poubout: 15" - $15,000.00 up; 18" - $20,000.00 up.

#242: (See photo in Series 5, pg. 137.) 18" - $4,800.00.

#247: 15" - $2,900.00; 18" - $4,700.00.

#248: Very pouty, glass eyes. 15" - $4,200.00; 18" - $5,800.00.

#251 Toddler: 17"- $1,800.00; 21" - $2,300.00; 25" - $2,800.00. **Baby:** 15" - $1,500.00; 21" - $2,300.00; 25" - $2,900.00.

#252 Toddler: 15" - $5,750.00; 19" - $7,700.00; 25" - $9,000.00. **Baby:** 10" - $2,000.00; 15" - $5,100.00; 21" - $7,600.00; 25" - $8,600.00.

#257: 17" - $2,700.00.

#266: 21" - $4,200.00.

#306: Princess Elizabeth. See Jumeau section.

Googly: See Googly section.

Kiss Throwing, Walking Doll: (See photo in Series 5, pg. 138.) Composition body with straight legs, walking mechanism. When it walks, arm goes up to throw kiss. Head moves from side to side. Flirty eyes and open mouth. In working condition, no damage to bisque head and nicely dressed. 21-22" - $2,200.00.

23" marked "S.F.B.J. 252 Paris 11." Closed mouth pouty on toddler body. 23" - **$7,900.00.** Courtesy Frasher Doll Auctions.

20" marked "Tete Jumeau S.F.B.J. 301." Label on body: "Bebe Vrai ('True') Modele Fabrication Jumeau." Has original leather gloves. 20" - **$1,800.00.** Courtesy Turn of Century Antiques.

Snow Babies were made in Germany and Japan. They can be excellent to poor in quality from both countries. Snow Babies have fired-on "pebble-textured" clothing. Many are unmarked and the features are painted. Prices are for good quality painted features, rareness of pose, and no damage to the piece.

Single Figure: 1½" - $50.00; 3" - $100.00-125.00.

Two Figures: Together. 1½" - $100-125.00; 3" - $150-195.00.

Three Figures: Together. 1½" - $145.00-185.00; 3" - $195.00-245.00.

One Figure On Sled: 2-2½" - $185.00. With reindeer: $200.00.

Two Figures On Sled: 2-2½" - $200.00.

Three Figures On Sled: (See photo in Series 6, pg. 180.) 2-2½" - $245.00.

Jointed: (See photo in Series 5, pg. 139.) Shoulders and hips. 3¼" - $165.00 up; 5" - $365.00 up; 7" - $450.00 up.

Shoulder head: Cloth body with china limbs. 9" - $385.00; 12" - $450.00.

On Sled in Glass: "Snow" scene - $225.00 up. Sled/dogs: 3-4" - $225.00.

With Bear: $200.00.

2" Snow Baby and bear (with front of ski broken off.) Both were made in Japan. 2" baby - $85.00; Bear - $95.00. Courtesy Stan Buler.

With Snowman: $185.00.

With Musical Base: $185.00 up.

Laughing Child: $150.00 up.

Snow Bear with Santa: $275.00.

With Reindeer: $225.00

Snow Baby Riding Polar Bear: $195.00.

Snow Angel: $125.00 up.

Igloo: $85.00.

Ice Skater: $185.00 up.

Steiff started business in 1894 and this German maker is better known for their plush/stuffed animals than for dolls.

Steiff Dolls: Felts, velvet or plush with seam down middle of face. Button-style eyes, painted features and sewn on ears. The dolls generally have large feet so they stand alone. Prices are for dolls in excellent condition and with original clothes. Second price is for dolls that are soiled and may not be original.

Adults: 16-17" - $1,900.00 up; 21-22" - $2,400.00 up.

Military Men: (See photo in Series 7, pg. 165.) 15" - $4,200.00 up; 17" - $4,600.00 up; 21" - $5,000.00 up.

Children: (See photo in Series 6, pg. 181.) 12" - $950.00 up; 15-16" - $1,500.00; 18-19" - $1,800.00 up.

Made is U.S. Zone Germany: Has glass eyes. 12" - $700.00 up; 16" - $900.00 up.

Comic Characters: Such as chef, elf, musician, etc. 14" - $2,400.00 up; 16" - $3,200.00 up.

Mickey Mouse: 9-10" - $1,000.00 up.

Minnie Mouse: 9-10" - $1,800.00 up.

Clown: 16" - $2,300.00 up.

14" Herm Steiner baby, mold #240. Closed mouth, cloth body, and celluloid hands (can also have composition hands). Baby: 14" - $285.00; 17" - $525.00, 21" - $700.00. Child: 8" - $135.00; 14" - $285.00; 17" - $385.00; 22" - $485.00; 26" - $600.00. Shown with a 24" William Goebel with a crown mark and "B5-11." Bent limb baby with sleep eyes and open mouth. 24" Goebel - $925.00. Courtesy Frasher Doll Auctions.

STEINER, JULES

Jules Nicholas Steiner operated from 1855 to 1892 when the firm was taken over by Amedee LaFosse. In 1895, this firm merged with Henri Alexander, the maker of Phenix Bébé and a partner, May Freres Cie, the maker of Bébé Mascotte. In 1899, Jules Mettais took over the firm and in 1906, the company was sold to Edmond Daspres.

In 1889, the firm registered the girl with a banner and the words "Le Petit Parisien" and in 1892, LaFosse registered "Le Parisien."

Marks:
(See body marks in Series 7, pg. 167.)

J. STEINER
STE. S.G.D.G.
FIRE A12
PARIS

STE C3
J. STEINER
B. S.G.D.G.

Bourgoin

"A" Series Child: 1885. Closed mouth, paperweight eyes, jointed body and cardboard pate. No damage and nicely dressed. 10" - $3,300.00; 14" - $4,550.00; 20" - $6,300.00; 24" - $7,350.00; 27" - $8,400.00.

"A" Series Child: Open mouth, otherwise same as above. 14" - $2,000.00; 20" - $3,200.00; 26" - $4,000.00.

"B" Series: Closed mouth. 22" - $4,850.00; 28" - $6,800.00.

"C" Series Child: Ca. 1880. Closed mouth, round face, paperweight eyes, no damage and nicely dressed. 17" - $5,400.00; 21" - $6,950.00; 26" - $8,900.00; 29" - $9,300.00.

Bourgoin Steiner: 1870's. With "Bourgoin" incised or in red stamp on head along with the rest of the Steiner mark. Closed mouth. No damage and nicely dressed. 16" - $5,500.00; 20" - $6,700.00; 25" - $8,450.00.

Wire Eye Steiner: Closed mouth, flat glass eyes that open and close by moving wire that comes out the back of the head. Jointed body, no damage and nicely dressed. **Bourgoin:** 17" - $5,250.00; 21" - $6,200.00; 26" - $7,600.00. **"A" Series:** 17" - $5,200.00; 21" - $6,100.00; 26" - $7,400.00. **"C" Series:** 17" - $5,100.00; 21" - $6,000.00; 26" - $7,400.00.

"Le Parisien" - "A" Series: 1892. Closed mouth: 13-14" - $3,600.00; 17" - $4,800.00; 21" - $5,700.00; 23" - $6,100.00; 26" - $7,500.00. Open mouth: 17" - $1,900.00; 21" - $2,700.00; 26" - $3,500.00.

Mechanical: See that section.

Right: 15" "A" series Steiner marked "J Steiner, SGDG Paris Fire A 7." Closed mouth, marked Steiner body. Left: 12" walking Bru marked "Bru Jne R 2." Closed mouth, wood and composition body, and one-piece arms and legs. Hip mechanism allows doll to "walk." 15" - $4,600.00; Bru - $5,000.00. Courtesy Frasher Doll Auctions.

23" early Steiner marked on head "5" and original body label "9 Medailles aux Expositions 1867-68-72-73-74-J. Terrene, 10 Rue du Mache's Honore Paris." White bisque round face with open mouth and two rows of teeth. Straight wrists. 23" - $6,800.00. Courtesy Frasher Doll Auctions.

Bisque Hip Steiner: Motschmann-style body with bisque head, shoulders, lower arms and legs and bisque torso sections. No damage anywhere. 18" - $6,700.00.

Early White Bisque Steiner: With round face, open mouth with two rows of teeth. Unmarked. On jointed Steiner body, pink wash over eyes. No damage and nicely dressed. 14" - $4,200.00; 18" - $5,900.00.

16" Jules Steiner "Le Petit Parisien." Marked with store name where purchased — "Au Bonheur des Enfants, Chaufour 43 Blvd Males Sherees Paris." Has pull string for "mama/papa" cryer box. 16" - $5,000.00. Courtesy Turn of Century Antiques.

14" very early Jules Steiner with Motschmann-style body with upper torso and upper limbs of cloth. Maybe original wig and clothes. 14" - $5,900.00. Courtesy Turn of Century Antiques.

28" marked "A No. 18. J. Steiner, Bte S.G.D.G. Paris." Closed mouth and wired eyes operated by wire in back of head. Jointed French Steiner body. 28" - $8,600.00. Courtesy Turn of Century Antiques.

"Tynie Baby" was made for Horsman Doll Co. in 1924. Doll will have sleep eyes, closed pouty mouth and "frown" between eyes. Its cloth body has celluloid or composition hands. Markings will be "1924/E.I. Horsman/ Made in Germany." Some will also be incised "Tynie Baby." Doll should have no damage and be nicely dressed.

Bisque head: 11" - $450.00; 16" - $800.00.

Composition head: 14" - $285.00.

All bisque: Glass eyes, swivel neck. 6" - $1,000.00; 9" - $1,700.00.

Beautiful little "Tynie Baby" with bent limb baby body and sleep eyes. All bisque and original. Courtesy Shirley Bertrand.

UNIS

"Unis, France" was a type of trade association or a "seal of approval" for trade goods to consumers from the manufacturers. This group of businessmen, who were to watch the quality of French exports, often overlooked guidelines and some poor quality dolls were exported. Many fine quality Unis marked dolls were also produced.

Unis began right after World War I and is still in business. Two doll companies are still members, "Poupee Bella" and "Petit Colin." Other type manufacturers in this group include makers of toys, sewing machines, tile, pens, etc.

22" bisque head, sleep eyes, and open mouth. Fully jointed French body and all original. Arm tag: "Poupee Jumeau Paris/ Unis France Jumeau." On head: "Unis France 301." 22" - $950.00. "Courtesy Jeannie Mauldin.

UNIS

Marks:

71   UNIS FRANCE   149

301

UNIS FRANCE

#60, 70, 71, 301: Bisque head with papier maché or composition body. Sleep or set eyes, open mouth. No damage and nicely dressed. 8-9" - $445.00; 15" - $650.00; 18" - $775.00; 22" - $875.00; 25" - $975.00. Closed mouth: 16" - $2,400.00; 20" - $3,000.00. Black or brown: 11-12" - $485.00; 16" - $700.00.

Bleuette: See S.F.B.J section.

Provincial Costume Doll: Bisque head, painted, set or sleep eyes, open mouth (or closed on smaller dolls.) Five-piece body. Original costume, no damage. 6" - $200.00; 12" - $350.00; 14" - $450.00.

Baby #272: Glass eyes, open mouth, cloth body, celluloid hands. 15" - $575.00; 18" - $975.00. Painted eyes, composition hands: 15" - $325.00; 18" - $500.00.

#251 Toddler: 16" - $1,500.00 up.

Princess Elizabeth: (See photo in Series 6, pg. 185.) 1938. Jointed body, closed mouth. (Allow more for flirty eyes.) 18" - $1,600.00; 23" - $1,900.00; 31" - $2,650.00.

12" "Bleuette" marked "71 Unis France 149 301." At base of socket - "1½" Body marked "2," feet marked "1." Sleep eyes, open mouth. Hat and coat are a late 1930's Gautier-Languereau fashion exclusive for "Bleuette." Handbag made for doll in 1930's; parasol in spring/summer 1938. 12" - $1,100.00 up.
Courtesy Billyboy™–Paris.

Left: 27" marked "Unis France 301." Open mouth and on fully jointed body. Right: 28" incised "A 18 Paris" and in red "Le Parisien." Open mouth, Steiner body. 28" - $4,400.00; 27" - $1,200.00.
Courtesy Frasher Doll Auctions.

27" doll with downcast look. Head turned slightly. Closed mouth and almond cut eyes. Flat underside to eyebrows. On kid body with bisque lower arms. Closed mouth: 16" - $850.00; 21" - $975.00; 24" - $1,400.00; 27" - $1,600.00. Open mouth: 16" - $500.00; 21" - $675.00; 24" - $875.00; 27" - $1,100.00. Courtesy Frasher Doll Auctions.

23" turned head lady. Bisque shoulder head with kid body and bisque lower arms. Open mouth, original mohair wig. Very flat undersides to eyebrows. 23" - $1,050.00. Courtesy Turn of Century Antiques.

Poured Wax: (See photos in Series 5, pg. 144; Series 7, pg. 174.) Cloth body with wax head, limbs and inset glass eyes. Hair is embedded into wax. Nicely dressed or in original clothes, no damage to wax, but wax may be slightly discolored (evenly all over.) Not rewaxed. 16" - $1,400.00; 19" - $1,700.00; 22" - $2,000.00; 25" - $2,600.00. Lady or Man: 20" - $2,600.00 up; 24" - $3,600.00.

Wax Over Papier Maché or Composition: (See photo in Series 6, pg. 189.) Cloth body with wax over papier maché or composition head and with wax over composition or wood limbs. Only minor scuffs with no chipped out places, good color and nicely dressed.

Early Dolls: 1860-on.

Molded hair: 14" - $285.00; 21" - $485.00; 24" - $565.00.

Squeeker body: 17-18" - $685.00.

"Alice:" Headband hairdo: 15" - $525.00. With wig: Excellent quality, with heavy wax. 12" - $265.00; 16" - $425.00; 21" - $575.00; 24" - $675.00; 29" - $725.00. Common quality: Wax worn or gone. 12" - $165.00; 16" - $325.00; 21" - $400.00; 24" - $485.00.

Later Dolls: 12" - $250.00; 16" - $450.00.

Bonnet or Cap: (See photo in Series 6, pg. 190.) Hat molded on forehead. 16" - $2,600.00. Derby-type hat: 22" - $2,100.00. Bonnet-style hat: 20" - $2,250.00. Round face, poke bonnet: 22" - $2,450.00. Baby: $16" - $1,400.00.

Pumpkin: Hair laced over ridged raised front area. 16" - $425.00; 20" - $525.00.

Slit Head Wax: (See photo in Series 6, pg. 189.) English, 1830–1860's. Glass eyes, some open and closed by an attached wire. 14" - $575.00 up; 18" - $865.00; 25" - $1,000.00 up.

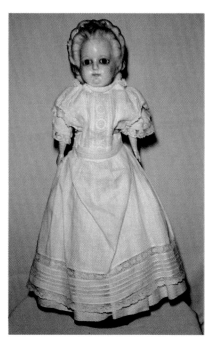

22" wax over papier maché with glass eyes, high molded hairdo, cloth body with wooden limbs. Original clothes. Ca. 1850's. 22" - $600.00.

31" wax over papier maché shoulder head with glass eyes. Straw filled cloth body and papier maché lower legs with molded-on shoes and stockings. 31" - $600.00. Courtesy Frasher Doll Auctions.

10½" poured wax lady from 1840's. Glass pupiless eyes and all original. 10½" - $1,000.00.
Courtesy Turn of Century Antiques.

WEGNER, HEINRICH

14" rare character by Heinrich Wegner of Sonneburg who made dolls from 1910-1914. Artist and designer Herr Wegner did not reapper on the manufacturing scene after World War I. Wonderful expression, closed mouth and intaglio eyes. It is thought the heads for this designer were actually made by Kley and Hahn. 14" - $2,700.00 up; 16" - $3,700.00 up; 18" - $4,800.00 up.
Courtesy Frasher Doll Auctions.

Norah Welling's designs were made for her by Victoria Toy Works in Wellington, Shropshire, England. These dolls were made from 1926 into the 1960's. The dolls are velvet as well as other fabrics, especially felt and velour. They will have a tag on the foot "Made in England by Norah Wellings."

Child: All fabric with stitch jointed hips and shoulders. Molded fabric face with oil painted features. Some faces are papier maché with a stockinette covering. All original felt and cloth clothes, clean condition. Painted eyes: 14" - $450.00; 17" - $700.00; 21" - $1,000.00; 23" - $1,400.00. Glass eyes: 14" - $600.00; 17" - $800.00; 21" - $1,200.00.

Mounties, Black Islanders, Scots, and Other Characters: These are most commonly found. Must be in same condition as child. 8" - $100.00; 12" - $165.00; 14" - $200.00.

Glass Eyes: White: 14" - $300.00; 17" - $450.00. Black: 14" - $250.00; 20" - $400.00; 26" - $650.00.

Babies: Same description as child and same condition. 15" - $500.00; 22" - $900.00.

12" Norah Wellings "Mountie" and girl. All velvet with felt clothes. Both are original. Mountie - $165.00; girl - $365.00. Courtesy Jeannie Maudin.

The Adolf Wislizenus doll factory was located at Waltershausen, Germany and the heads he used were made by Bahr & Proschild, Ernst Heubach of Koppelsdorf, and Simon & Halbig. The company was in business starting in 1851, but it is not known when they began to make dolls.

Marks:

Child: 1890's into 1900's. Bisque head on jointed body, sleep eyes, open mouth. No damage and nicely dressed. 12" - $225.00; 14" - $425.00; 17" - $500.00; 22" - $550.00; 25" - $625.00.

Baby: Bisque head in perfect condition and on five-piece bent limb baby body. No damage and nicely dressed. 17" - $525.00; 21" - $685.00; 26" - $1,000.00.

#110, 115: 16" - $1,100.00. Glass eyes: 16" - $1,850.00 up.

24" marked "A.W." child with open mouth and on fully jointed body. Original wig. 24" - $600.00. Courtesy Private Collection.

WOOD

English: William & Mary Period, 1690's-1700. Carved wooden head, eyes. Eyebrow and eyelashes are painted with tiny lines. Colored cheeks, human hair or flax wig. Wood body, carved wood hands shaped like forks. Legs are wood and jointed. Upper arms are cloth. In medium to fair condition: 15-18" - $55,000.00 up.

English: Georgian Period, 1750's-1800. Round wooden head with gesso coating, inset glass eyes. Eyelashes and eyebrows made up of dots. Human or flax wig. Jointed wood body with pointed torso. Medium to fair condition: 13" - $2,950.00; 16" - $4,600.00; 18" - $5,200.00; 24" - $6,550.00.

English: 1800's-1840's. Gesso, coated wooden head, painted eyes. Human hair or flax wig. Original gowns generally longer than wooden legs. 12-13" - $1,350.00; 15" - $1,950.00; 20" - $2,800.00.

German: 1810's-1850's. Hair is delicately carved and painted with little curls around face. All wood doll with pegged or ball jointed limbs. Some have decorations carved in hair. Features are painted. 7" - $765.00; 12-13" - $1,400.00; 16-17" - $1,700.00.

German: 1850's-1900. All wood with painted plain hairstyle. Some may have spit curls around face. 5" - $150.00; 8" - $235.00; 12" - $375.00. Same, except wooden shoulder head, more elaborate carved hair such as buns. Wood limbs and cloth body. 9-10" - $400.00; 16-17" - $600.00; 23" - $875.00.

German: After 1900. Turned wood head with carved nose. Hair painted and painted lower legs with black shoes. Peg jointed. 10-11" - $100.00. Child: All wood, body is fully jointed. Glass eyes, open mouth. 14-15" - $450.00; 18" - $700.00; 23" - $900.00.

6½" jointed wood doll, maker unknown. Extremely fine quality. Fully articulated, swivel neck and waist. Jointed ankles and wrists. Maybe early artist's model. 6½" - $300.00. Courtesy Frasher Doll Auctions.

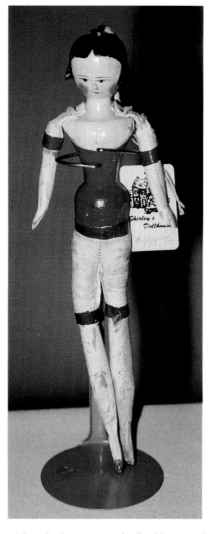

10" early "penny wooden" with carved hair with tucks on sides. Cloth upper arms and legs. Germany, ca. 1850's. 10" - $1,350.00. Courtesy Shirley Bertrand.

MODERN DOLLS

Back Row: 18" composition "Little Lady," 14" P-90 "Toni" in original box. Center: 18" "Sweet Sue" walker. 13" "Shirley Temple" in box. Front Row: 17" "Alice in Wonderland," 12" "Mortimer Snerd," and two 8" "Alexanderkins." Courtesy Frasher Doll Auctions.

The author's separate price guide covering over 1,000 Madame Alexander dolls is available from book dealers or Collector Books.

1953–1954: 7½-8" straight leg, non-walker, heavy hard plastic. **Party Dress:** Mint and all correct - $350.00 up. Soiled, dirty hair mussed or parts of clothing missing - $95.00. **Ballgown:** Mint and correct - $700.00 up. Soiled, dirty, bad face color, not original - $150.00. **Nude:** Clean and good face color. $250.00. Dirty and bad face color - $40.00.

1955: 8" straight leg walker. **Party Dress:** Mint and all correct. $450.00. Soiled, dirty, parts of clothes missing - $80.00. **Ballgown:** Mint and all correct - $700.00 up. Dirty, part of clothing missing, etc. - $150.00. **Basic sleeveless dress:** Mint - $175.00. Dirty - $40.00. **Nude:** Clean and good face color - $200.00. Dirty, not original, faded face color - $65.00.

1956–1965: Bend knee walker. **Party Dress:** Mint and all correct - $350.00. Dirty, part of clothes missing, etc. - $65.00. **Ballgown:** Mint and correct - $950.00 up. Soiled, dirty, parts missing, etc. - $150.00. **Nude:** Clean, good face color - $150.00. Dirty, faded face color - $40.00. **Basic sleeveless dress:** Mint - $165.00. Dirty, faded face color - $45.00. **Internationals:** $375.00. Dirty, parts missing - $65.00.

1965–1972: Bend knee, non-walkers: **Party Dress:** Mint and original - $250.00. Dirty, parts missing, etc. - $50.00. **Internationals:** Clean and mint - $125.00. Dirty or soiled - $45.00. **Nude:** Clean, good face color - $95.00. Dirty, faded face color - $30.00.

1973–1976: "Rosies." Straight leg, non-walker, rosy cheeks and marked "Alex." **Bride or Ballerina:** Bend knee walker - $300.00 up. Bend knee only - $125.00. Straight leg - $65.00. **Internationals:** $65.00. **Storybook:** $65.00.

7½" 1953–1954 straight leg non-walker in mint condition. Gown is variation of "Day In The Country." 7½" - $700.00 up. Courtesy Chris McWilliams.

Mint set of "Little Women" and "Laurie" using the 8" Alexander-kin dolls. All have bend knees. 8" "Little Women," each - $225.00 each; Laurie - $225.00. Courtesy Turn of Century Antiques.

1977–1981: Straight leg, non-walker marked "Alexander." **Bride or Ballerina:** $50.00-60.00. **International:** $50.00-60.00. **Storybook:** $50.00-60.00.

1982–1987: Straight leg, non-walker with deep indentation over upper lip that casts a shadow and makes the doll look as if it has a mustache. **Bride or ballerina:** $45.00-55.00.

International: $50.00-60.00. **Storybook:** $50.00-60.00.

1988–1989: Straight leg, non-walker with new face that is more like the older dolls than others and still marked with full name "Alexander." **Bride or ballerina:** $45.00-55.00. **International:** $45.00-55.00. **Storybook:** $50.00-60.00.

8" bend knee walker "Bride" of 1961. Mint condition. Bride - $450.00 up. Courtesy Shirley Bertrand.

MADAME ALEXANDER – BABIES

Prices are for mint condition dolls.

Baby Brother or Sister: 1977–1982. 14" - $85.00; 20" - $95.00.

Baby Lynn: 1973–1975. 20" - $60.00.

Baby McGuffey: Composition. 22" - $175.00. Soiled - $50.00.

Bonnie: Vinyl. 19" - $100.00. Soiled - $30.00.

Genius, Little: Composition. 18" - $125.00. Soiled - $45.00.

Genius, Little: Vinyl, may have flirty eyes. 19" - $150.00. Soiled - $45.00.

Genius, Little: 8" - $125.00 up. Soiled - $45.00.

Happy: Vinyl. 20" - $275.00. Soiled - $80.00.

Honeybun: Vinyl. 19" - $150.00. Soiled - $35.00.

Huggums, Big: 1963–1979. 25" - $90.00. **Lively:** 1963. 25" - $110.00.

Kathy: Vinyl. 19" - $125.00; 26" - $165.00. Soiled: 19" - $35.00; 26" - $45.00.

Kitten, Littlest: Vinyl. 8" - $125.00 up. Soiled - $40.00.

Mary Cassatt: 1969–1970. 14" - $200.00; 20" - $250.00.

Mary Mine: 14" - $85.00. Soiled - $30.00.

Pinky: Composition. 23" - $150.00. Soiled - $60.00.

Precious: Composition. 12" - $125.00. Soiled - $55.00.

Princess Alexandria: Composition. 24" - $300.00. Soiled - $95.00.

Pussy Cat: Vinyl. 14" - $55.00-85.00. Black: 14" - $100.00. Soiled: $8.00-35.00.

Rusty: Vinyl. 20" - $300.00. Soiled - $55.00.

Slumbermate: Composition. 21" - $500.00. Soiled - $165.00.

Sweet Tears: 9" - $65.00. With layette - $135.00. Soiled - $25.00.

Victoria: 20" - $60.00. Soiled - $20.00.

16" "Sweet Tears" with plastic body and vinyl head and limbs. Rooted hair, open mouth/nurser. Marked "Alexander Doll Co., 1965" on head. Made from 1965–1971. 16" - $85.00. Courtesy Jeannie Mauldin.

14" "Baby McGuffey" with cloth body, vinyl head and limbs. All original, made 1972–1978. 14" - $165.00. Courtesy Shirley Bertrand.

This 10-11" high heel doll named "Cissette" was made from 1957 to 1963, but the mold was used for other dolls later. She is made of hard plastic, and clothes will be tagged "Cissette."

First prices are for mint condition dolls; second prices are for soiled, dirty or faded clothes, tags missing and hair messy.

Street Dresses: $125.00-175.00, $40.00-60.00

Ballgowns: $200.00-500.00, $100.00-150.00.

Ballerina: $385.00, $100.00.

Gibson Girl: $950.00, $225.00.

Jacqueline: $500.00 up, $175.00.

Margot: $450.00 up, $160.00.

Portrette: $400.00, $150.00.

Wigged in case: $1,200.00 up, $500.00.

Seven "Cissette" dolls used as "Jenny Lind," "Scarlett," "Melanie," "Ballerina," "Sleeping Beauty" (made for Disney), a nude doll, and "Godey." Jenny Lind - $325.00; Scarlett - $425.00; Melanie, mint - $450.00; Ballerina - $385.00; Sleeping Beauty - $400.00; Nude doll - $125.00; Godey - $400.00. Courtesy Turn of Century Antiques.

"Cissy" was made 1955–1959 and had hard plastic with vinyl over the arms, jointed at elbows, and high heel feet. Clothes are tagged "Cissy."

Street Dress: $225.00–275.00.
Ballgown: $475.00–1,000.00.
Bride: $525.00–600.00.
Queen: $600.00–700.00.
Portrait: "Godey," etc. 21" - $1,400.00 up.
Scarlett: $985.00.
Flora McFlimsey: Vinyl head, inset eyes. 15" - $525.00.

20" "Cissy." The one on the left was made in 1957; on the right, 1958. Hard plastic with bend knees and vinyl over-sleeved arms that are jointed at elbows. Both dolls - $275.00. Courtesy Gary Green, Madame Alexander Museum.

MADAME ALEXANDER – CLOTH DOLLS

The Alexander Company made cloth and plush dolls and animals and also oil cloth baby animals in the 1930's, 1940's and early 1950's. In the 1960's, a few were made.

First prices are for mint condition dolls; second prices are for ones in poor condition, dirty, not original, played with or untagged.

Animals: $200.00 up, $75.00.
Dogs: $225.00, $90.00.
Alice in Wonderland: $850.00, $250.00.
Clarabelle, The Clown: 19" - $400.00-500.00.
David Copperfield or Other Boys: $700.00-800.00.
Funny: $65.00, $15.00,

Little Shaver: 7" - $400.00; 10" - $425.00.
Little Women: $625.00-700.00 each, $225.00.
Muffin: 14" - $125.00, $30.00.
So Lite Baby or Toddler: 20" - $500.00, 175.00.
Susie Q: $650.00, $200.00.
Tiny Tim: $500.00-700.00.
Teeny Twinkle: Has disc floating eyes. $550.00, 140.00.

13½" "Bunny" with pink cloth torso and arms, striped legs. Dotted swiss dress with felt flowers, attached organdy slip and matching undies. Non-removable felt shoes. Painted face mask, turquoise yarn hair with "buns" on sides. Yellow felt ears lined with pink. Tagged and mint. "Bunny" - $325.00. Courtesy Turn of Century Antiques.

MADAME ALEXANDER – COMPOSITION

First prices are for mint condition dolls; second prices are for dolls that are crazed, cracked, dirty, soiled clothes or not original.

Alice in Wonderland: 9" - $245.00, $75.00; 14" - $400.00, $85.00; 21" - $800.00, $250.00.

Babs Skater: 1948. 18" - $650.00, 200.00.

Baby Jane: 16" - $950.00, $325.00.

Brides or Bridesmaids: 7" - $225.00, $85.00; 9" - $245.00, $90.00; 15" - $285.00, $75.00; 21" - $600.00, $200.00.

Dionne Quints: 8" - $150.00, $50.00; Set of five - $1,000.00. 11" - $300.00, $125.00; Set of five - $1,800.00. Cloth Baby: 14" - $425.00, $140.00; Set of five - $2,500.00. Cloth Baby: 16" - $650.00, $150.00. 19-20" - $600.00,

$200.00; Set of five - $3,200.00.

Dr. DeFoe: 14-15" - $1,000.00, $450.00.

Fairy Princess: 1939. 15" - $565.00; 21" - $900.00 up.

Flora McFlimsey: (Marked Princess Elizabeth) Freckles: 15" - $400.00-475.00, $150.00; 22" - $600.00-650.00, $200.00.

Flower Girl: (Princess Elizabeth) 1939–1947. 16" - $400.00, $100.00; 20" - $575.00, $200.00; 24" - $700.00, $300.00.

Internationals/Storybook: 7" - $245.00, $50.00; 11" - $325.00, $100.00.

Jane Withers: 13" - $950.00 up, $400.00; 18" - $1,100.00, $550.00.

Kate Greenaway: (Marked Princess Elizabeth) Very yellow blonde wig. 14" - $525.00, $175.00; 18" - $725.00, $275.00.

Little Colonel: 9" - $350.00, $125.00; 13" - $550.00, $225.00; 23" - $800.00, $400.00.

Madelaine DuBain: 1937–1944. 14" - $525.00, $200.00; 17" - $675.00, $300.00.

Margaret O'Brien: 15" - $645.00, $250.00; 18" - $850.00, $285.00; 21" - $1,100.00, $500.00.

Marionettes: Tony Sarg: 12" Disney - $350.00, $165.00. Others: 12" - $245.00, $95.00.

McGuffey Ana: (Marked Princess Elizabeth) 13" - $450.00, $165.00; 20" - $700.00, $300.00.

Military Dolls: 1943–1944. 14" - $675.00, $285.00.

Nurse: 1936–1940. 14-15" - $400.00 up.

Portrait Dolls: 1939–1941, 1946: 21" - $1,900.00 up, $800.00.

Princess Elizabeth: Closed mouth. 13" - $450.00, $150.00; 18" - $600.00, $250.00; 24" - $700.00, $350.00.

Scarlett: 9" - $375.00, $125.00; 14" - $700.00, $200.00; 18" - $965.00, $400.00; 21" - $1,900.00, $800.00.

Snow White: (Princess Elizabeth) 1939–1942. 13" - $325.00, $100.00; 18" - $550.00, $165.00.

Sonja Henie: 17" - $800.00, $300.00; 20" - $975.00, $400.00. Jointed waist: 14" - $625.00, $285.00.

Wendy Ann: 11" - $350.00, $125.00; 15" - $500.00, $175.00; 18" - $600.00, $200.00.

14" "Bride" made of all composition and using the "Wendy Ann" doll. 1930's. All original. 14" - $285.00 up.
Courtesy Sharon McDowell.

21" portrait doll of 1946, "Princess Flavia." All original, except replaced crown very much like original. 21" - $1,900.00 up. Courtesy Kris Lundquist.

14" "Nurse" (using "Betty" doll) and 14" "Dr. DeFoe." Both made from 1937–1939. Shown with set of 8" "Dionne Quints" in original basket. 14" nurse - $400.00 up; 14" doctor - $1,000.00 up; 8" quints, each - $150.00, set - $1,500.00 up.   Courtesy Shirley Bertrand.

MADAME ALEXANDER – HARD PLASTIC

First prices are for mint condition dolls; second prices are for dolls that are dirty, played with, soiled clothes or not original.

Alice in Wonderland: 14" - $500.00, $185.00; 17" - $565.00, $200.00; 23" - $750.00, $300.00.

Annabelle: 15" - $500.00, $200.00; 18" - $600.00, $200.00; 23" - $750.00, $300.00.

Babs: 20" - $675.00, $250.00.

Babs Skater: 18" - $650.00, $225.00; 21" - $750.00, $375.00.

Ballerina: 14" - $375.00, $165.00.

Brenda Starr: 1942. 12". Dress - $225.00; Gown - $225.00 up; Bride - $225.00.

Binnie Walker: 15" - $185.00, $90.00; 25" - $375.00, $125.00.

Cinderella: 14" - $850.00, $325.00. 14" in "poor" outfit - $600.00, $225.00.

Cynthia: Black doll. 15" - $800.00, $350.00; 18" - $1,000.00, $500.00; 23" - $1,200.00, $600.00.

Elise: Street dress. 16½" - $165.00, $80.00. Ballgown: $350.00, $160.00.

Bride: 16" - $325.00, $165.00.

Fairy Queen: 14½" - $650.00, $300.00.

Godey Lady: 14" - $1,400.00, $650.00.

Man/Groom: 14" - $950.00, $400.00.

Kathy: 15" - $600.00, $200.00.

Kelly: 12" - $450.00, $150.00; 16" (Marybel): $250.00, $100.00.

Lissy: Street dress: 12" - $275.00, $165.00. Bride: $285.00, $150.00. Ballerina: $365.00, $195.00.

Little Women: 8" - $125.00, $60.00; Set of five (bend knee) - $700.00; Set of five (straight leg) - $400.00. 12" Lissy:

$350.00, $135.00; Set of five - $1,500.00. 14" - $450.00; Set of five - $1,800.00.

Laurie: Bend knee. 8" - $125.00 up, $60.00; 12" - $475.00, $195.00.

Madeline: 1950–1953. Jointed knees and elbows. 18" - $700.00, $350.00.

Maggie: 15" - $450.00, $175.00; 17" - $585.00, $200.00; 23" - $700.00, $300.00.

Maggie Mixup: 8" - $400.00 up, $150.00; 16½" - $325.00, $135.00. 8" angel: $1,000.00, $400.00.

Margaret O'Brien: 14½" - $825.00, $400.00; 18" - $985.00, $425.00; 21" - $1,100.00, $500.00.

Mary Martin: Sailor suit or ballgown. 14" - $900.00 up, $450.00; 17" - $750.00, $385.00.

18" all original "Maggie Teenager." All hard plastic. Made between 1951 and 1953. 18" - $485.00 up. Courtesy Sharon McDowell.

McGuffey Ana: 1948–1950. Hard plastic/vinyl. 21" - $800.00, $400.00.

Peter Pan: 15" - $600.00, $300.00.

Polly Pigtails: 14" - $785.00, $350.00; 17" - $950.00, $450.00.

Prince Charming: 14" - $700.00, $325.00; 18" - $850.00, $375.00.

Queen: 18" - $1,200.00, $600.00.

Shari Lewis: 14" - $295.00, $165.00; 21" - $465.00, $295.00.

Sleeping Beauty: 16½" - $500.00, $150.00; 21" - $800.00, $350.00.

Wendy (Peter Pan Set): 14" - $800.00, $400.00.

Wendy Ann: 14½" - $600.00, $200.00; 17" - $800.00, $350.00; 22" - $850.00, $350.00.

Winnie Walker: 15" - $225.00, $95.00; 18" - $350.00, $150.00; 23" - $400.00, $185.00.

21" "Cynthia" using the "Margaret" doll. Caracul (lamb's wool) wig. All original. Made in 1952 only. Can have variation to dress color. 21" - $1,000.00. Courtesy Sharon McDowell.

15" beautiful blue ballerina using the "Margaret" face doll. Early 1950's. Ballerina - $575.00 up. Courtesy Shirley Bertrand.

MADAME ALEXANDER – PLASTIC AND VINYL

First prices are for mint condition dolls; second prices are for dolls that are played with, soiled, dirty and missing original clothes.

Bellows' Anne: 1987 only. 14" - $55.00-65.00.

Bonnie Blue: 1989 only. 14" - $120.00.

Bride: 1982-1987. 17" - $120.00.

Caroline: 15" - $350.00, $125.00.

Cinderella: Pink: 1970–1981. Blue: 1983–1986. 14" - $90.00.

Edith, the Lonely Doll: 1958–1959. 16" - $225.00; 22" - $300.00.

Elise: 1966. 17" in street dress. $165.00. Formal: 1966, 1976–1977. $170.00. Bride: 1966–1986. $120.00.

First Ladies: First set of six - $775.00. Second set of six - $650.00. Third set of six - $650.00. Fourth set of six - $565.00. Fifth set of six - $550.00. Sixth set of six - $560.00.

Grandma Jane/Granny, Little: 1970–1972. 14" - $200.00, $95.00.

Ingres: 1987 only. 14" - $55.00-65.00.

Isolde: 1985 only. 14" - $55.00-65.00.

Jacqueline: Street Dress. 21" - $675.00, $250.00. Ballgown: $800.00 up, $350.00. Riding Habit: $675.00, $275.00.

Janie: 12" - $250.00, $125.00.

Joanie: 36" - $325.00, $145.00.

Leslie: Black doll. Ballgown: 17" - $350.00, $100.00. Ballerina: $350.00, $100.00. Street Dress: $300.00, $100.00.

Little Shaver: Vinyl, 1963 only. 12" - $185.00.

Nancy Drew: 1967 only. 12" - $400.00, $150.00.

Napoleon: 1980–1986. 12" - $60.00-70.00.

Marybel: 16" - $235.00, $95.00; In case - $325.00; $185.00.

Mary Ellen: 31" - $500.00, $200.00.

Melinda: 14" - $265.00, $125.00; 16" - $450.00, $200.00.

Michael with Bear: Peter Pan set. 11" - $475.00, $175.00.

Peter Pan: 14" - $250.00, $95.00.

Polly: 17" - $250.00, $100.00.

Renoir Girl: 14" - $85.00-95.00. With watering can: 1986–1987. $55.00-65.00. With hoop: 1986–1987. $55.00-65.00.

Scarlett: White gown, green ribbon. 1969–1986. 14" - $100.00, 50.00.

Smarty: 12" - $285.00, $100.00.

Sound of Music: Small set: $1,900.00. Large set: $2,600.00. **Liesl:** 10" - $375.00, $100.00; 14" - $375.00, $100.00. **Louisa:** 10" - $375.00, $100.00; 14" - $375.00, $100.00. **Brigitta:** 12" - $245.00, $95.00; 14" - $375.00, $100.00. **Maria:** 12" - $450.00, $150.00; 17" - $475.00, $160.00; **Marta:** 8" - $265.00, $75.00; 11" - $350.00, $165.00. **Gretl:** 8" - $265.00, $95.00; 11" - $350.00, $165.00. **Friedrich:** 8" - $265.00, $95.00; 11" - $285.00, $125.00.

Wendy: Peter Pan set. 14" - $275.00, $125.00.

29" "Alice in Wonderland" using the "Barbara Jane" doll. Cloth body with stuffed early vinyl head and limbs. 1952 only. All original except hair bow. 29" - **$500.00 up.** Courtesy Kris Lundquist.

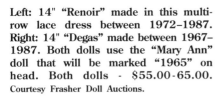

Left: 14" "Renoir" made in this multi-row lace dress between 1972–1987. Right: 14" "Degas" made between 1967–1987. Both dolls use the "Mary Ann" doll that will be marked "1965" on head. Both dolls - $55.00-65.00. Courtesy Frasher Doll Auctions.

Prices are for mint condition dolls. The 21" Portrait dolls are many and all use the Jacqueline face with the early ones having jointed elbows and then all having one-piece arms. All will be marked "1961" on head.

Agatha: 1967–1980. $325.00-550.00.
Bride: 1965. $1,350.00.
Coco: 1966. 21" Portrait: $2,500.00. Street Dress: $2,500.00. Ballgown (other than portrait series): $2,500.00.
Cornelia: 1972–1978. $325.00-500.00.
Gainsborough: 1968–1978. $375.00-700.00.
Godey: 1965, 1967–1977. $700.00, $300.00-500.00.
Jenny Lind: 1969. $1,600.00.
Lady Hamilton: 1968: $550.00.
Madame Pompadour: 1970. $1,000.00.
Magnolia: 1977: $360.00. 1988: $250.00.
Manet: 1982–1983. $300.00.
Melanie: 1967–1989. $250.00-600.00.
Mimi: 1971. $600.00.
Monet: 1984. $225.00.
Morisot: 1985–1986. $265.00.
Queen: 1965. $800.00 up.
Renoir: 1965–1973. $625.00-850.00.
Scarlett: 1965–1989. $300.00-1,000.00.
Toulouse-Lautrec: 1986–1987. $245.00.

21" "Magnolia" made in 1988 only. Uses the "Jacqueline" doll that will be marked "1961" on the head. "Magnolia" - $250.00. Courtesy Lee Crane.

21" "Scarlett" wearing all dark green velvet. Made between 1979–1985. Uses the "Jacqueline" doll that will be marked "1961" on the head. "Scarlett" - $350.00.

All American Character dolls are very collectible and all are above average in quality of doll material and clothes. Dolls marked "American Doll and Toy Co." are also made by American Character, and this name was used from 1959 until 1968 when the firm went out of business. Early dolls will be marked "Petite." Many will be marked "A.C."

First prices are for mint dolls; second prices are for dolls that have been played with, dirty, with soiled clothes or not original.

"A.C." marked child: Composition. 14" - $145.00, $50.00; 20" - $200.00, $75.00.

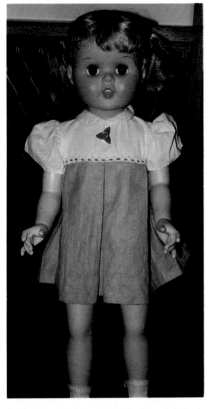

30" "Little Miss Echo." Plastic/vinyl, battery operated talker. Knob to operate comes through original dress in front. Open/closed mouth with painted teeth. **30" - $200.00.** Courtesy Gloria Anderson.

Annie Oakley: 1955. 17" hard plastic. $375.00, $100.00.

Betsy McCall: See Betsy McCall section.

Butterball: 1961. 19" - $185.00, $85.00.

Cartwright: Ben, Joe or Hoss. 1966. 8" - $85.00, $40.00.

Chuckles: 1961. 23" - $185.00, $90.00. Baby: 18" - $145.00, $60.00.

Composition Babies: 1930's – 1940's. Cloth bodies, marked "A.C." 14" - $95.00, $25.00. 22" - $145.00, $60.00. Marked "Petite." 1920's–1930's: 14" - $165.00, $80.00; 22" - $250.00, $100.00.

Cricket: 1964. 9" - $30.00, $10.00. Growing hair: $35.00, $15.00.

Eloise: 1950's. A cloth character, yarn hair, crooked smile. (See photo in Series 7, pg. 212.) 21" - $365.00.

Freckles: 1966. Face changes. 13" - $45.00, $20.00.

Hedda-Get-Betta: 1960. 21" - $95.00, $40.00.

Miss Echo, Little: 1964. 30" talker: $200.00, $90.00.

"Petite" marked child: Composition. 14" - $165.00, $70.00; 20" - $250.00, $100.00; 23" - $300.00, $125.00.

Preteen: 14" child, marked "AM. Char. 63" (1963). Grow hair. $28.00, $12.00.

Puggy: All composition, painted eyes, frown, marked "Petite." 13" - $450.00, $150.00.

Ricky, Jr.: 1955–1956. 13" - $85.00, $40.00; 20" - $145.00, $60.00.

Sally: 1929–1935. Composition, molded hair in "Patsy" style: 12" - $160.00, $50.00; 14" - $185.00, $75.00. 16" - $250.00, $75.00; 18" - $275.00, $100.00.

Sally Says: 1965. Talker, plastic/vinyl. 19" - $95.00, $40.00.

Sweet Sue/Toni: 1949–1960. Hard plastic, some walkers, some with extra joints at knees, elbows and/or ankles, some combination hard plastic and vinyl. Marked "A.C. Amer.Char.Doll," or "American Character" in circle. Must have excellent face color and be original. **Ballgown:** 10½" (1958) - $145.00, $60.00; 15" - $265.00, $85.00; 18" - $325.00, $125.00. **Street dress:** 10½" (1958) - $110.00, $40.00; 15" - $185.00, $60.00; 18" - $325.00, $125.00; 22" - $375.00, $145.00; 24" - $450.00, $165.00; 30" - $565.00, $200.00. **Vinyl:** 10½" - $135.00, $40.00; 17" - $265.00, $60.00; 21" - $350.00, $100.00; 25" - $465.00, $175.00; 30" - $550.00, $200.00. **Groom:** 20" - $450.00, $150.00.

Talking Marie: 1963. 18", vinyl/plastic. Record player in body, battery operated. $95.00, $25.00.

Tiny Tears: Hard plastic/vinyl: 1955–1962. 8" - $45.00, $15.00; 13" - $125.00, $45.00; 17" - $165.00, $85.00. **All vinyl:** 1963. 8" - $35.00, $10.00; 12" - $65.00, $30.00; 16" - $100.00, $45.00.

Toodles: 1956–1960. Baby: 14" - $125.00, $50.00. Tiny: 10½" - $150.00, $50.00. Toddler with "follow me eyes": 22" - $250.00, $90.00; 28" - $350.00, $150.00; 30" - $400.00, $185.00.

Toodle-Loo: 1961. 18" - $200.00, $75.00.

Tressy: 12½". Grow Hair: 1963–1964. (#1 heavy makeup). $45.00, $15.00. #2 Mary/Magic Makeup: 1965–1966. Pale face, no lashes, bend knees. $30.00, $10.00.

Whimette/Little People: 1963. 7½" - $30.00, $10.00.

Whimsey: 1960. 19" - $110.00, $45.00.

14" "Sweet Alice" In Wonderland using the "Sweet Sue" doll of 1953–1955. All hard plastic and original. 14" - $265.00 up. Courtesy Sharon McDowell.

14" early "Sweet Sue" with suntan. 1948–1950. All hard plastic and original. 14" - $265.00 up. Courtesy Kris Lundquist.

28" "Sweet Sue." 1950's, hard plastic with vinyl arms jointed at elbows and knees. 28" - $465.00 up.

14" "Sweet Sue Sophisticate" with vinyl head, hard plastic body and limbs, rooted hair, earrings, painted nails, and high heel feet. "American Beauty" gown. All original. 14" - $265.00 up. Courtesy Ann Wencel.

30" "Sweet Sue Sophisticate" in mint condition in original box. 1957. Hard plastic with jointed knees and elbows, vinyl head and arms. 30" - $500.00 up. Courtesy Sharon McDowell.

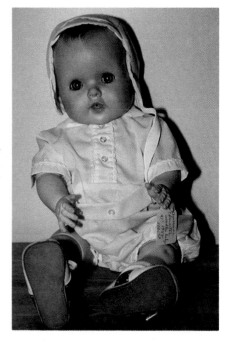

21" heavy vinyl "Toodles" toddler baby with extra joints at elbows and knees. Molded hair and sleep eyes. 21" - $225.00 up. Courtesy Jeannie Mauldin.

ARRANBEE DOLL COMPANY

The Arranbee Doll Company began making dolls in 1922 and was purchased by the Vogue Doll Company in 1959. Vogue used the Arranbee marked molds until 1961. Arranbee used the initials "R & B."

First prices are for mint condition dolls; second prices are for dolls that have been played with, are cracked, crazed, dirty or do not have original clothes.

Angeline: 1951–1952. Hard plastic, mohair wig. 14" - $245.00; 18" - $300.00.

Babies: Bisque heads. See Armand Marseille section.

Babies: 1930's–1940's. Composition/cloth bodies. 16" - $95.00, $45.00; 22" - $145.00, $60.00.

Bottletot: 1932–1935. Has celluloid bottle molded to celluloid hand. 18" - $200.00, $90.00.

Debu-Teen: 1940. Composition girl with cloth body. 14" - $165.00, $60.00; 18" - $225.00, $80.00; 21" - $300.00, $125.00.

Dream Baby, My: (See Armand Marseille section for bisque heads.) Composition, 1934–1944: 14" - $250.00, $100.00. Vinyl/cloth, 1950: 16" - $75.00, $35.00; 26" - $175.00, $75.00.

Francine: Hard plastic, waist length saran wig, 1955. 14" - $235.00; 18" - $285.00.

Kewty: 1934–1936. Composition "Patsy" style molded hair. 10" - $125.00, $45.00; 16" - $165.00, $80.00.

Littlest Angel: 1956, all hard plastic: 10" - $50.00, $15.00. Vinyl head: 10" - $45.00, $15.00. Red hair/freckles, 1960: 10" - $95.00, $40.00.

Miss Coty: 1958. Vinyl, marked "Ⓟ." 10" - $125.00, $45.00.

My Angel: 1961, plastic/vinyl. 17" - $55.00, $20.00; 22" - $75.00, $35.00; 36" - $195.00, $90.00. 30" walker: 1957–1959. $95.00. Oil cloth body/vinyl: 1959. 22" - $85.00.

Nancy: 1936–1940. Composition, molded hair or wig. 12" - $185.00, $65.00; 17" - $350.00, $140.00; 19" - $400.00, $165.00; 23" - $450.00, $165.00. Hard plastic, vinyl arms/head: 1951–1952 only. Wig. 14" - $135.00, $70.00; 18" - $185.00, $90.00; 24" Walker - $225.00, $100.00.

Nancy Lee: 1939. Composition. 14" - $225.00, $100.00. Hard plastic: 1950–1959. 14" - $265.00, $100.00; 20" - $465.00, $150.00.

Nancy Lee: 1954. Unusual eyebrows/vinyl. 15" - $145.00, $65.00.

Nancy Lee: 1952. Baby, painted eyes, "crying" look. 15" - $125.00, $60.00.

Nancy Lee: 1934–1939. Baby with composition head and limbs, open mouth with upper and lower teeth. 25" - $300.00, $100.00.

Nanette: 1949–1959. Hard plastic. 14" - $200.00, $85.00; 17" - $285.00, $100.00; 21" - $350.00, $150.00; 23" - $450.00, $165.00. Walker: Jointed knees, 1957–1959. 18" - $300.00, $100.00; 25" - $465.00, $200.00. Plastic/vinyl walker: 1955–1956. 30" - $195.00, $95.00.

Sonja Skater: 1945. Composition. 14" - $200.00, $90.00; 18" - $245.00, $100.00; 21" - $400.00, $150.00.

Storybook Dolls: 1930–1936. All composition. Molded hair, painted eyes. 10" - $165.00, $45.00.

Taffy: 1956. Looks like Alexander's "Cissy." 23" - $95.00, $50.00.

14" "Nanette." All hard plastic and has flosss styled wig. All original, 1952. 14" ballgown - $250.00. Courtesy Kris Lundquist.

14" "Nanette" from 1954. Dressed in one of the many outfits available on this doll. Floss style wig. 14" - $200.00 up. Courtesy Kris Lundquist.

28" "Nanette" with hard plastic body and limbs. Vinyl head with rooted hair. All original. 28" - $195.00 up. Courtesy Kris Lundquist.

14" "Nanette" from 1953. Original gown, all hard plastic and glued-on wig. 14" - $200.00 up. Courtesy Sharon McDowell.

10" "Littlest Angel." Hard plastic with vinyl head. Had a vast wardrobe available for her. This same doll, called "Lil' Imp," came with red hair, green eyes and freckles. 10" - $50.00. Courtesy Marie Ernst.

ARTISAN NOVELTY CO.

19" "Miss Gadabout" dolls from 1953. All hard plastic of excellent quality. Both are original and childhood dolls of owner. Dresses are tagged "Michelle of California." Made by the Artisan Novelty Co. who also made the "Raving Beauty" dolls using same mold. 19" - $300.00 up. Courtesy Kris Lundquist.

BETSY McCALL

First prices are for mint condition dolls; second prices are for played with, dirty, soiled or not original dolls.

8": 1958. All hard plastic, jointed knees. Made by American Character Doll Co. Street Dress: $165.00, $70.00. Ballgown: $200.00, $90.00. Bathing Suit or Romper: $150.00, $60.00. Ballerina: $175.00; $65.00. Riding Habit: $185.00, $80.00.

11½": Brown sleep eyes, reddish rooted hair, vinyl/plastic and made by Uneeda, but unmarked. $100.00, $40.00.

13": Made by Horsman in 1975, although doll is marked "Horsman Dolls, Inc. 1967" on head. $65.00, $35.00.

14": 1961. Vinyl with rooted hair, medium high heels, round sleep eyes and made by American Character Doll Company and will be marked "McCall 1958." $265.00, $100.00.

14": Vinyl head, rooted hair, rest hard plastic marked "P-90 body." Made by Ideal Doll Company. $285.00, $85.00.

22": Unmarked. Has extra joints at waist, ankles, wrists and above knees. Made by American Character. $300.00, $100.00.

20": Vinyl with rooted hair, slender limbs and made by American Character Doll Company. (Allow more for flirty eyes.) $285.00, $95.00.

22": Vinyl/plastic with extra joints and made by Ideal Doll Company. $300.00, $100.00.

29-30": All vinyl, rooted hair and made by American Character Doll Company. $450.00, $175.00.

29": Marked "McCall 1961." Has extra joints at ankles, knees, waist and wrists. Made by American Character. $500.00, $165.00.

29": Marked "B.M.C. Horsman 1971." $250.00, $80.00.

36": All vinyl with rooted hair and made by American Character Doll Company. $650.00, $300.00.

36": Marked "McCall 1959." Made by Ideal Doll Company. $550.00, $225.00.

39": Boy called "Sandy McCall." Marked same as above girl. Made by Ideal Doll Company. $675.00, $325.00.

11" "Toni" and 8" "Betsy McCall" wearing "Sunday Best" from 1959. Both made by American Character. 11" is #A910; 8" is #B99. 8" - $165.00 up; 11" - $135.00 up. Courtesy Peggy Pergande.

14" "Betsy McCall" in "Schooldays" outfit #214 from 1959. Right photo shows back of hat. 14" - $265.00 up. Courtesy Peggy Pergande.

20" American Character "Betsy McCall" in "Coat Ensemble" #320. Has flirty eyes. 20" - $285.00 up. Courtesy Peggy Pergande.

14" American Character "Betsy McCall" that is all original and never played with from 1958. 14" - $265.00. Courtesy Peggy Pergande.

8" Betsy McCall Fashion Designers Studio #B490 from 1959. Doll only - $165.00; Fashion set - $250.00. Courtesy Peggy Pergande.

14" American Character "Betsy McCall" from
1958. Mint condition in original box. 14"
ballgown - $285.00 up.

BUDDY LEE

"Buddy Lee" dolls were made in composition to 1949, then changed to hard plastic and discontinued in 1962–1963. "Buddy Lee" came dressed in two "Coca-Cola" uniforms. The tan with green stripe outfit matched the uniforms worn by delivery drivers while the white with green stripe uniforms matched those of plant workers. (Among Coca-Cola employees the white uniform became more popular and in warmer regions of the country, the white outfit was also worn by outside workers.)

"Buddy Lee" came in many different outfits.

Engineer: $300.00 up.

Gas Station attendant: $250.00 up.

Cowboy: $350.00 up.

Coca-Cola uniform: White with green stripe - $350.00 up. Tan with green stripe - $400.00 up.

Other soft drink companies uniforms: $350.00 up.

Hard Plastic: Original clothes. $325.00 up.

BUDDY LEE

13" "Buddy Lee" made with all composition with joints at shoulders only. Painted hair and features. Original clothes. Composition, original - $300.00 up; Not original - $125.00. Hard plastic, original - $325.00 up; Not original - $140.00. Courtesy Jeannie Mauldin.

CAMEO DOLL COMPANY

Annie Rooney, Little: 1926. All composition, legs painted black, molded shoes. 16" - $700.00.

Baby Bo Kaye: 1925. Bisque head, open mouth. 17-18" - $2,800.00. All bisque: 4½" - $1,275.00; 6½" - $1,675.00. Celluloid head: 15-16" - $900.00. Composition head, mint: 18" - $700.00. Light craze and not original: 18" - $375.00.

Baby Mine: 1962–1964. Vinyl/cloth, sleep eyes. Mint: 16" - $145.00; 19" - $185.00. Slightly soiled and not original: 16" - $75.00; 19" - $100.00.

Bandy: Wood/composition. Ad doll for General Electric. Large ears. Majorette uniform painted on. Tall hat (non-removable). 17" - $475.00 up.

Betty Boop: 1932. Composition head, wood jointed body. Mint: 12" - $625.00. Light craze and a few paint chips: 12" - $300.00.

Champ: 1942. Composition/freckles. Mint: 16" - $600.00. Light craze, not original: 16" - $300.00.

Giggles: 1946. Composition, molded loop for ribbon. Mint: 11" - $285.00; 14" - $525.00. Light craze: 11" - $165.00; 14" - $325.00.

Ho-Ho: 1940. Plaster in excellent condition. 4" - $60.00. Vinyl in excellent condition: 4" - $15.00.

Joy: 1932. Composition, wood jointed body. Mint: 10" - $285.00; 15" - $380.00. Slight craze: 10" - $160.00; 15" - $285.00.

Kewpie: See Kewpie section.

Margie: 1935. Composition. Mint: 6" - $185.00; 10" - $245.00. Slight craze and not original: 6" - $80.00; 10" - $125.00. Segmented wood/composition: 1929. 9½" - $285.00.

Miss Peep: 1957 and 1970's. Pin jointed shoulders and hips. Vinyl. Mint and original: 1960's. 18" - $60.00. Black: 18" - $95.00. Slightly soiled and not original: 18" - $28.00. Black, 1972: 18" - $35.00. Ball jointed shoulders and hips: 1970's–1980's. 17" - $95.00; 21" - $115.00.

Miss Peep, Newborn: 1962. Plastic and vinyl. Mint and original: 18" - $50.00. Slight soil and not original: 18" - $20.00.

Peanut, Affectionately: 1958. Vinyl. Mint and original: 18½" - $90.00. Slight soil and not original: 18½" - $40.00.

Pete the Pup: 1930–1935. Composition, wood jointed body. Mint: 8" - $250.00. Slight craze and few paint chips: 8" - $100.00.

Pinkie: 1935. Composition. Mint and original: 10" - $285.00. Slight craze: 10" - $125.00. Wood jointed body: 10" - $300.00. Vinyl/plastic: 1950's. Mint: $185.00. Slight soil and not original: 10" - $125.00.

Plum: 1952–1954. Body hinged like "Miss Peep." Dimples. 18" - $65.00; 23" - $90.00.

Scootles: 1925, 1930's. Composition. Mint and original: 8" - $400.00 up; 12" - $400.00 up; 15" - $550.00 up. Light craze and not original: 8" - $100.00; 12" - $225.00; 15" - $285.00. Composition with sleep eyes: Mint: 15" - $600.00; 21" - $800.00 up. Slight craze: 15" - $350.00; 21" - $385.00. Black, composition: Mint: 15" - $700.00. Slight craze: 15" - $300.00. Vinyl: 1964. Mint, original: 14" - $165.00 up; 19" - $325.00 up; 27" - $475.00 up. Lightly soiled and not original: 14" - $80.00; 19" - $125.00; 27" - $200.00.

12" **"Skootles" dolls. Both are all composition and original with one missing shoes and socks. Black has painted eyes; white has sleep eyes. Sleep eyes - $485.00; Black, painted eyes - $600.00. Not shown: White, painted eyes - $400.00.** Courtesy Shirley Bertrand.

CAMEO DOLL COMPANY

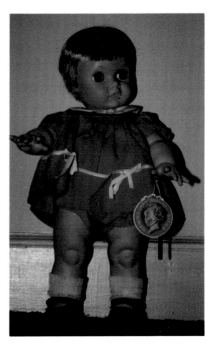

Tiny 8" all composition "Skootles." Still in original box. All original. 8" - $400.00. Courtesy Shirley Bertrand.

22" "Baby Mine" of 1950. All vinyl and original. Rooted hair, large sleep eyes, and uses the "Skootles" body. 22" - $165.00. Courtesy Jeannie Mauldin.

CLOTH

20" oil cloth face doll with cloth body and yarn hair. This style doll was very popular during World War II and the years that followed. 20" - $85.00. Courtesy Sandra Cummins.

15" "Campbell Kid" made of all cloth. Printed face with back of head all yellow and has yarn hair on sides only. Tag marked "The Campbell Kids/Trademark of the Campbell Soup Co." Also "A & S (or G * S) International Services. N.Y." Designed by Grace Drayton. 15" - $65.00.

14" "Snuffy Smith" made of all cloth with pressed face mask. Felt ears, sewn-on shoes. Tag marked "Copyright King Features Syndicate, Inc. Columbia Products/Kansas City, Missouri." 14" mint - $225.00; 14" played with condition: $100.00. Courtesy Virginia Jones.

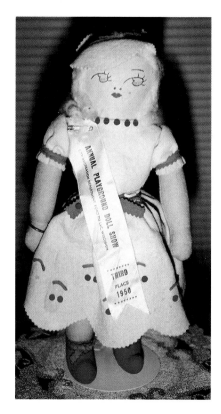

15" cloth and felt doll with mohair wig and embroidered face. Ca. early 1930's. Commerically made and most likely English. 15" - $100.00.

15" black stockinette doll that was commerically made. Felt and embroidered face. Maybe original dress. 15" - $95.00.
Courtesy Gloria Anderson.

18" "Pippi Longstocking" made by Applause in 1988. All cloth with rooted yarn hair, painted features with freckles. 18" - $45.00. Courtesy Jeannie Mauldin.

4 foot tall "Big Bertha" by Mattel, 1969. All cloth, all original. Pull string talker and has foot straps so child could dance with her. Yarn hair and painted purple eyes. There is a coloring book and crayons in pockets. "Big Bertha" - $85.00 up. Courtesy Jeannie Mauldin.

8" "Ginger." All hard plastic in #442 of Holiday Series. 8" - $65.00 up. Courtesy Maureen Fukushima.

8" "Ginger" #331 of the Novelty Series, "Girl Scout." 8" - $125.00 up. Courtesy Maureen Fukushima.

8" "Ginger" in #441 of the Holiday Series. 8" - $65.00 up. Courtesy Maureen Fukushima.

8" "Ginger" in Holiday Series outfit #443. 8" - $65.00 up. Courtesy Maureen Fukushima.

8" "Ginger" in outfit #552 of the Activity Series. 8" - $65.00 up. Courtesy Maureen Fukushima.

8" "Ginger" in outfit #664. Made of all hard plastic. 8" - $65.00 up. Courtesy Maureen Fukushima.

COSMOPOLITAN

8" "Ginger" in outfit #776 of the Party Series. 8" - $100.00 up. Courtesy Maureen Fukushima.

8" "Ginger" in outfit #774 of the Party Series. 8" - $125.00 up. Courtesy Maureen Fukushima.

DELUXE TOPPER

8" "Penny Brite." All vinyl, painted features with open/closed mouth and four painted teeth. Marked "A9/Deluxe Reading Corp./ 1963" on head; "Deluxe Reading Corp./ Elizabeth N.J./Pat. Pending" on back. Both dolls are original. Pink gown is often found on "Betsy McCall" dolls but is original to "Penny Brite." 8" - $22.00. Courtesy Karen Geary.

Left: 6" "Dawn" in original box, made in 1970. (The dolls of the "Dawn" series are becoming highly collectible, especially when mint in box.) In box - $18.00; Doll only - $12.00. Right: This "Dawn Model Agency" is one of the most desirable dolls in the series. 1970–1971. In box - $45.00; Doll only - $35.00. Courtesy Gloria Anderson.

One of the many boxed outfits available for the 6" "Dawn" doll, 1970–1971. Boxed outfit - $8.00 up. Courtesy Gloria Anderson.

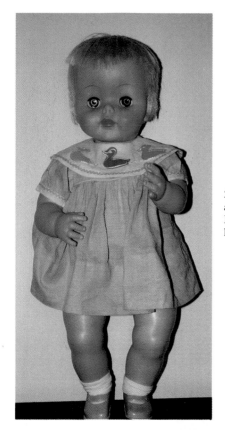

20" "Tickles" is made of plastic and vinyl and has battery operated talker/laugher. Marked "1963 Deluxe Reading/38" on head. 20" - $50.00. Courtesy Gloria Anderson.

18" "Smarty Pants" made of plastic and vinyl has battery operated talker. Black doll is original; other doll is redressed. Marked "Topper Co. 1971" White doll - $40.00; Black doll - $60.00. Courtesy Marie Ernst.

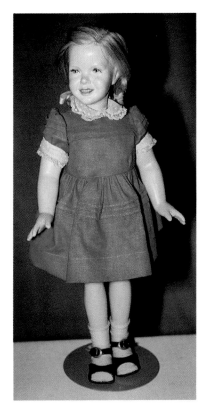

17" "Melissa" made by Lenox, limited to 750. All bisque with glass eyes. $1,200.00 up. Courtesy Shirley Bertrand.

14" "Smoky" made by Dewees Cochran during 1930's. All painted latex, embedded eyelashes, open/closed smiling mouth. Original. Sold through Marshall-Fields. $1,000.00 up. Courtesy Shirley Bertrand.

Beautiful "Romeo and Juliet" pair of all bisque with painted features. Made in 1981 by Mary Ann Oldenburg. One of a kind; price unavailable. Courtesy Shirley Bertrand.

Carved wood and cloth dolls by Avis Lee in 1943. Sold through Marshall-Fields. Left: 10" "Organ Grinder" and "Mrs. O'Leary." Right: 12" "John Kinzie" (one of the first businessmen in Chicago, 1804). $325.00 each. Courtesy Shirley Bertrand.

25" Indians that are wood with cloth bodies. Made in Homosassa, Florida, carver unknown. Each - $165.00 up. Courtesy Jeannie Mauldin.

Original "Madonna and Child" by Susan Durham of Durham Arts. For more information, see credits for address.

Large 24" "Father Christmas" that is wax over papier maché with inset glass eyes. Made by Louis Sorenson. $1,200.00 up. Courtesy Shirley Bertrand.

Left to right: "Dale Evans," "Annie Oakley," and "Roy Rogers." All hard plastic with one-piece body and legs. He has painted hair and all have painted-on shoes. Clothes are stapled on except vests and hats. Made by Dutchess Dolls. Each - $15.00 up. Courtesy Gloria Anderson.

Typical 7-8" Dutchess Dolls made during 1950's. All hard plastic, sleep eyes, jointed neck and shoulders. Clothes stapled on. Each - $4.50. Courtesy Gloria Anderson.

7" Dutchess Doll with stapled on clothes. Plastic-like material with pockets that hold crayons. Sleep eyes, mohair hairdo, and jointed at neck and shoulders only. $8.00. Courtesy Shirley Bertrand.

7" "Tinkerbelle," "Peter Pan," and "Captain Hook." All original in original box. All hard plastic, jointed at neck and shoulders only. Have sleep eyes, painted-on shoes and socks, and stapled-on clothes. "Tinkerbelle," "Peter Pan" - $15.00 each; "Captain Hook" - $20.00. Courtesy Sandra Cummins.

The name of this company was made up from the name of the founder E.G. Goldberger. Founded in 1917, the early dolls were marked "E.G.", then E. Goldberger" and now the marks of "Eegee" and "Goldberger" are used.

Andy: Teen type. 12" - $35.00.

Annette: Teen type. 11½" - $50.00. 1966, marked "20/25M/13." 25" - $55.00; 28" - $75.00; 36" - $95.00.

Annette: 1966, plastic/vinyl walker. 25" - $50.00; 28" - $60.00; 36" - $85.00.

Baby Luv: 1973, cloth/vinyl, marked "B.T. Eegee." 14" - $50.00.

Baby Susan: 1958, name marked on head. 8½" - $20.00.

Baby Tandy Talks: 1960, foam body, rest vinyl, pull string talker. $65.00.

Babette: 1962, Barbie look-a-like. 11½" - $85.00 up.

Ballerina: 1958, hard plastic/vinyl head. 20" - $60.00.

Ballerina: 1964, hard plastic/vinyl head. 31" - $125.00.

Ballerina: 1967. Foam body and limbs, vinyl head. 18" - $50.00.

Boy Dolls: Molded hair, rest vinyl. 13" - $35.00; 21" - $50.00.

Composition: Sleep eyes, open mouth girls. 14" - $165.00 up; 18" - $225.00 up. Babies: Cloth and composition. 16" - $100.00 up; 20" - $160.00 up.

Debutante: 1958, vinyl head, rest hard plastic, jointed knees. 28" - $100.00.

Dolly Parton: 1980. 12" - $30.00; 18" - $70.00.

Flowerkins: 1963, plastic/vinyl, marked "F-2" on head. (7 in set.) 16" - $90.00 in box.

Gemmette: 1963, teen type. 14" - $45.00.

Georgie or Georgette: 1971, red-headed twins. Cloth and vinyl. 22-23" - $65.00.

Gigi Perreaux: 1951, hard plastic, early vinyl head. 17" - $250.00 up.

Granny: from "Beverly Hillbillies." Old lady modeling, grey rooted hair, painted or sleep eyes. 14" - $85.00.

13½" "Gemmette" called "Emerald" made by Eegee. Green sleep eyes, rooted green hair, flat feet. Original, marked "Eegee Co. 1963." 13½" - $45.00. Courtesy Marie Ernst.

Miss Charming: 1936, all composition Shirley Temple look-alike. 19" - $385.00 up. Pin - $25.00.

Miss Sunbeam: 1968, plastic/vinyl, dimples. 17" - $50.00.

Musical Baby: 1967, has key wind music box in cloth body. 17" - $25.00.

My Fair Lady: 1956, all vinyl, jointed waist, adult type. 10½" - $55.00; 19" - $95.00.

Posey Playmate: 1969, foam and vinyl. 18" - $25.00.

Puppetrina: 1963. 22" - $40.00.

Shelly: 1964, "Tammy" type. Grow hair. 12" - $35.00.

Sniffles: 1963, plastic/vinyl nurser. Marked "13/14 AA-EEGEE." 12" - $28.00.

Susan Stroller: 1955, hard plastic/vinyl head. 20" - $50.00; 23" - $65.00; 26" - $75.00.

Tandy Talks: 1961, plastic/vinyl head, freckles, pull string talker. 20" - $85.00.

EFFANBEE DOLL COMPANY

First prices are for mint condition dolls; second prices for dolls that are played with, soiled, dirty, cracked or crazed or not original. Dolls marked with full name or "F & B."

Alyssia: 1958, walker. Hard plastic/vinyl head. 20" - 285.00, $100.00.

American Children: 1938. Marked with that name, some have "Anne Shirley" marked bodies, others are unmarked. All composition, painted or sleep eyes. Closed Mouth Girls: 18-19" - $1,400.00. Closed Mouth Boy: 15" - $1,200.00; 17" - $1,300.00. Open Mouth Girl: 15" (Barbara Joan) - $750.00; 18" (Barbara Ann) - $900.00; 21" (Barbara Lou) - $1,100.00.

Anne Shirley: 1936-1940. Marked with name. All composition. 15" - $250.00; 17" - $265.00; 21" - $350.00; 27" - $475.00.

Babyette: 1946, cloth/composition. Sleeping. 12" - $350.00, $175.00.

Babykin: 1940, all composition. 9-12" - $185.00, $85.00. All vinyl: 10" - $50.00.

Baby Cuddleup: 1953, vinyl coated cloth body, rest vinyl. Two lower teeth. 20" - $60.00, $30.00; 23" - $95.00, $45.00.

Baby Dainty: 1912–1925. Marked with name. Composition/cloth. 15" - $250.00, $95.00; 17" - $300.00, $125.00.

Baby Evelyn: 1925, marked with name. Composition/cloth. 17" - $300.00, $125.00.

Baby Grumpy: See Grumpy.

Baby Tinyette: 1933–1936. Composition. 8-9" - $225.00, $100.00. Toddler: 8-9" - $250.00; $100.00.

Betty Brite: 1933, marked with name. All composition, fur wig, sleep eyes. 16-17" - $250.00, $100.00.

19" **"American Child"** made of all composition with painted latex arms. Hands have separated fingers and it wears original gloves. Painted features, all original clothes. 19" - $1,400.00.
Courtesy Shirley Bertrand.

17" extremely rare key wound "Happy Birthday" musical "American Child." Has music box in body. All original. Sleep eyes and all composition. 17" - $1,400.00. Courtesy Shirley Bertrand.

24" "Candy Walker" with hard plastic body and limbs. Vinyl head with sleep eyes and rooted hair. Marked "Effanbee" on head. 24" - $85.00. Courtesy Jeannie Mauldin.

8" "Tinyette Button Nose" toddlers. All composition and from 1936–1937. First one has brown painted eyes; the others have blue eyes. All original except shoes. 8" - $235.00 each. Courtesy Gloria Anderson.

Bright Eyes: 1938, 1940's. Same doll as Tommy Tucker and Mickey. Composition/cloth, flirty eyes. 16" - $275.00; 18" - $325.00; 22-23" $375.00.

Brother or Sister: 1943. Composition head and hands, rest cloth, yarn hair, painted eyes. 12" - $175.00, $70.00; 16" - $200.00, $80.00.

Bubbles: 1924, marked with name. Composition/cloth. 16" - $285.00, $125.00; 20" - $365.00, $145.00; 23" - $450.00, $200.00; 26" - $500.00, $200.00. Black: 16" - $550.00; 20" - $850.00.

Button Nose: 1936–1943. Composition. 8-9" - $235.00, $75.00. Vinyl/cloth: 1968. 18" - $55.00, $25.00.

Candy Kid: 1946, all composition. White: 12" - $300.00, $95.00. Black: 12" - $375.00, $95.00.

Charlie McCarthy: Composition/cloth. 19-20" - $525.00, $200.00.

Composition Dolls: Molded hair, all composition, jointed neck, shoulders and hips. Painted or sleep eyes. Open or closed mouth. Original clothes. All composition in perfect condition. Marked "Effanbee." 1930's. 9" - $165.00, $50.00; 15" - $200.00, $90.00; 18" - $265.00, $100.00; 21" - $350.00, $150.00.

Composition Dolls: 1920's. Cloth body, composition head and limbs, open or closed mouth, sleep eyes. Original clothes and in perfect condition. Marked "Effanbee." 18" - $200.00, $90.00; 22" - $250.00, $125.00; 25" - $350.00, $125.00; 27-28" - $400.00, $150.00.

Currier & Ives: Plastic/vinyl. 12" - $50.00, $25.00.

Disney Dolls: 1977–1978. Cinderella, Snow White, Alice in Wonderland and Sleeping Beauty. 14" - $250.00, $95.00.

Emily Ann: 1937. 13" puppet, composition. $145.00, $50.00.

Dydee Baby: 1933 on. Hard rubber head, rubber body. Perfect condition. 14" - $165.00, $60.00.

Dydee Baby: 1950 on. Hard plastic/vinyl: 15" - $150.00, $50.00; 20" - $225.00, $150.00.

Fluffy: 1954. All vinyl. 10" - $45.00, $15.00. Girl Scout: 10" - $50.00, $15.00. Black: 10" - $50.00, $15.00. Molded hair (Katie), 1957. 8½" - $65.00, $25.00.

Gumdrop: 1962 on. Plastic/vinyl. 16" - $45.00, $20.00.

Grumpy: 1912–1938. Frown, painted features, cloth and composition. 12" - $225.00, $95.00; 14" - $285.00, $100.00; 18" - $375.00, $165.00. Black: 12" - $300.00, $125.00; 14-15" - $385.00, $150.00.

Half Pint: 1966 on. Plastic/vinyl. 10" - $40.00, $15.00.

Happy Boy: 1960. All vinyl, freckles, molded tooth. 10" - $60.00, $25.00.

Historical Dolls: 1939. All composition, original. 14" - $600.00, $250.00; 21" - $1,400.00, $675.00.

Honey: All composition. 14" - $200.00, $95.00; 20" - $350.00, $150.00; 27" - $500.00, $200.00.

Honey: 1949–1955. All hard plastic, closed mouth. 14" - $245.00, $90.00; 18" - $325.00, $150.00; 21" - $400.00, $175.00.

Honey: 1947–1948. Composition, flirty eyes: 21" - $450.00, $125.00. Walker: 14" - $245.00, 19" - $345.00. Jointed knees: 19" - $365.00.

Ice Queen: 1937. Skater outfit, composition, open mouth. 17" - $800.00, $250.00.

Lamkin: 1930, cloth/composition. 16" - $425.00 up; 21" - $625.00 up.

Lil Sweetie: 1967. Nurser with no lashes or brow. 16" - $60.00, $30.00.

Limited Edition Club:
1975: Precious Baby - $550.00. **1976:** Patsy - $375.00. **1977:** Dewees Cochran - $235.00. **1978**: Crowning Glory - $200.00. **1979:** Skippy - $350.00. **1980:** Susan B. Anthony - $200.00. **1981:** Girl with watering can - $200.00. **1982:** Princess Diana - $165.00. **1983:** Sherlock Holmes - $185.00. **1984:** Bubbles - $125.00. **1985:** Red Boy - $145.00. **1986:** China head - $125.00.

Little Lady: 1939–1947. All composition. 15" - $265.00, $90.00; 18" - $400.00, $125.00; 21" - $485.00, $165.00; 27" - $600.00, $225.00.

24" "Honey" walker, all original. All hard plastic, sleep eyes, excellent face color. 24" - $550.00. Courtesy Kris Lundquist.

20" "Honey" as majorette. All original with mohair wig. Strung body is made of all hard plastic. Majorette - $500.00. Courtesy Peggy Pergande.

14" "Patsy" dolls that are completely original, including the hair ribbons. All composition. Came in trunk with wardrobe. 14" - $350.00 up; In trunk - $1,000.00. Courtesy Shirley Bertrand.

Little Lady: 1943. Cloth body, yarn hair: 21" - $350.00 up. Pink cloth body, wig: 17" - $265.00 up. With magnets in hands: 15" doll only. $350.00. Doll and accessories: $450.00.

Lovums: Marked with name. Composition/cloth, open mouth smiling. 15-16" - $275.00, $100.00. 22" - $350.00, $150.00.

Mae Starr: Marked with name. Composition/cloth. Record player in torso. 30" - $450.00, $200.00.

Marionettes: Composition/wood. 14" - $175.00, $80.00.

Martha and George Washington: 1976. 11" - $200.00.

Mary Ann or Lee: 1928–1937. Marked with name. Open smile mouth, composition and cloth and all composition. 16" - $275.00, $95.00; 18" - $350.00, $125.00; 20" - $400.00, $150.00; 24" - $465.00, $175.00.

Marilee: 1920's. Marked with name. Composition/cloth, open mouth. 14" - $245.00, $100.00; 17" - $295.00, $125.00; 22" - $345.00, $150.00; 25" - $445.00; $200.00.

Mary Jane: 1960. Plastic/vinyl, walker and freckles. 31" - $265.00, $100.00.

Mary Jane: 1920's. Composition, jointed body or cloth, "Mama" type. 20-22" - $275.00.

Mickey: 1946. (Also Tommy Tucker and Bright Eyes.) Composition/cloth, flirty eyes. 16" - $275.00; 18" - $325.00, $100.00; 22-23" - $375.00, $125.00.

Mickey: 1956. All vinyl. Some with molded on hats. 11" - $100.00, $45.00.

Miss Chips: 1965 on. Plastic/vinyl. White: 18" - $65.00. Black: 18" - $85.00.

Pat-O-Pat: Composition/cloth, painted eyes. Press stomach and pats hands together. 13-14" - $165.00, $70.00.

Patricia: 1932–1936. All composition. 14" - $385.00, $145.00.

Patricia-kin: 1929–1930's. 11" - $325.00, $125.00.

Patsy: 1927–1930's. All composition. 14" - $350.00, $125.00. Composition/cloth: 14" - $325.00, $145.00.

15" "Little Lady" with magnets in hands to hold items shown in box. All composition and original. Human hair wig. Doll only - $350.00; With accessories - $450.00. Courtesy Ellen Petersen.

Patsy Babyette: 1930's, 1940's. 9-10" - $245.00, $90.00.

Patsyette: 1930's. 9" - $275.00, $100.00.

Patsy Ann: 1930's. 19" - $465.00, $165.00. Vinyl: 1959. 15" - $165.00, $60.00.

Patsy Joan: 1927–1930. Reissued 1946–1949. 16" - $450.00, $175.00. Black: 16" - $525.00 up, $225.00.

Patsy, Jr.: 11" - $285.00, $100.00.

Patsy Lou: 1929–1930's. 22" - $485.00, $175.00.

Patsy Mae: 1932. 30" - $785.00, $325.00.

Patsy Ruth: 1935. 26-27" - $765.00, $325.00.

Patsy, Wee: 1930's. 5-6" - $345.00, $125.00.

Polka Dottie: 1953. 21" - $200.00, $80.00.

Portrait Dolls: 1940. All composition. 12" - $245.00, $90.00.

Prince Charming or Cinderella: All hard plastic. 16" - $400.00 up, $165.00.

Left: 18-19" "Patsy Ann" boy and girl. All composition and original. Girl - $465.00 up; Boy - $575.00 up. Right: 9" "Patsy Babyette" boy and girl, 1940's. All composition with sleep eyes and all original. 9" each - $245.00 up. Above dolls courtesy Shirley Bertrand.

6" "Colleen Moore" doll house dolls using the "Wee Patsy" dolls. All composition and original with original buttons. Painted eyes, shoes, and socks. 6" each - $485.00 up. Courtesy Shirley Bertrand.

Pum'kin: 1966 on. All vinyl, freckles. 10½" - $35.00, $15.00.

Rootie Kazootie: 1953. 21" - $200.00, $80.00.

Rosemary: 1925 on. Marked with name. Composition/cloth. 14" - $265.00, $125.00; 17" - $295.00, $150.00; 22" - $350.00, $150.00; 28" - $475.00, $200.00.

Skippy: 1929, 1940's. All composition. 14" - $445.00, $165.00. Soldier: $500.00. Sailor: $565.00.

Suzanne: 1940. Marked with name. All composition. 14" - $275.00, $125.00.

Suzie Sunshine: 1961 on. Freckles. White: 17-18" - $55.00-30.00. Black: 17-18" - $85.00, $45.00.

Suzette: 1939. Marked with name. All composition. 12" - $200.00, $95.00.

Sweetie Pie: 1938–1940's. Composition/cloth. 14" - $175.00, $50.00; 19" - $250.00, $90.00; 24" - $350.00, $125.00.

Tommy Tucker: 1946. (Also Mickey and Bright Eyes.) Composition/cloth, flirty eyes. 16" - $275.00, 18" - $325.00, 22-23" - $375.00, $125.00.

W.C. Fields: 1938. Composition/cloth. 22" - $695.00, $200.00. Plastic/vinyl: 15" - $265.00.

19" very unique and rare "Santa Claus" that is all composition with molded hat and beard. He is jointed at neck, shoulders and hips. Original, head marked "F & B." Late 1930's. 19" - $1,000.00. Courtesy Shirley Bertrand.

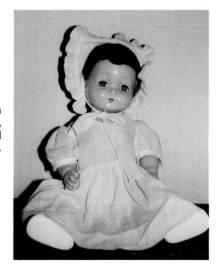

20" "Sweetie Pie" of 1940's. Cloth with composition head and limbs. Sleep eyes, caracul (lamb's wool) wig and original clothes except shoes. 20" - $250.00. Courtesy Sharon McDowell.

14" "Skippy" sailor and soldier. All composition and original. Painted eyes, molded hair. Sailor's button marked "Blue Bird/Effanbee/Dolls/ Finest & Best." Soldier's button marked "Effanbee/Dolls/Skippy/The real American Boy." Soldier - $500.00; Sailor - $565.00. Courtesy Shirley Bertrand.

15" and 15¼" "Humphrey Bogart" made in 1988. The one on the right is a prototype for the marketed doll, shown on the left. The prototype has a black hat and larger head; the other has a brown hat. Prototype - no price; 15" - $95.00. Courtesy Shirley Bertrand.

16" "Eleanor Roosevelt" and "F.D. Roosevelt" made by Effanbee in 1985. Both original. Plastic and vinyl. Part of the Presidential Series. 16" - $85.00 each. Courtesy Jeannie Mauldin.

224

20" "Clement" with wax-like vinyl head and limbs, cloth body. Original. Doll unmarked but has body tag "Clodrey Made in France." Doll that was made for the "CR Club" (Clodrey Club) in 1971. 20" - $225.00. Courtesy Marie Ernst.

16" very character faced advertising doll made in Germany for "Wickuler Beer." Holds mug and other hand holds shaft of sword. Vinyl and plastic, all original. 16" - $300.00. Courtesy Shirley Bertrand.

Right: 18" Zanini & Zambelli made doll of Italy. Original, came with rocker, needles, and yarn. Rooted hair, vinyl. 18" - $95.00. Courtesy Marie Ernst.

A wonderful 18" large "Donald Duck" that is original and made of excellent quality rigid vinyl. Marked "Italy." "Donald Duck" - $875.00 up. Courtesy Shirley Bertrand.

Original 24" fashion doll of the 1960's made in Italy. All hard plastic with flirty sleep eyes and glued-on human hair wig. Marked on head "Ottolini C&D/Mod. Dep./Made in Italy." 24" - $150.00.

14" "Lela" is made of all cloth and has mask face with painted features. Original, made in Italy in 1950. 14" - $95.00. Courtesy Gloria Anderson.

HARTLAND INDUSTRIES

Hartland Industries made many figures with horses during the mid to late 1950's. These are extremely collectible as they are rare, especially when the horses have saddles. Most came from the Warner Brothers productions on television. The figures included:

James Arness as "Matt Dillon" on *Gunsmoke*. (Sept. 1955 to Sept. 1975)

John Lupton as "Tom Jefords" on *Broken Arrow*. (Sept. 1956 - Sept. 1960)

Gail Davis as "Annie Oakley." (April 1953 - Dec. 1956)

Hugh O'Brien as "Wyatt Earp." (Sept. 1955 - Sept. 1961)

Dale Robertson as "Jim Hardie" on *Wells Fargo*. (March 1957 - Sept. 1962)

Pat Conway as "Clay Hollister" on *Tombstone Territory*. (Oct. 1957 - Oct. 1959)

Wayde Preston as "Capt. Chris Colt" on *Colt 45*. (Oct. 1957 – Sept. 1960)

Richard Boone as "Paladin" on *Have Gun Will Travel*. (Sept. 1957 – Sept. 1963)

John Payne as "Vint Bonner" on *The Restless Gun*. (Sept. 1957 – Sept. 1959)

Clint Walker as "Cheyenne" (Sept. 1955 – Sept. 1963)

Ward Bond as "Major Seth Adams" on *Wagon Train*. (Sept. 1957 – Sept. 1965)

Chief Thunderbird with horse "Northwind."

Robert E. Lee with horse "Traveler."

General George Custer and horse "Bugler."

Brave Eagle with horse "White Cloud."

General George Washington with horse "Ajax."

"Lone Ranger" with horse "Silver."

"Tonto" with horse "Scout."

Jim Bowie with horse "Blaze."

"Sgt. Preston of the Yukon" with horse.

Roy Rogers with horse "Trigger."

Dale Evans with horse "Buttercup."

Cochise with pinto horse.

Buffalo Bill with horse.

Other figures made by the company include baseball notables Mickey Mantle, Ted Williams, Stan Musial, Henry Aaron, Ed Mathews, and George "Babe" Ruth.

Figure and horse: $200.00 up.

Figure in box with horse and accessories: $300.00.

Figure alone: $95.00.

Horse alone: $100.00.

Baseball figure: $250.00 up.

Left: 7-8" "Bret Maverick" (James Garner). Right: 7-8" "Tonto" (Jay Silverheels). Figures are molded in one piece with very good quality plastic. Figures marked "Hartland Industries." Horses marked inside hind leg "Hartland Industries." Horses have unique stand-up manes and removable saddles. $200.00 each up. Courtesy Shirley Bertrand.

All prices are for mint condition dolls.

Adam: 1971. Boy for World of Love series. 9" - $18.00.

Aimee: 1972. Plastic/vinyl. 18" - $60.00.

Charlie's Angels: 1977. 8½" Jill, Kelly, or Sabrina. $18.00 each.

Defender: 1974. One-piece arms and legs. 11½" - $75.00 up.

Dolly Darling: 1965. 4½" - $9.00.

Flying Nun: Plastic/vinyl, 1967. 5" - $40.00.

G.I. Joe, #1: 12", marked "G.I. Joe Copyright 1964 by Hasbro Patent Pending Made in U.S.A." **1964-1966:** (4 models.) White only. Scar, molded hair, no beard. #1 marking. $85.00 up. **1965-1966:** (5 models.) Black, #1 marking. $90.00 up. **1966-1967:** No scar on face. $90.00 up.

G.I. Joe, #2: 1967-1974. 12", marked "G.I. Joe Copyright 1964 by Hasbro Pat. No. 3,277,602 Made in U.S.A." **1967:** (6 models) #2 marking. Design same as #1. Talking Commander: No scar, blonde, brown eyes. $80.00 up.

G.I. Joe, #3: 1975. 12", body marked same as #2 model; head marked "Hasbro Ind. Inc. 1975 Made in Hong Kong." **1968:** Same style (6 models). Scar on face. #2 marking. $75.00 up.

G.I. Joe, #4: 1975. 12", marked in small of back "Hasbro Pat. Pend. Par. R.I." Talking 1975 version has #2 marked body. **1970:** (9 models.) Flocked hair and/or beard. Black and white. **Land Adventurer:** $175.00 up. **Sea Adventurer:** $200.00 up. **Air Adventurer:** $250.00 up. **Astronaut:** $250.00 up. **Talking:** $250.00 up.

G.I. Joe, #5: 1974. (8 models.) #2 & #3 markings. Kung Fu grip. $200.00 up.

G.I. Joe, #6: 1975. (7 models.) #3 and #4 markings. White. **Mike Powers, Atomic Man:** $95.00 up. **Eagle Eye:** $90.00. **Fire Fighter:** $100.00. **West Point:** $200.00 up. **Military Police:** $100.00 up. **Ski Patrol:** $185.00 up.

Secret Agent: Unusual face, mustache. $250.00 up. **Foreign:** (See photo in Series 7, page 235.) $235.00 up. **Green Beret:** $85.00 up. **Negro Adventurer:** No beard. $350.00 up. **Frogman:** 1973. With 17" sled. $300.00 up. **G.I. Joe Nurse:** $750.00 up.

G.I. Joe Accessories:

Space Capsule: $55.00 up. **Foot Locker:** $30.00 up. **Sea Sled:** $80.00 up. **Tank:** $175.00 up. **Jeep:** $145.00 up. **Helicopter:** $200.00 up. **All Terrain Vehicle:** $150.00 up.

G.I. Joe Boxed Uniforms:

Boxed figure in uniform: $125.00 up. **Adventure Team outfit:** $300.00 up. **Diver:** "Eight Ropes of Danger." $200.00 up. **Scuba Diver:** "Jaws of Death." $200.00 up. **Safari:** "White Tiger Hunt." $200.00 up.

12" "G.I Joe" sailor with flocked hair and no beard. $95.00 up.

HASBRO

Leggy: 1972. 10" - $15.00.
Little Miss No Name: 1965. 15" - $85.00.
Mamas and Papas: 1967. $40.00 each.
Monkees: Set of four. 4" - $95.00 up.

Show Biz Babies: 1967. $35.00 each. Mama Cass: $45.00.
Storybooks: 1967. 3" - $35.00-50.00 in boxes.
Sweet Cookie: 1972. 18" - $35.00.
That Kid: 1967. 21" - $85.00.
World of Love Dolls: 9", 1971. White: $10.00. Black: $15.00.

4" "Mamas and Papas." Left to right: Cass Elliot, Denny Daheaty, and Michelle Gillian. All marked "1967" and came with a 33⅓ record telling about the person. $35.00-45.00 each. Courtesy Virginia Jones.

HEMSTEDT

1987 "Barefoot Children." Right: "Ellen" in the white pinafore was first issue. Left: Dressed in pink pinafore was second issue. The first issues have chamois skin bodies. Later issues have regular cloth bodies. Designed by Annette Hemstedt and imported by Mattel. $900.00. Courtesy Shirley Bertrand.

The "Barefoot Children" doll on the left is a first issue. The one on the right is a second issue with a darker and different styled pinafore. $800.00 each. Courtesy Shirley Bertrand.

"Fatou" on the right is from the first set of the "Barefoot Children." The one on the left has braided hair and was made for the African market. Both are original. $800.00. With braids - $950.00. Courtesy Shirley Bertrand.

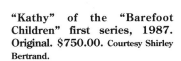

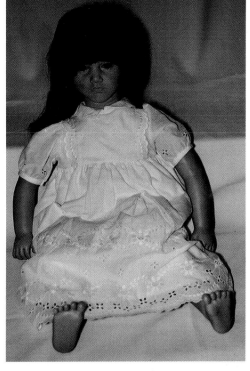

"Kathy" of the "Barefoot Children" first series, 1987. Original. $750.00. Courtesy Shirley Bertrand.

"Liza" from the first set of "Barefoot Children" with wide open/closed laughing mouth. Original first issue pinafore. $800.00. Courtesy Shirley Bertrand.

"Baston" from the first set of "Barefoot Children" in original first issue clothes. $700.00. Courtesy Shirley Bertrand.

First prices are for mint condition dolls; second prices for ones that have been played with, are dirty and soiled or not original. Marked "Horsman" or "E.I.H."

Angelove: Made for Hallmark, 1974. Plastic/vinyl. 12" - $40.00.

Answer Doll: 1966. Button in back moves head. 10" - $20.00, $10.00.

Billiken: Composition head, slant eyes, plush or velvet body. 1909. 12" - $365.00, $125.00; 16" - $450.00.

Baby Bumps: 1912. Composition/cloth. 11" - $185.00, $75.00; 16" - $245.00, $85.00. Black: 11" - $275.00, $90.00; 16" - $300.00, $125.00.

Baby First Tooth: 1966. Cloth/vinyl, cry mouth with one tooth, tears on cheeks. 16" - $50.00, $20.00.

Baby Tweaks: 1967. Cloth/vinyl, inset eyes. 20" - $40.00, $18.00.

Ballerina: 1957. Vinyl, one-piece body and legs, jointed elbows. 18" - $75.00.

Betty: All composition. 16" - $225.00, $90.00. All vinyl, one-piece body and limbs. 1951. 14" - $65.00. Plastic/vinyl: 16" - $30.00, $15.00.

Betty Jo: All composition. 16" - $225.00, $90.00. Plastic/vinyl, 1962: 16" - $30.00, $15.00.

Betty Ann: All composition. 19" - $300.00, $150.00. Plastic/vinyl: 19" - $50.00, $25.00.

Betty Jane: All composition. 25" - $350.00, $150.00. Plastic/vinyl: 25" - $75.00, $40.00.

Bye-Lo Baby: Cloth/vinyl. 100th anniversary for Wards, 1972. 14" - $55.00. Reissued 1980–1990's. 14" - $25.00.

Body Twist: 1929–1930. All composition. Top of body fits down into torso. 11" - $175.00, $65.00.

Bright Star: 1937–1946. All composition. 18-19" - $375.00, $125.00. All hard plastic, 1952: 15" - $275.00, $95.00.

Brother: Composition/cloth. 22" - $250.00 up, $100.00. Vinyl: 13" - $45.00, $20.00.

14" **"Bright Star"** made of all hard plastic with sleep eyes, open mouth and glued-on saran wig. 1956, all original except hairbow. $250.00 up.
Courtesy Sharon McDowell.

Campbell Kids: Marked "E.I.H." Ca. 1911. Composition/cloth, painted features. 13" - $550.00 up. 12": 1930–1940's. "Dolly Dingle" style face. All composition. $400.00 up.

Celeste Portrait Doll: In frame. Eyes painted to side. 12" - $35.00, $10.00.

Christopher Robin: 11" - $45.00, $10.00.

Child Dolls: 1930–1940's. All composition: 15" - $200.00, $80.00; 19" - $300.00, $100.00. All composition, very chubby toddler: 16" - $175.00, $70.00.

All hard plastic: 14" - $125.00, $50.00; 18" - $250.00 up, $100.00.

Cindy: Marked "170." All hard plastic. 1950's. 15" - $125.00 up, $50.00; 17" - $185.00 up, $80.00. All early vinyl (1953): 18" - $65.00, $15.00. Lady type, jointed waist, 1959: 19" - $85.00, $40.00.

Cindy Kay: All vinyl, long legs. Child, 1950-on. 15" - $75.00, $40.00.

Cinderella: 1965, plastic/vinyl. Painted eyes to side. 11½" - $45.00, $15.00.

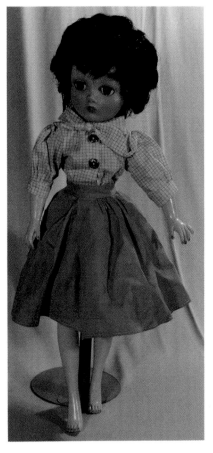

18" "Cindy" has a rigid vinyl body, high heel feet, jointed knees, and swivel waist. Vinyl head has sleep eyes, rooted hair, and pierced ears. All original. Skirt has attached slip. Marked "Horsman/83" on head and "B-18" on back. 18" - $65.00. Courtesy Marie Ernst.

Composition Dolls: 1910's–1920's. "Can't Break Em" composition/cloth body, marked "E.I.H." 12" - $165.00, $60.00; 16" - $195.00, $100.00. 1930's: 16" - $160.00, $70.00; 18" - $225.00, $90.00; 22" - $285.00, $125.00.

Crawling Baby: Vinyl, 1967. 14" - $40.00, $18.00.

Dimples: 1928–1933. Composition/cloth. 14" - $185.00, $90.00; 20" - $300.00, $125.00; 24" - $350.00, $145.00. Toddler: 20" - $365.00, $145.00; 24" - $400.00, $165.00. Laughing, painted teeth: 22" - $375.00, $165.00.

Disney Exclusives: "Cinderella," "Snow White," "Mary Poppins," "Alice in Wonderland." 1981. 8" - $45.00 each.

Gold Medal Doll: 1930's. Composition/cloth, upper & lower teeth. 21" - $200.00, $90.00. Vinyl/molded hair, 1953: 26" - $185.00, $85.00. Vinyl Boy, 1954: 15" - $75.00, $30.00.

Ella Cinders: 1925. Comic character. Composition/cloth. 14" - $375.00; 18" - $650.00.

Elizabeth Taylor: 1976. 11½" - $75.00, $40.00.

Floppy: 1965. Foam body and legs/vinyl. 18" - $35.00.

Flying Nun: (Sally Field) 1965. 12" - $65.00, $30.00.

Hansel & Gretel: 1963. Sleep eyes, unusual faces. (See photo in Series 7, pg. 238.) $185.00 each.

Hebee-Shebee: All composition. 10½" - $525.00, $225.00

Jackie Coogan: 1921. Composition/cloth, painted eyes. 14" - $500.00, $200.00.

Jackie Kennedy: 1961. Marked "Horsman J.K." Adult body, plastic/vinyl. 25" - $185.00, $80.00.

Jeanie Horsman: 1937. All composition. 14" - $225.00, $90.00. Composition/cloth: 16" - $185.00, $80.00.

Jojo: 1937. All composition. 12" - $200.00, $90.00. 16" - $265.00, $125.00.

Life-size Baby: Plastic/vinyl. 26" - $250.00, $100.00.

Lullabye Baby: 1964, 1967. Cloth/vinyl. Music box in body. 12" - $20.00, $8.00. All vinyl: 12" - $15.00, $5.00.

Mary Poppins: 1964. 12" - $45.00, $20.00; 16" - $85.00, $30.00; 26" (1966) - $185.00, $100.00; 36" - $350.00, $175.00. In box with Michael and Wendy: 12" & 8" - $150.00.

Mama Style Babies: 1920's and 1930's. Composition/cloth. Marked "E.I.H" or "Horsman." 16" - $175.00, $85.00; 22" - $245.00, $100.00. Hard plastic/cloth: 16" - $75.00; $35.00; 22" - $90.00, $40.00. Vinyl/cloth: 16" - $20.00, $8.00; 22" - $30.00, $15.00.

Michael: (Mary Poppins) 1965. 8" - $35.00, $15.00.

Mouseteer: 1971. Boy or girl. 8" - $35.00, $15.00.

Patty Duke: 1965. Posable arms. 12" - $45.00, $18.00.

Peggy: 1957. All vinyl child, one-piece body and legs. 25" - $65.00, 35.00.

Peggy Pen Pal: 1970. Multi-jointed arms. Plastic/vinyl. 18" - $55.00, $25.00.

Pippi Longstockings: 1972. Vinyl/cloth. 1972. 18" - $45.00, $20.00.

Polly & Pete: 1957. Black dolls, molded hair. All vinyl. 13" - $225.00, $60.00.

Poor Pitiful Pearl: 1963, 1976. 12" - $50.00, $25.00; 17" - $100.00, $50.00.

Peterkin: 1915–1930. All composition, painted googly-style eyes. 12" - $350.00, $125.00.

Pudgie Baby: 1978. Plastic/vinyl. 12" - $35.00, $15.00. 24" (1980) - $50.00, $30.00.

Three "Poor Pitiful Pearl" dolls. Left: 10½" by Tri-Star. Vinyl/plastic with sleep eyes, cloth body. Doll unmarked but body tagged "1955 Wilbur Steig." Center: 13" all vinyl by Brookglad. Good quality, marked "A Brookglad Creation." Right: 11" Horsman made of rigid vinyl. Vinyl head has sleep eyes, rooted hair. Marked "Horsman Dolls Inc/1963 W. Steig" on head; "Horsman Dolls Inc. 10." on back. On box: "Designed by Irene Szor." 10½" - $40.00; 13" - $75.00; 11" - $50.00.
Courtesy Marie Ernst.

Pudgy: 1974. All vinyl, very large painted eyes. 12½" - $40.00, $20.00.

Roberta: 1928. All composition. Molded hair or wigs, 1937. 14" - $250.00, $90.00; 20" - $325.00, $125.00. 24" - $325.00, $150.00.

Rosebud: 1928. Composition/cloth. Marked with name, dimples and smile. Sleep eyes, wig. 14" - $250.00, $90.00; 18" - $300.00, $125.00. 24" - $325.00, $150.00.

Ruthie: 1958–1966. All vinyl or plastic/vinyl. 14" - $22.00, $8.00; 20" - $38.00, $12.00.

Sleepy Baby: 1965. Vinyl/cloth, eyes molded closed. 24" - $50.00, $25.00.

Tuffie: 1966. All vinyl. Upper lip molded over lower. 16" - $85.00, $30.00.

15" "Kindergarten Kathy" has plastic body and legs with vinyl arms and head. Rooted hair and sleep eyes. Marked "Horsman/ T14." 1961, original dress. 15" - $20.00.

All composition and original "Campbell Kid" of 1940's. Painted-on shoes and socks, painted eyes. $400.00.

236

The Mary Hoyer Doll Mfg. Co. operated in Reading, Pa. from 1925. The dolls were made in all composition, all hard plastic, and last ones produced were in plastic and vinyl. Older dolls are marked in a circle on back "Original Mary Hoyer Doll" or "The Mary Hoyer Doll" embossed on lower back.

First price is for perfect doll in tagged factory clothes. Second price for perfect doll in outfits made from Mary Hoyer patterns and third price is for redressed doll in good condition with only light craze to composition or slight soil to others.

Composition: 14" - $500.00, $400.00 up, $165.00.

Hard Plastic: 14" - $485.00, $450.00 up, $185.00; 17" - $600.00 up, $525.00 up, $300.00.

Plastic and Vinyl: 14-15" (Margie) Marked "AE23." 12" - $145.00, $70.00, $15.00; 14" - $200.00, $95.00; $30.00.

14" **"Mary Hoyer"** that is all composition and is marked with name in circle on back. Outfit made from Hoyer pattern. $500.00. Courtesy Sharon McDowell.

This 14" **"Mary Hoyer"** is made of all hard plastic and has sleep eyes and saran wig. Original factory dress and center snap shoes. $485.00. Courtesy Kris Lundquist.

First prices are for mint condition dolls. Second prices are for cracked, crazed, dirty, soiled or not original dolls.

April Showers: 1968. Battery operated, splashes with hands, head turns. (See photo in Series 7, pg. 242.) 14" - $30.00, $15.00.

Baby Belly Button: 1970. 9" plastic/vinyl. White: $15.00, $7.00; Black: $20.00, $12.00.

Baby Crissy: 1973–1975. 24", pull string to make hair grow. White: $85.00, $35.00. Black: $100.00, $45.00. 1981 re-issue: No grow hair. 24" - $40.00, $15.00.

Baby Snooks and Other Flexies: Wire and composition. 12" - $325.00, $125.00.

Bam-Bam: 1963. Plastic/vinyl or all vinyl. 12" - $20.00, $8.00; 16" - $30.00, $10.00.

Batgirl and Other Super Women: Vinyl. (See photo in Series 7, pg. 243.) 12" - $125.00, $45.00.

Betsy McCall: See that section.

Betsy Wetsy: 1937 on. Composition head, excellent rubber body. 16" - $125.00, $20.00. Hard plastic/vinyl: 12" - $75.00, $20.00; 14" - $90.00, $35.00. All vinyl: 12" - $25.00, $9.00; 18" - $75.00, $30.00.

Betty Big Girl: 1968. Plastic/vinyl. 30" - $225.00, $100.00.

Betty Jane: 1930's–1944. Shirley Temple type. All composition, sleep eyes, open mouth. 14" - $185.00, $90.00; 18" - $300.00, $145.00; 26" - $385.00, $175.00.

Blessed Event: 1951. Called "Kiss Me." Cloth body with plunger in back to make doll cry or pout. Vinyl head with eyes almost squinted closed. 21" - $125.00, $50.00.

20" "Baby Big Eyes" with stuffed vinyl body and limbs. Vinyl head, sleep eyes, rooted hair. Original dress. Marked "Ideal Doll/VS 18/20" on head; "Ideal Doll/P-19" on back. 20" - $55.00.

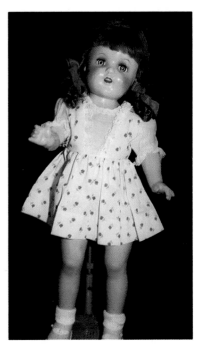

21" "Betty Jane" using the "Mary Jane" doll. All composition with sleep eyes, open mouth with teeth. Original dress, replaced shoes. 21" - $385.00. Courtesy Sharon McDowell.

Bonnie Braids: 1951. Hard plastic/vinyl head. (See photo in Series 7, pg. 245.) 13" - $60.00, $25.00. Baby: 13" - $50.00; $10.00.

Bonnie Walker: 1956. Hard plastic, pin jointed hips, open mouth, flirty eyes. Marked "Ideal W-25." 23" - $100.00, $45.00.

Brandi: 1972. Of Crissy family. 18" - $80.00, $40.00.

Brother/Baby Coos: 1951. Composition/cloth with hard plastic head. 25" - $125.00, $70.00. Composition head/latex: 24" - $35.00, $10.00. Hard plastic head/vinyl: 24" - $50.00, $15.00.

Busy Lizy: 1971. 17" - $35.00, $15.00.

Bye Bye Baby: 1960. Lifelike modeling. 12" - $165.00, $50.00; 25" - $365.00, $175.00.

Captain Action: 1966. Extra joints. 11½" - $65.00. As Batman, etc.: $85.00.

Cinnamon: 1971. Of Crissy family. 12" - $70.00, $30.00. Black: $125.00, $50.00. Hair Doodler - $60.00. Curly Ribbons - $65.00.

Composition Child: All composition girl with sleep eyes, some flirty, open mouth, original clothes and excellent condition. Marked "Ideal" and a number or "Ideal" in a diamond. 14" - $175.00, $70.00; 18" - $300.00, $90.00; 22" - $325.00, $100.00. Cloth body with straight composition legs. 14" - $145.00, $45.00; 18" - $195.00, $70.00; 22" - $225.00, $80.00.

Composition Baby: Composition head and limbs with cloth body and closed mouth. Sleep eyes (allow more for flirty eyes), original and in excellent condition. 18" - $165.00, $85.00; 22" - $185.00, $90.00; 25" - $250.00, $100.00. Flirty eyes: 16" - $200.00, $90.00; 18" - $275.00, $100.00.

Cricket: 1970–1971. Of Crissy family. 18" - $60.00, $30.00. Black: $85.00, $40.00. Look-a-round: $60.00, $30.00.

Crissy: 1968–1971. 18" - $60.00, $20.00. Black: $85.00, $40.00. Look-a-round (1972): $60.00, $25.00. Talking (1971): $80.00, $35.00. First, floor length hair (1968): $145.00, $60.00. Moving: $75.00, $30.00. Swirls Curler (1973): $60.00, $20.00. Twirly Beads (1974): $50.00, $15.00; Hair Magic, no ponytail. (1977): $45.00, $10.00.

Daddy's Girl: 1961–1962. 42" - $850.00, $300.00.

Deanna Durbin: 1939. All composition. 14" - $475.00, $200.00; 17" - $525.00, $185.00; 21" - $625.00, $300.00; 24" - $750.00, $325.00; 27" - $900.00, $400.00.

Dianna Ross: Plastic/vinyl. 18" - $165.00, $80.00.

Dina: 1972. Of Crissy family. 15" - $90.00, $40.00.

Doctor Evil: 1965. Multi joints. Came with face masks. 11" - $45.00, $15.00.

Dodi: 1964. Of Tammy family. Marked "1964-Ideal-D0-9E." 9" - $40.00, $10.00.

42" **"Daddy's Girl"** shown with 25" **"Miss Ideal."** The multi-jointed bodies have similar design. Faces are so much alike they look like sisters. Original. 42" - $850.00 up; 25" - $350.00 up. Courtesy Ann Wencel.

Dorothy Hammill: 1977. 11½" - $25.00, $8.00.

Eric: 1976. Tuesday Taylor's boyfriend. 12½" - $30.00, $15.00.

Flatsy: 1968–1970. Set of nine in frames. 5" - $9.00 each, $3.00. Fashion: 1969. 8" - $15.00, $6.00.

Flexies: 1940's. Composition and wire, soldier, children, Fanny Brice, etc. 12" - $325.00, $125.00.

Flossie Flirt: 1938–1945. Composition/cloth. Flirty eyes: 22" - $300.00, $100.00. Black: $400.00, $150.00.

Giggles: Plastic/vinyl. 16" - $50.00, $20.00; 18" - $85.00, $35.00. Black: 18" - $150.00, $75.00. Baby: 16" - $50.00, $20.00.

Goody Two Shoes: 1965. 18" - $125.00, $45.00. Walking/talking: 27" - $225.00, $70.00.

Harmony: 1971. Battery operated. 21" - $70.00, $40.00.

Harriet Hubbard Ayer: 1953. Hard plastic/vinyl. 14½" - $250.00, $70.00; 18" - $350.00, $125.00.

Honey Moon: 1965. From "Dick Tracy." White yarn hair, magic skin body. 15" - $60.00, 10.00. Cloth/vinyl: $65.00, $30.00

Joan Palooka: 1952. 14" - $75.00, $45.00.

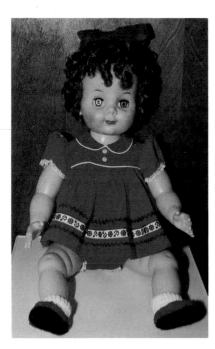

24" "Dew Drop" of 1959. Cloth body with vinyl head and limbs. Rooted hair, sleep eyes, dimples. Marked "Ideal Doll B-23." Original clothes. 24" mint in box - $100.00. Doll only - $65.00. Courtesy Jeannie Mauldin.

20" "Howdy Doody" from late 1940's. First ventriloquist's dummy made of this personality. Composition head with floating disc eyes. Composition/cloth body. Original cowboy outfit. Mouth moves by string in back of head. Made by Ideal Doll & Novelty Co. $200.00 - 300.00. Courtesy Frasher Doll Auctions.

Joey Stivic (Baby): 1976. One-piece body and limbs. Sexed boy. 15" - $50.00, $25.00.

Jiminy Cricket: 1939–1940. Composition/wood. 9" - $300.00, $145.00.

Judy Garland: 1939. All composition. 14" - $1,000.00, $400.00; 18" - $1,200.00 up, $500.00. Marked with backward "21" (1941): 21" - $500.00, $200.00.

Judy Splinters: 1951. Cloth/vinyl/latex, yarn hair, painted eyes. 18" - $125.00, $45.00; 22" - $200.00, $75.00; 36" - $350.00, $125.00.

Katie Kachoo: 1968. Raise arm and she sneezes. $50.00; $25.00.

Kerry: 1971. Of Crissy family. 18" - $75.00, $35.00.

King Little: 1940. Composition/wood. 14" - $300.00, $100.00.

Kiss Me: 1951. See Blessed Event.

Kissy: 22" - $65.00, $35.00. Black: $175.00, $60.00. Cuddly: 1964. Cloth/vinyl. 17" - $50.00, $25.00.

Kissy, Tiny: 1962. 16" - $55.00, $25.00. Black: $100.00, $50.00. Baby: 1966. Press stomach, all vinyl. 12" - $45.00, $20.00.

Liberty Boy: 1918. 12" - $300.00, $100.00.

Little Lost Baby: 1968. Three-faced doll. (See photo in Series 7, pg. 249.) 22" - $75.00, $40.00.

Magic Lips: 1955. Vinyl coated cloth/vinyl. Lower teeth. 24" - $85.00, $40.00.

Mama Style Dolls: 1920–1930's. Composition/cloth. 18" - $200.00, $85.00; 23" - $275.00, $100.00. Hard plastic/cloth: 18" - $85.00, $35.00; 23" - $125.00, $45.00.

Mary Hartline: 1952 on. All hard plastic. 15" - $400.00, $100.00; 21-23": $550.00 up, $200.00.

Mary Jane or Betty Jane: All composition, sleep and/or flirty eyes, open mouth. Marked "Ideal 18": 18" - $300.00 up, $100.00. 21" - $385.00, $175.00.

Mia: 1970. Of Crissy family. 15½" - $75.00, $30.00.

15" mint and original "Mary Hartline." Extra makeup around eyes. Marked "P-90." $400.00 up. Courtesy Jeannie Mauldin.

Mini Monsters: (Dracky, Franky, etc.) 8½" - $30.00, $10.00.

Miss Clairol (Glamour Misty): 1965. Marked "W-12-3." 12" - $50.00, $20.00.

Miss Curity: 1952 on. Hard plastic. 14" - $350.00 up, $100.00. Composition: 21" - $450.00, $125.00.

Miss Ideal: 1961. Multi-jointed. 25" - $350.00 up, $90.00; 28" - $400.00, $145.00.

Miss Revlon: 1956 on. 10½" - $95.00, $40.00; 17" - $175.00 up, $80.00. 20" - $225.00, $95.00. In box or trunk: 20" - $450.00; $125.00.

Mitzi: 1960. Teen. 12" - $85.00, $45.00.

Mortimer Snerd and Other Flexie Dolls: 1939. Composition and wire. 12" - $300.00, $100.00.

Left: All original hard plastic "Mary Hartline" with rare blue dress. Marked "P-90." Right: Very rare vinyl head "Mary Hartline" that is all original in white dress. Hard plastic body and a walker. Marked "V-91" and made in 1954. Fitted boots are original. "P-90" - $400.00; "V-91" - $500.00. Courtesy Ann Wencel.

14" "Miss Curity." Extra eye makeup, uses "Toni" P-90 doll. Box marked "Sponsored by Baur & Black, Division of Kendell Company, Chicago 6, Il. Copyright by The Kendell Co." $350.00 up. Courtesy Marie Ernst.

18" "Miss Revlon" with rigid vinyl body, swivel waist, and high heel feet. Vinyl head, sleep eyes, rooted hair. All original. 18" - $175.00 up.

Patti Playpal: 1960-on. 30" - $185.00, $95.00; 36" - $285.00, $125.00. Black: 30" - $350.00, $150.00; 36" - $450.00, $200.00.

Pebbles: 1963. Plastic/vinyl and all vinyl. 8" - $18.00, $8.00; 12" - $30.00, $15.00; 15" - $45.00, $25.00.

Penny Playpal: 1959. 32" - $200.00, $95.00.

Pepper: 1964. Freckles. Marked "Ideal - P9-3." 9" - $35.00, $20.00.

Pete: 1964. Freckles. Marked "Ideal - P8." 7½" - $35.00, $20.00.

Peter Playpal: 1961. 38" - $400.00, $175.00.

Pinocchio: 1938–1941. Composition/wood. 11" - $300.00, $100.00; 21" - $600.00, $200.00.

Pixie: 1967. Foam body. 16" - $35.00, $15.00.

10" extremely mint "Pinocchio." Composition and wood with felt hat. Marked "Des. & Copyright by Walt Disney/Made by Ideal Novelty & Toy Co." 10" mint condition - $485.00; 10" near mint condition - $300.00. Courtesy Shirley Bertrand.

12" "Tammy" and 9" "Pepper" from 1962. Both made of plastic/vinyl, have painted features and rooted hair. Both are original. "Pepper" is wearing extra packaged outfit available for her. 12" - $50.00; 9" - $35.00. Courtesy Karen Geary.

Posey (Posie): 1953–1956. Hard plastic/vinyl head, jointed knees. Marked "Ideal VP-17." 17" - $125.00, $50.00.

Real Live Baby: 1965. Head bobs. 20" - $40.00, $20.00.

Sally-Sallykins: 1934. Cloth/composition, flirty eyes, two upper and lower teeth. 14" - $150.00, $75.00; 19" - $225.00, $95.00; 25" - $300.00, $125.00.

Samantha, The Witch: 1965. Green eyes. Marked "M-12-E-2." 12" - $95.00, $35.00.

Sandy McCall: See Betsy McCall section.

Sara Ann: 1952 on. Hard plastic. Marked "P-90." (See photo in Series 7, pg. 248.) Saran wig: 14" - $245.00 up, $90.00. 21" marked "P-93": $400.00 up, $150.00.

Saralee: 1950. Cloth/vinyl. Black. 18" - $265.00, $125.00.

Sara Stimson: (Little Miss Marker) 1980, marked "1979." $20.00, $8.00.

Saucy Walker: 1951 on. 16" - $125.00, $50.00; 19" - $165.00, $60.00; 22" - $185.00, $70.00. Black: 18" - $265.00, $100.00.

Shirley Temple: See that section.

Snoozie: 1933. Composition/cloth, molded hair, sleep eyes, open yawning mouth. Marked "B Lipfert." 13" - $165.00, $50.00; 16" - $245.00, $100.00; 20" - $300.00, $150.00.

Snow White: 1937 on. All composition, black wig, on marked Shirley Temple body, sleep and/or flirty eyes. 12" - $475.00, $200.00; 18" - $545.00, $225.00. Molded hair, eyes painted to side (1939): 14" - $185.00, $85.00; 18" - $450.00, $145.00.

Sparkle Plenty: 1947. 15" - $70.00, $40.00.

Suzy Playpal: 1960–1961. Chubby, vinyl body and limbs. Marked "Ideal O.E.B. 24-3." 24" - $175.00, $75.00.

Tabitha: 1966. Cloth/vinyl. Eyes painted to side. Marked "Tat-14-H-62" or "82." 15" - $65.00, $25.00.

15" "Tiny Thumbelina." Cloth body with vinyl head and limbs. Painted eyes, rooted hair and original outfit #9606 purchased separately. Marked "Ideal Toy Corp./OTT-14" on head. 15" - $30.00 up. Courtesy Marie Ernst.

Tara: 1976. Grows hair. Black. 16" - $50.00, $25.00.

Tammy: 1962. 12" - $50.00, $20.00. Black: $60.00, $25.00. Grown-up (1965): 12" - $45.00, $20.00.

Tammy's Mom: 1963. Eyes to side. Marked: "Ideal W-18-L." 12" - $55.00, $30.00.

Ted: 1963. Tammy's brother. Molded hair. Marked "Ideal B-12-U-2." 1963. 12½" - $50.00, $25.00.

Thumbelina: 1962 on. Kissing: 10½" - $20.00, $8.00. Tearful: 15" - $30.00, $12.00. Wake Up: 17" - $45.00, $20.00. Black: 10½" - $50.00, $20.00.

Tickletoes: 1930's. Composition/cloth. 15" - $185.00, $85.00; 21" - $285.00, $100.00. Magic Skin body: 1948. Hard plastic head. 15" - $95.00, $20.00.

Tiffany Taylor: 1973. Top of head swivels to change hair color. 18" - $80.00, $35.00. Black: 18" - $95.00, $50.00.

20-21" "Toni" marked "P-93." Original. $485.00. Courtesy Sharon McDowell.

20-21" "Toni" marked "P-93." Original. $485.00 up. Courtesy Sharon McDowell.

20-21" "Toni" marked "P-90." Original. $300.00 up. Courtesy Sharon McDowell.

15½-16" "Toni" marked "P-91." Original. $350.00 up. Courtesy Sharon McDowell.

Tippy or Timmy Tumbles: 16" - $35.00, $15.00. Black: $50.00, $25.00.

Toni: 1949 on. 14" (P-90): $300.00 up, $100.00. 15" (P-91): $350.00 up, $150.00. 17-18" (P-92): $450.00 up, $135.00. 21" (P-93): $485.00 up, $185.00. 23" (P-94): $600.00 up, $185.00. Walker: $285.00 up, $135.00.

Tressy: Of Crissy family. 18" - $75.00, $35.00. Black $125.00, $45.00.

Tribly: 1951. 3 faced baby. Cloth/vinyl. 20" - $65.00, $20.00.

Tubbsy: 1966. Plastic/vinyl, battery operated. 18" - $50.00, $20.00.

Tuesday Taylor: 1977. 11½ - 12" - $45.00, $15.00.

Upsy Dazy: 1972. Foam body, stands on head. 15" - $20.00, $8.00.

Velvet: 1970–1971. Of Crissy family. 16" - $60.00, $20.00. Black: $125.00, $45.00. Look-a-round: $70.00, $30.00. Talking: $70.00, $35.00. Moving: $65.00, $20.00. Beauty Braider: 1973. $55.00, $20.00. Surely Daisy: 1974. $50.00, $20.00.

17-18" "Toni" marked "P-92." Original. $450.00 up. Courtesy Sharon McDowell.

15-16" "Toni" marked "P-91." Original. $350.00 up. Courtesy Sharon McDowell.

14" "Toni" marked "P-90." Wearing cowgirl outfit made from Toni pattern. $225.00 up. Courtesy Sharon McDowell.

14" "Wingy," a character from the Dick Tracy comic strip at the same time as "Honey Moon" and "Sparkle Plenty." Walker doll with hard plastic toddler body and pin jointed hips. Vinyl head with dimples in both cheeks and blue eyes. When head is twisted, her face glows blue in the dark. Marked "CPR 1953/Chicago Tribune/Ideal Doll/11 (unclear number) A." Marked "Ideal Doll" on back. Doll redressed. Courtesy Alice Arthur.

IRWIN

The Oolong Island group includes seven children from various nations that were placed on the island as the protectors of the jewels. The children have protectors, "Lady Potunia," and "Colonel Kettleby." The beautiful "Valerian" steals the jewels and turns into an old hag.

The children were packaged separately according to toy reference material. It is assumed that each of their teapots were also sold separately. There is also a teapot bridge and a tall bridge where the jewels are kept. It is not known if these teapot items were marketed. The set is dated 1987 and made by Irwin Toys. The box is printed in both English and French.

Lady Potunia or Colonel Kettleby: $40.00 each.

Children: $220.00 each.

Tea Pots: $18.00 each.

Valerian: $45.00.

10" pudgy "Lady Potunia" has all plastic body and limbs. Her large head is vinyl with painted features, rooted hair, and attached eyeglasses. Marked "China" on head; box marked "Irwin Toys, Ltd." She is fully dressed with purse over shoulder. The plastic teapot is hinged so doll can be removed. There is also an old man, "Colonel Kettleby." They are guardians of the Oolong Island jewels. $40.00.

According to the tale, "Valerian" became evil and turned into an ugly old hag. Packaged doll comes with mask head and outfit. 11½" doll is plastic with vinyl head and legs. Knees bend. Face is painted with "pout" look to lips. All dolls come with large poster with one side in English and the other side in French. $45.00.

13" "Busy Timmy" is all vinyl with sleep eyes and marked "Jolly Toys 1962" on head. Designed by Eloise Wilkins who also illustrated the *Little Golden Book* shown with doll. All original except replacement shoes. 13" - $250.00 up. Courtesy Cheryl and Wayne Koenig.

KAYSTAN

14" "Miss Teenage America" pageant doll, original. Plastic and vinyl with painted features, high heel feet and marked "3428/Kaystan Co./1972/Hong Kong" on back. Medal marked "Miss Teenage America." 14" - $95.00 up. Courtesy Marie Ernst.

First prices are for mint condition dolls; second prices are for played with, dirty or missing clothing and accessories.

Baby Bundles: 16" - $20.00, $10.00. Black: $28.00, $15.00.

Baby Yawnie: Cloth/vinyl, 1974. 15" - $25.00, $15.00.

Big Foot: All rigid vinyl. (See photo in Series 7, pg. 253.) 13" - $20.00, $9.00.

Butch Cassidy or Sundance Kid: 4" - $18.00, $7.00 each.

Blythe: 1972. Pull string to change the color of eyes. 11½" - $45.00, $20.00.

Charlie Chaplin: All cloth with walking mechanism. 1973. 14" - $80.00, $45.00.

Cover Girls (Darci, Erica, Dana, etc.): 12½" White: $35.00, $12.00. Black: $40.00, $15.00.

Crumpet: 1970. Plastic/vinyl. 18" - $40.00, $15.00.

Dana: Black doll, 1978. 12½" - $40.00, $15.00.

Darci: Blonde, 1978. 12½" - $35.00, $12.00.

Dusty: 12". $25.00, $10.00.

Erica: Red hair, 1978. 12½" - $35.00, $12.00.

Gabbigale: 1972. 18" - $45.00, $20.00. Black: $60.00, $25.00.

Garden Gals: 1972. Hand bent to hold watering can. 6½" - $10.00, $4.00.

Hardy Boys: 1978. Shaun Cassidy and Parker Stevenson. 12" - $20.00, $8.00.

International Velvet: 1976. (Tatum O'Neill) 11½" - $20.00, $9.00.

18" "Crumpet" with sleep eyes, swivel waist and wrists. Pours tea and offers dish. Battery operated. Marked "1970 Kenner Products Co./235-225" on head. 18" - $40.00. Courtesy Jeannie Mauldin.

Jenny Jones and Baby: All vinyl, 1973. 9" Jenny and 2½" baby: $15.00, $6.00. Set: $25.00, $8.00.

Skye: Black doll. 12" - $25.00, $10.00.

Star Wars: 1974–1978. Large size figures. R2-D2: 7½" - $90.00 up, $30.00. C-3PO: 12" - $95.00 up, $35.00. Darth Vader: 15" - $90.00 up, $25.00. Boba Fett: 13" - $125.00 up, $30.00. Jabba: 8½" - $55.00, $20.00. IG-88: 15" - $150.00 up, $50.00. Stormtrooper: 12" - $85.00 up, $25.00. Leia: 11½" - $90.00 up, $25.00. Hans Solo: 12" - $85.00, $25.00. Luke Skywalker: 13½" - $85.00, $25.00. Chewbacca: 15" - $85.00 up, $25.00. Obi Wan Kenobi: 12" - $90.00, $30.00.

Strawberry Shortcake: 1980's. 4½ - 5": $10.00 each up. Sleep eyes: $35.00 each. 9" characters ("Sour Grapes", etc.): $12.00.

Steve Scout: 1974. 9" - $20.00, $8.00. Black: $30.00, $10.00.

Sweet Cookie: 1972. 18" - $35.00, $15.00.

5" "Belle" figures in roller skating and ballerina outfits. All rigid vinyl and fully jointed. Painted features, removable clothes. Kenner produced many different outfits for "Belle" and "Snoopy." 5" - $8.00 each. Courtesy Marie Ernst.

KEWPIE

First prices are for mint condition dolls; second prices are for dolls played with, crazed or cracked, dirty, soiled or not original.

Bisque Kewpies: See antique Kewpie section.

All Composition: Jointed shoulder only. 9" - $135.00, $50.00; 14" - $225.00, $90.00. Jointed hips, neck and shoulder: 9" - $200.00, $80.00; 14" - $325.00, $130.00. Black: 12" - $350.00.

Talcum Powder Container: 7-8" - $195.00.

Celluloid: 2" - $45.00; 5" - $90.00; 9" - $165.00. Black: 5" - $145.00.

Bean Bag Body: 10" - $45.00, $15.00.

Cloth Body: Vinyl head and limbs. 16" - $200.00, $95.00.

Kewpie Gal: With molded hair/ribbon. 8" - $65.00, $25.00.

Hard Plastic: 1950's. One-piece body and head. 8" - $95.00, $25.00; 12" - $225.00, $95.00; 16" - $350.00, $145.00. Fully jointed at shoulder, neck and hips: 12-13" - $385.00, $175.00; 16" - $500.00, $225.00.

Ragsy: 1964. Vinyl one-piece, molded-on clothes with heart on chest. 1964. 8" - $60.00, $28.00. Without heart, 1971: 8" - $45.00, $19.00.

Thinker: 1971. One-piece vinyl, sitting down. 4" - $15.00, $8.00.

Kewpie: Vinyl, jointed at shoulder only. 9" - $55.00, $15.00; 12" - $85.00, $20.00; 14" - $100.00, $30.00. Jointed at neck, shoulders and hips: 9" - $75.00, $25.00; 12" - $125.00, $35.00; 14" -

$175.00, $50.00; 27" - $300.00, $165.00. Not jointed at all: 9" - $35.00, $10.00; 12" - $50.00, $15.00; 14" - $65.00, $20.00. Black: 9" - $50.00, $15.00; 12" - $75.00, $25.00; 14" - $125.00, $45.00. Bean Bag Type Body: 1970's. Vinyl head. 10" - $45.00, $15.00.

Ward's Anniversary: 1972. 8" - $80.00, $25.00.

All Cloth: Made by Kreuger. All one-piece including clothing. 12" - $185.00, $90.00; 16" - $285.00, $100.00; 20" - $265.00, $175.00; 25" - $925.00, $300.00. Removable dress and bonnet: 12" - $225.00, $85.00; 16" - $350.00, $145.00; 20" - $565.00, $200.00; 25" - $1,000.00, $400.00.

Kewpie Baby: 1960's. With hinged joints. 15" - $195.00, $80.00; 18" - $265.00, $95.00.

Kewpie Baby: With one-piece stuffed body and limbs. 15" - $165.00, $80.00; 18" - $185.00, $70.00.

Plush: Usually red with vinyl face mask and made by Knickerbocker. 1960's. 6" - $60.00, $20.00; 10" - $85.00, $25.00.

13" vinyl "Kewpie" made exclusively for Shirley's Doll House, Wheeling, IL. Under 50 made. 13" - **$145.00 up.**

12" black and white composition "Kewpie" with original paper label on chests. Jointed shoulders only. Kewpie on left has original ribbon. One on right has original wrist tag. White Kewpie - **$225.00 up;** Black Kewpie - **$350.00 up.** Courtesy Shirley Bertrand.

Right: 6" all celluloid "Kewpie" with original chest sticker in original box.

Left: Top of box for 6" celluloid "Kewpie." In original box - $165.00; "Kewpie" alone - $95.00. Courtesy Shirley Bertrand.

Left: 10" Klumpe made during the time Effanbee was importing them from Spain. Holds ring with key and burglar instruments. 10" - $85.00. Courtesy Shirley Bertrand.

Right: 12" Klumpe doctor. Made of all flannel felt with oil-painted features. Body can be posed on wire frame. Made in 1960's when Effanbee was importing the figures from Spain. 12" - $65.00 Courtesy Shirley Bertrand.

First prices are for mint condition dolls; second prices are for dolls played with, crazed or cracked, dirty, soiled or not original.

Alexander: All composition, painted hair and features. 9" - $375.00, $125.00.

Bozo Clown: 14" - $45.00; 24" - $85.00.

Cinderella: With two heads; one sad; the other with tiara. 16" - $25.00.

Clown: Cloth. 17" - $35.00.

Composition Child: 1938 on. Bent right arm at elbow. 15" - $225.00 up.

Daddy Warbucks: 1982. 7" - $20.00, $9.00.

Dagwood: Composition, painted hair and features. 14" - $650.00, $275.00.

Flintstones: 17" - $45.00 each.

Kewpie: See Kewpie section.

Levi Rag Doll: All cloth. 15" - $20.00.

Little House on the Prairie: 1978. 12" - $20.00 each.

Little Orphan Annie: 1982. 6" - $15.00, $6.00.

Lord of Rings: 5" - $20.00 each.

Mickey Mouse: 1930–1940's. 18" - $1,600.00.

Miss Hannigan: 7" - $20.00, $9.00.

Molly: 5½" - $20.00, $15.00.

Pinocchio: All plush and cloth. 13" - $145.00 up. All composition: 13" - $300.00 up.

Punjab: 7" - $20.00, $9.00.

Scarecrow: Cloth. 23½" - $150.00 up.

Seven Dwarfs: 10", all composition. Each - $250.00 up.

Sleeping Beauty: 1939. All composition, bent right arm. 15" - $285.00 up.

Snow White: 1937. All composition, bent right arm. Black wig. 15" - $285.00 up; 20" - $350.00 up.

Soupy Sales: 1966. Vinyl and cloth, non-removeable clothes. 13" - $165.00.

Two-headed Dolls: 1960's. Vinyl face masks; one crying, one smiling. 12" - $20.00.

17" "Bozo The Clown" with vinyl head, painted features, and cloth body. Marked "Capitol Records. Made in Taiwan 23." Tag marked "Larry Harmon's/Bozo The Clown/ Capitol Records, Inc./Knickerbocker Toy Co." 17" - $50.00.
Courtesy Sandra Cummins.

18" "Donald Duck" made of all foam over wire armature. Marked "Walt Disney Productions/Mfg. by Lakeside Ind. Inc. by Neufield of England." 18" - $250.00 up. Courtesy Shirley Bertrand.

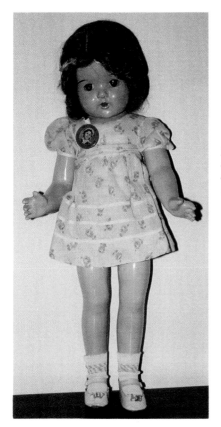

23" unmarked composition with sleep eyes, mohair wig, open mouth and all original except pin. Ca. 1935–1939. 23" - $285.00. Courtesy Gloria Anderson.

36" unmarked "Patti Playpal" look-a-like. Original clothes. Plastic with rigid vinyl arms, vinyl head, sleep eyes and rooted hair. 36" - $165.00. Courtesy Gloria Anderson.

18" unmarked composition with factory clothes, mohair wig, sleep eyes and closed mouth. 18" - $185.00. Courtesy Kris Lundquist.

18" unmarked all composition doll that was made either by Ideal or Horsman for Mollye International. Original with sleep eyes, open mouth with teeth, and mohair wig. Ca. 1945–1948. 18" - $225.00. Courtesy Sharon McDowell.

7" "Tom Corbett" and "Dr. Joan Dale" made by the Marcie Co. in the 1950's. Dolls are shown with original box. Jointed at neck and shoulders only, painted-on shoes. Clothes are stapled on. *Tom Corbett, Space Cadet* was first telecast in October 1950 and ran until September 1952. Frankie Thomas played "Tom Corbett" and Margaret Garland played "Dr. Joan Dale." Set - $200.00. Courtesy Carol Turpen.

7" "Marcie Majorette" doll, ca. 1954, that is all hard plastic and jointed at neck and shoulders only. Clothes cannot be removed. Mohair wig and painted features. This style doll was sold extensively through Sears and Wards during the 1950's. Courtesy Gloria Anderson.

11½" "Beverly Johnson, Real Model." Plastic body and arms, vinyl head and legs. Bending knees. Painted features, excellent quality. Matchbox discontinued dolls in 1989. Few dolls reached the market. Marked "Beverly Johnson" on head and "Matchbox, 1989, Made in China" on lower back. $50.00

11½" "Cheryl Tiegs, Real Model." Same construction as Beverly Johnson and body marked the same. Head marked "Cheryl Tiegs." Made in 1989. Discontinued. $35.00.

11½" "Christie Brinkley, Real Model." Same construction as Beverly Johnson doll and body is marked the same. Head marked "Christie Brinkley." $35.00.

MATTEL, INC.

First prices are for mint condition dolls; second prices are for dolls that have been played with, are dirty, soiled, not original and/or do not have accessories.

Allen: 12" in box - $200.00 up.

Baby First Step: 1964. 18" - $35.00, $12.00. Talking: $45.00, $15.00.

Baby Go Bye Bye: 1968. 12" - $20.00, $10.00.

Baby's Hungry: 1966. 17" - $40.00, $15.00.

Baby Love Light: 1970. Battery operated. 16" - $35.00, $15.00.

Baby Pataburp: 13" - $40.00, $15.00.

Baby Play-A-Lot: 1971. 16" - $38.00, $16.00.

Baby Say 'n See: 1965. 17" - $35.00, $12.00.

Baby Secret: 1965. 18" - $45.00, $15.00.

Baby Small Talk: 1967. 11" - $20.00, $8.00. As Cinderella: $25.00, $10.00. Black: $35.00, $15.00.

Baby Tenderlove: 1969. Newborn. 13" - $15.00, $5.00. Talking: 1969. 16" - $20.00, $10.00. Living: 1970. 20" - $30.00. Molded hair piece: 1972. 11½" - $35.00. Brother: 1972. Sexed. 13" - $40.00.

Baby Teenie Talk: 1965. 17" - $40.00, $10.00.

Baby Walk 'n Play: 1968. 11" - $30.00, $10.00.

Baby Walk 'n See: 18" - $35.00, $15.00.

Barbie: 1958-1959: #1, holes in feet with metal cylinders. $2,500.00 in box. Doll only: $1,500.00 up.

1960: #3, curved brows, marked 1959 body. $300.00 up.

1961: #4, marked "Pat. Pend. 1961." $250.00 up.

1963: Fashion Queen with 3 wigs. $200.00 up. Bubble cut: $125.00 up. Gift sets: $350.00 up.

1964: Ponytail with swirl bangs. No curly bangs. $200.00 up.

1965: Color 'n Curl, 2 heads and accessories. $450.00 up. First bend knees, Dutch boy style hair, full bangs. $250.00 up.

1968: Spanish Talking - $200.00 up.

1969: Twist 'n Turn - $95.00 up.

1971: Growing Pretty Hair, bendable knees. $250.00 up.

1972: Ward Anniversary - $200.00 up.

1973: Quick Curl - $95.00 up.

1974: Newport - $45.00 up. Sun Valley - $75.00 up. Sweet Sixteen - $85.00 up.

1975: Free Moving - $65.00 up. Funtime - $65.00 up. Gold Medal Skater - $50.00 up. Winter Sports - $35.00 up. Olympic Sports - $40.00 up.

1976: Ballerina - $50.00 up. Deluxe Quick Curl - $50.00. Free Moving - $60.00 up.

1977: Super Star - $70.00 up.

1978: Super Size Barbie - $100.00. Fashion Photo - $40.00. In The Spotlight - $75.00.

1979: Pretty Changes - $70.00 up. Kissing - $50.00 up. Sunloving Malibu - $20.00 up.

1980: Beauty Secrets - $75.00 up. Black Barbie - $45.00 up. Roller Skater - $25.00 up.

1981: Western - $35.00 up.

1982: Pink & Pretty - $35.00. Magic Curl - $50.00. Fashion Jeans - $25.00.

1983: Twirly Curls: White - $35.00 up; Black, Hispanic - $75.00. Happy Birthday - $30.00. My First Barbie - $20.00. My First Barbie: short dress,

#3 "Barbie." Left: In nurse's uniform. Center: Candy Striper. Right: In barbeque outfit. #3 "Barbie" - $300.00 up. Courtesy Jeannie Mauldin.

second issue - $25.00. Horse Loving - $35.00. Golden Dream (Dept. store) - $50.00 up. Dream Date - $20.00. Angel Face - $25.00.

1984: Loving You - $15.00. Sun Gold Malibu - $15.00. Great Shape - $25.00. Crystal - $30.00.

1985: Peaches & Cream - $45.00. Dreamtime - $25.00. Day To Night - $30.00.

1986: Dream Glow - $35.00. Rockers - $40.00 up. Gift Giving - $20.00. Tropical - $15.00. Astronaut: Red/silver suit. $70.00. Magic Moves - $20.00.

Barbie Special Internationals:

1981: Royal, Parisian, Italian - $50.00 up.

1982: Scottish - $150.00. Oriental - $100.00.

1983: Hawaiian - $50.00. Eskimo - $150.00. India - $150.00.

1984: Spanish - $150.00. Swedish - $75.00.

1985: Swiss, Irish - $150.00.

1986: Japanese - $100.00. Greek - $35.00. Peruvian - $35.00. German - $85.00. Canadian - $30.00. Korean - $35.00. Hispanic - $75.00.

Barbie Clothes: 1958: Easter Parade - $400.00. Gay Parisienne - $400.00. Roman Holiday - $400.00. Solo In Spotlight - $150.00 up. Enchanted Evening (pink gown) - $165.00. Plantation Belle - $200.00. Picnic Set - $125.00.

1963: Drum Majorette - $85.00. Cheerleader - $85.00. Little Theatre outfits - $70.00-100.00. Travel outfits - $60.00-80.00. Masquerade - $90.00.

1964: Astronaut - $165.00. Holiday Dance - $45.00. Campus Sweetheart - $80.00. Junior Prom - $60.00. Skin Diver - $35.00.

1965: Golden Glory - $60.00. Benefit Performance - $80.00. Debutante Ball - $100.00. Riding in the Park - $65.00.

Barbie Items: Roadster - $265.00 up. Sports Car - $200.00. Dune Buggy - $80.00 up. Clock - $40.00. Family House -

"Feelin' Groovy Barbie" designed by Billyboy™ includes accessories such as sunglasses, jewelry, gloves, shoulder bag, travel case, camera, hanger, passport, and theater tickets. **$225.00 up.**

$150.00 up. Watches - $20.00-40.00. Airplane - $500.00 up. Horse "Dancer" (brown) - $125.00 up. Wardrobe - $45.00 up. First Barbie stand (round with two prongs) - $165.00 up.

Bozo: 18" - $45.00, $15.00.

Bucky Love Notes: 1974. Press body parts for tunes. 12" - $28.00.

Buffie: 1967. With Mrs. Beasley. 6" - $65.00, $12.00. 10" - $85.00, $20.00.

Capt. Lazer: 1967. 12½" - $250.00, $50.00.

Casey: 1975. 11½". $165.00 up.

Casper, The Ghost: 1964: 16" - $40.00, $20.00. 1971: 5" - $20.00, $5.00.

Charlie's Angels: 1978, marked "1966." 11½" - $15.00, $6.00.

Charmin' Chatty: 1961. 25" - $125.00, $40.00.

Chatty Brother, Tiny: 1963. 15" - $40.00, $10.00. Baby: 1962. $40.00, $10.00. Black: $55.00, $20.00.

Chatty Cathy: 1962 on. 20" - $95.00, $40.00. Brunette/brown eyes: $125.00, $50.00. Black: $225.00, $55.00.

Cheerleader: 1965. 13" - $20.00, $9.00.

Cheerful Tearful: 1965. 13" - $25.00, $8.00. Tiny: 1966. 6½" - $15.00, $6.00.

Christie: 1968. Black doll. 11½" - $95.00 up.

Cynthia: 1971. 20" - $60.00, $25.00.

Dancerina: 1968. 24" - $50.00, $20.00. Black: $70.00, $30.00. Baby: Not battery operated. $40.00, $15.00. Black: $60.00, $25.00.

Debbie Boone: 1978. 11½" - $25.00, $9.00.

Dick Van Dyke: 25" - $125.00, $50.00.

Donny Osmond: 1978, marked "1968." 12" - $15.00, $9.00.

Drowsy: 1966. Pull string talker. 15" - $25.00, $10.00.

Dr. Doolittle: 1967. Talker. Cloth/vinyl: 22½" - $60.00, $25.00. All vinyl: 6" - $25.00, $7.00.

Fluff: 9" - $60.00 up.

Francie: 1966. 11½" - $90.00 up. Black: $400.00 up. Malibu: $30.00. Twist n' Turn: 1967. $75.00. Busy Hands: 1972. $60.00. Quick Curl: 1973. $45.00.

Grandma Beans: 11" - $20.00, $9.00.

Gorgeous Creatures: 1979. Mae West style body/animal heads. $25.00 each, $10.00.

Grizzly Adams: 1971. 10" - $20.00, $8.00.

Guardian Goddesses: 1979. 11½", each - $185.00 up.

Herman Munster: 16" - $45.00, $15.00.

Heros In Action: (Set of 14) 1975. Marked "Mattel Hong Kong. Pat Pending." 3" - $15.00 each.

25" "Charmin' Chatty" from 1961. Both are all original. The one on the left is dressed like girl on book cover. $125.00 up. Courtesy Jeannie Mauldin.

Hi Dottie: 1969. 17" - $35.00, $15.00.

Honey Hill Bunch: 1975. (Set of 6) 6" - $12.00, $3.00.

How West Was Won: 1971. 10" - $25.00. Indians: 10" - $30.00.

Hush Lil Baby: 15" - $20.00, $9.00.

Jamie, Walking: With dog, 1969. 11½" - $325.00 up.

Jimmy Osmond: 1979. 10" - $30.00, $10.00.

Julia: 1969. 11½" nurse - $200.00 up. Talking: $225.00 up.

Lil Big Guy: 13" - $15.00, $8.00.

Kelley: Quick Curl: 1973. $75.00. Yellowstone: 1974. $70.00.

Ken: Flocked hair - $125.00 up. Molded hair/non-bending knees - $125.00 up. Malibu - $30.00 up. Live Action - $60.00 up. Mod hair - $30.00 up. Busy - $45.00 up. Talking - $150.00 up.

Kiddles: 1966 on. With cars - $45.00 up. With planes - $50.00 up. In ice cream cones - $20.00 up. In jewelry - $30.00 up. In perfume bottles - $20.00 up. In bottles - $20.00 up. With cup and saucer - $100.00 up. Storybooks with accessories - $100.00 up. Baby Biddle in carriage - $175.00 up. Santa - $50.00 up. Animals - $40.00. Circus necklace: 1968. $50.00 each.

Kitty O'Neill: 1978. 11½"" - $25.00, $9.00.

Midge: 1963. 11½", freckles. $150.00 up. Bendable legs, 1965: $85.00 up.

Mother Goose: 20" - $50.00, $20.00.

Mrs. Beasley: Talking, 16". $60.00, $25.00.

Peachy & Puppets: 1972. 17" - $25.00, $10.00.

"Walking Jamie" and dog from "Jamie Furry Friends" gift set made exclusively for Sears, 1970–1971. Hair came in various colors. Doll marked "1967 Mattel Inc. U.S. Patented/Pat'd Canada 1967/ Other Pats. Pending/Japan." Fuzzy poodle has wired body for posing. Plastic eyes, felt nose/tongue. Dog unmarked. $325.00 up. Courtesy Bessie Carson.

1969 "Francie" with "grow pretty" hair. $90.00 up. Courtesy Gloria Anderson.

One of the "Kola Kiddles." This one is "Kleo." Original. Bottle drops down over doll and is plastic. $20.00 up.

1969 "Talking P.J." with pull string in back of head. Long eyelashes and bend knees. $95.00 up. Courtesy Gloria Anderson.

14" "Myrtle" of 1969. Hand puppet and pull string talker. From "My Three Sons" television program. Vinyl head and hands, yarn hair, and painted features. 14" - $60.00. Courtesy Jeannie Mauldin.

P.J.: 11½" - $75.00 up. Talking: $95.00 up.

Randy Reader: 1967. 19" - $40.00, $20.00.

Real Sister: 14" - $25.00, $15.00.

Ricky: 1965, red hair and freckles. $125.00 up.

Rockflowers: 1970. 6½" - $30.00, $10.00.

Rose Bud Babies: 6½" - $25.00, $10.00.

Saucy: 1972. 16" - $65.00. Black: $95.00.

Scooby Doo: 1964. 21" - $85.00, $30.00.

Shaun: 1979. 12" - $15.00, $9.00.

Shrinking Violet: 1962. Pull string talker, features move. Cloth, yarn hair. 15" - $50.00 up, $15.00.

Skediddles: 1966 on. 4" - $50.00 up. Disney - $125.00 up. Cherry Blossom: 1967. $125.00. Cartoon: $85.00.

Skooter: 1963, freckles. $85.00 up.

Skipper: 1963 - $125.00 up. Growing up, 1976: $65.00 up.

Singing Chatty: 1964. Pull string. 17" - $45.00, $15.00.

Sister Belle: 1961. 17" - $50.00, $20.00.

Small Talk: 1967. Pull string. 11" - $20.00, $8.00. Sister: 1967. 10" - $20.00, $8.00. Cinderella: 1968. $25.00, $10.00.

Small Walk, Sister: 1967. 11½" - $25.00, $10.00.

Stacey, Talking: $150.00.

Swingy: 20" - $45.00, $20.00.

Tatters: 10" - $45.00, $20.00.

Teachy Keen: 1966. 17" - $35.00, $12.00.

Teeners: 4" - $45.00, $10.00.

Timey Tell: (Chatty Tell) 1964, watch attached to wrist. 17" - $45.00, $15.00.

Tinkerbelle: 19" - $45.00, $15.00.

Tippy Toes: 1967. 16" - $25.00, $9.00. Tricycle or horse: $20.00, $5.00.

Truly Scrumptious: 11½" - $250.00 up. Doll only: $175.00 up. Talking (1968): $200.00.

"Sensational Malibu Skipper" and "Western Skipper," both from 1981. $65.00 up. Courtesy Gloria Anderson.

MATTEL, INC.

Tutti: 1965. 6" - $65.00 up. Packaged sets: $100.00 up.
Todd: 1965. 6" - $65.00 up.
Twiggy: 1967. 11½" - $175.00 up.
Upsy-Downsy: 1969. 3" - $30.00, $6.00.
Welcome Back, Kotter: 1973. 9" figures: $15.00-30.00.

23½" "Shogun Warriors." Left: "Great Mazinga." Right: "Raydeen." $265.00 up.
Courtesy Margaret Mandel.

MEGO CORPORATION

First prices are for mint condition dolls; second prices are for ones that are dirty or not original. For full listings, see *Modern Collector Dolls*, Volume 4, page 172-177.

Action Jackson: 1971–1972. Beard and no beard. 8" - $185.00 up.
Batman: 1974. Action figure. 8" - $20.00, $8.00. Arch enemy set: (4 in series) 8" - $20.00, $8.00.
Camelot: 1974. (5 in series) 8" - $50.00, $15.00.
Captain & Tenille: 1977. 12" - $20.00, $9.00.
Cher: 12" - $15.00 up, $6.00. Dressed in Indian outfit: $20.00, $10.00.
CHIPs: Ponch and Jon, 1977. 8" - $15.00, $6.00.
Diana Ross: 12½" - $45.00 up, $15.00.
Dinah Mite: 1973. 7½" - $15.00, $6.00. Black: $20.00, $9.00.

12½" "Cher" with grow hair feature. Outfit is "Genie" designed by Bob Mackie and not shown in fashion booklets or on box. $15.00 up. Courtesy Marie Ernst.

268

Haddie Mod: 1971. Teen type, 11½" - $15.00, $6.00.

Happy Days Set: 1974. Fonzie - $15.00, $6.00. Others - $10.00, $3.00.

Jaclyn Smith: 1975. 12½" - $20.00, $9.00.

Joe Namath: 1971. 12" - $85.00, $25.00.

Kiss: 1978. (4 in series) 12½" - $45.00, $10.00.

Lainie: 1973. Jointed waist, battery operated. 19" - $50.00, $20.00.

Laverne & Shirley: 1977. 11½" - $20.00, $9.00. Lenny & Squiggy: 12" - $25.00, $10.00.

One Million BC: 1974–1975. (5 in series) 8" - $15.00, $6.00.

Our Gang Set: 1975. 5" (6 in series). Mickey - $22.00, $10.00. Others - $12.00, $6.00.

Planet of Apes: 1974–1975. (5 in series) 8" - $15.00, $7.00.

Pirates: 1971. (4 in series) 8" - $50.00, $15.00.

Robin Hood Set: 1971. (4 in series) 8" - $45.00, $10.00.

Soldiers: 8" - $20.00, $8.00.

Sonny: 12" - $20.00 up, $9.00.

Starsky or Hutch: 1975. $15.00, $6.00. Captain or Huggy Bear: $20.00, $8.00.

Star Trek Set: 1974–1975. (6 in series) 8" - $30.00, $10.00.

8" "Captain Kirk" (William Shatner) and "Mr. Spock" (Leonard Nimoy) from **1975** *Star Trek* action figure set made by Mego. All original with accessories. Other figures include "Klingon" and "Dr. McCoy." Each - **$30.00 up.**

MEGO CORPORATION

Star Trek Aliens: 1974–1977. (4 in set) 8" - $15.00, $6.00.

Super Women: 1973. Action figures (4 in series). 8" - $15.00, $6.00.

Suzanne Somers: 1975. 12½" - $20.00, $9.00.

Waltons: 1975–1975. (6 in series) 8" - $15.00, $6.00.

Wild West Set: 1974. (6 in series) 8" - $00.00.

Wonder Woman: (Lynda Carter) 1975. 12½" - $20.00, $9.00.

World's Greatest Super Heros: 1974–1975. (8 in series) 8" - $20.00, $8.00. Arch Enemy Set: (8 in series) 8" - $20.00, $8.00.

World's Greatest Super Heros: 1975–1976. Second set (6 in series.) $15.00, $7.00.

Wizard of Oz: 1974. Dorothy - $25.00, $9.00. Munchkins - $15.00, $6.00. Wizard - $20.00, $8.00. Others - $10.00 - $4.00. 15" size: Cloth/vinyl. $100.00, $40.00.

MOLLYE DOLLS

First prices are for mint condition dolls; second prices are for crazed, cracked, dirty dolls or ones without original clothes.

Mollye Goldman of International Doll Company and Hollywood Cinema Fashions of Philadelphia, PA made dolls in cloth, composition, hard plastic and plastic and vinyl. Only the vinyl dolls will be marked with her name, the rest usually have paper wrist tag. Mollye purchased unmarked dolls from many other firms and dressed them to be sold under her name. She designed clothes for many makers, including Horsman, Ideal and Eegee (Goldberger).

Airline Doll: Hard plastic. 14" - $250.00 up, $100.00; 18" - $350.00 up, $125.00; 23" - $385.00 up, $100.00; 28" - $500.00 up, $200.00.

Babies: Composition: 15" - $150.00, $65.00; 21" - $225.00, $95.00. Composition/cloth: 18" - $85.00, $40.00. All composition toddler: 15" - $175.00, $80.00; 21" - $250.00, $100.00.

Babies: Hard plastic: 14" - $95.00, $65.00; 20" - $165.00, $90.00. Hard plastic/cloth: 17" - $95.00, $55.00; 23" - $165.00, $85.00.

Babies: Vinyl: 8½" - $15.00, $7.00; 12" - $20.00, $8.00; 15" - $35.00, $12.00.

Cloth: Children: 15" - $145.00, $65.00; 18" - $185.00, $75.00; 24" - $225.00, $80.00; 29" - $300.00, $100.00.

Cloth: Young ladies: 16" - $185.00, $80.00; 21" - $275.00, $100.00.

Cloth: Internationals: 13" - $90.00 up, $40.00; 15" - $150.00 up, $50.00; 27" - $275.00 up, $85.00.

Composition: Children: 15" - $150.00, $45.00; 18" - $185.00, $75.00.

Composition: Young lady: 16" - $365.00, $100.00; 21" - $525.00, $150.00.

Composition: Jeanette McDonald: 27" - $800.00 up, $250.00.

Composition: Thief of Bagdad Dolls: 14" - $275.00, $85.00; 19" - $475.00, $125.00. Sultan: 19" - $650.00, $200.00. Sabu: 15" - $600.00, $200.00.

Vinyl Children: 8" - $30.00, $10.00; 11" - $50.00, $20.00; 16" - $75.00, $25.00.

Hard Plastic: Young ladies. 17" - $265.00 up, $85.00; 20" - $300.00 up, $100.00; 25" - $350.00, $125.00.

Little Women: 9" vinyl. $40.00, $15.00.

Lone Ranger/Tonto: Hard plastic/latex. 22" - $200.00, $75.00.

Raggedy Ann or Andy: See that section.

Beloved Belindy: See Raggedy Ann section.

7½" nude doll, jointed at shoulders only with painted-on slippers and mohair wig. All hard plastic and in original box. Patterns were available to make clothes for the doll. $20.00 in box.

17" all hard plastic doll made for Mollye. Sleep eyes, not original. Mollye used this doll with may style wigs and clothes. 1950's. 17" - $125.00 up. Courtesy Glorya Woods.

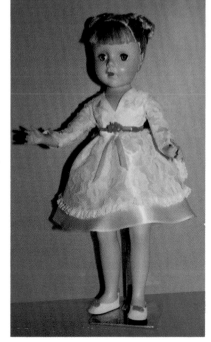

Right: 19" "Monica" made of all composition with hair rooted into composition head, painted features. Not original. ("Monica": 10½" - $285.00; 17" - $500.00; 21" - $585.00.) Center: 18" "Skating Doll/Sonja" by Arranbee. All composition and original. Left: 22" "Miss Curity" made by Ideal. All composition and marked on body "P-94." Redressed "Monica" - $350.00; 18" "Sonja" - $200.00 up; 22" - "Miss Curity" - $500.00 up. Courtesy Turn of Century Antiques.

NANCY ANN STORYBOOK

The painted bisque Nancy Ann Dolls will be marked "Storybook Doll U.S.A." and the hard plastic dolls marked "Storybook Doll U.S.A. Trademark Reg." The only identity as to who the doll represents is a paper tag around wrist with the doll's name on it. The boxes are marked with the name, but many of these dolls are found in the wrong box. Dolls were made 1937–1948.

First prices are for mint condition dolls; second prices are for played with, dirty dolls.

Bisque: 5" - $65.00-75.00 up, $15.00; 7½-8" - $60.00 up, $15.00. Jointed hips: 5" - $70.00 up, $18.00; 7½-8" - $75.00 up, $18.00. Swivel neck: 5" - $75.00 up, $20.00; 7½-8" - $80.00 up, $20.00. Swivel neck and jointed hips: 5" - $75.00, $20.00; 7½-8" - $85.00, $20.00. Black: 5" - $125.00 up, $35.00; 7½-8" - $150.00 up, $40.00.

Plastic: 5" - $45.00 up, $10.00; 7½-8" - $50.00, $15.00. Black: $65.00, $20.00.

Bisque Bent Leg Baby: 3½-4½" - $125.00 up, $35.00.

Plastic Bent Leg Baby: 3½-4½" - $85.00 up, $20.00.

Judy Ann: Incised with name on back. 5" - $325.00 up, $100.00.

Audrey Ann: 6" heavy doll, toddler legs, marked "Nancy Ann Storybook 12." $1,000.00 up, $300.00.

Margie Ann: 6" bisque, in school dress. $150.00 up, $45.00.

Debbie: Name on wrist tag/box. Hard plastic in school dress. $145.00 up, $40.00.

Debbie: Hard plastic with vinyl head. $90.00, $30.00.

Debbie: In dressier type Sunday dress and all hard plastic. $165.00, $45.00. Same with vinyl head. $100.00, $20.00.

Teen Type (Margie Ann): Marked "Nancy Ann." All vinyl. 10½" - $90.00 up, $20.00.

Muffie: 8", all hard plastic. Dress: $185.00 up, $85.00. Ballgown: $200.00 up, $95.00. Riding Habit: $200.00 up, $95.00. Walker: $145.00 up.

Muffie: 8" hard plastic, reintroduced doll. $95.00 up, $25.00.

Nancy Ann Style Show Doll: 17-18" unmarked. All hard plastic. All in ballgown. $500.00 up, $200.00.

7½" "Muffie" of the International Series. All hard plastic and one of the reintroduced dolls. Completely unmarked. Sleep eyes and all original. $95.00 up. Courtesy Margaret Mandel.

17-18" "Style Show" from 1954. All hard plastic with sleep eyes. $500.00 up. Courtesy Sharon McDowell.

These four "Muffie" dolls have no eyebrows and are strung. Marked "Storybook Dolls/Calif." Each - $185.00 up. Courtesy Maureen Fukushima.

Group of mint in box "Nancy Ann Storybook" dolls. All are 5" and bisque. Most are from Storybook series. Nine dolls - $400.00 – 600.00. Courtesy Frasher Doll Auctions.

4" christening babies that are painted bisque and all original. Box is marked "Hush A Bye" Baby. 4" - $125.00 up. Courtesy Joanne Brunken.

First prices are for mint condition dolls; second prices are for played with, dirty, missing clothes or redressed dolls.

Designed by Johnny B. Gruelle in 1915, these dolls are still being made. Early dolls will be marked "Patented Sept. 7, 1915." All cloth, brown yarn hair, tin button eyes (or wooden ones), thin nose, painted lashes far below eyes and no white outline around eyes. Some are jointed by having knees or elbows sewn. Features of early dolls are painted on cloth. 15-16" - $800.00 up; 23-24" - $1,050.00 up; 30" - $1,500.00. Worn and dirty: 15-16" - $565.00; 23-24" - $800.00; 30" - $975.00.

Applause Dolls: Will have tag sewn in seam. 1981. 12" - $25.00; 17" - $45.00; 25" - $60.00; 36" - $85.00 up.

Averill, Georgene: Red yarn hair, painted features and have sewn cloth label in side seam of body. Mid-1930's. 15" - $400.00 up - $125.00. **Asleep/Awake:** 13-14" - $600.00 up. Worn and dirty: $250.00 up. **1940's:** 18" - $165.00. **1950's:** 18" - $135.00. **1960-1963:** 15" - $75.00; 18" - $95.00.

Beloved Belindy: Knickerbocker: 1965. (See photo in Series 7, pg. 276.) Black doll. 15" - $500.00 up, $300.00. **Volland Co.:** Red/white legs, red feet. 15" - $1,500.00-800.00. **Averill:** 15" - $1,000.00 up.

Hasbro: 1983 to date. Under Playskool label. Still available.

Knickerbocker Toy Co.: 1963-1982. Printed features, red yarn hair. Will have tag sewn to seam. **1960's:** 12" - $165.00; 16" - $225.00; 23-24" - $350.00; 30-36" - $400.00-500.00. **1970's:** 12" - $45.00; 16" - $60.00; 23-24" - $100.00; 30-36" - $195.00-250.00. **1980's:** 16" - $25.00; 23-25" - $60.00; 30-36" - $85.00-125.00. **Talking:** 1974. 12" - $45.00. 1960's - $265.00.

Mollye Dolls: Red yarn hair and printed features. Heavy outlined nose. Lower lashes closer to eyes. Most will have multicolored socks and blue shoes.

Will be marked in printed writing on front of torso "Raggedy Ann and Andy Doll/Manufactured by Mollye Doll Outfitters." First company to imprint solid red heart on chest. 15" - $700.00 up, $185.00; 22" - $900.00 up, $200.00.

Nasco/Hobbs-Merrill: 1973. Plastic/vinyl with rooted yarn hair. 24" - $165.00-60.00.

Vinyl Dolls: 8½" - $12.00, $3.00; 12" - $18.00, $6.00; 16" - $22.00, $8.00; 20" - $28.00, $10.00.

Volland Co.: 1920-1934. Lashes low on cheeks. Feet turn outward. Can have brown yarn hair. Some have oversized hands with free-standing thumbs. Long thin nose, lines low under eyes. Different mouth appearances are:

15" - $800.00 up; 18" - $950.00 up; 22" - $1,000.00 up; 24" - $1,100.00 up; 29" - $1,400.00 up.

Georgene Averill "Beloved Belindy" dolls. **Left: 15" doll in an unusual color that is light with pink feet, blouse and bandana. Right: Early 18" doll that is all original with shoe button eyes. 15" - $1,000.00 up.** Courtesy Mimi Hiscox.

15" all original Raggedy Ann made by Volland. Dated with patent date number. Nose repainted a long time ago. 15" - $800.00 up. Courtesy Mimi Hiscox.

15" all original Raggedy Andy made by Volland. 15" - $800.00 up. Courtesy Mimi Hiscox.

18" all original Raggedy Ann and Andy made by Georgene Averill. Have black outlined noses. Each - $400.00 up. Courtesy Mimi Hiscox.

Left: 15" Volland "Raggedy Ann" that is all original. Right: 15" Volland "Beloved Belindy" that is all original except missing apron. "Raggedy Ann" - $800.00 up. "Beloved Belindy" - $1,500.00 up. Courtesy Mimi Hiscox.

18" Mollye Internationals that are all original. Each - $800.00 up. Courtesy Mimi Hiscox.

First prices are for mint condition dolls; second prices are for played with, dirty or not original dolls.

Addams Family: 5½" - $20.00, $8.00.

Baby Crawlalong: 1967. 20" - $25.00, $10.00.

Baby Grow A Tooth: 1969. 14" - $30.00, $10.00. Black: $35.00, $12.00.

Baby Know It All: 1969. 17" - $30.00, $15.00.

Baby Laugh A Lot: 1970. (See photo in Series 7, pg. 277.) 16" - $20.00, $7.00. Black: $30.00, $15.00.

Baby Sad or Glad: 1966. 14" - $30.00, $15.00.

Baby Stroll-A-Long: 1966. 15" - $25.00, $10.00.

Dave Clark 5: 1964. 4½" - $50.00, $20.00.

Heidi: 1965. 5½" - $9.00, $3.00. Herby: 4½" - $12.00, $5.00. Spunky (glasses): 5½" - $14.00, $5.00.

Winking Heidi: 1968. $10.00, $4.00.

Jeannie, I Dream Of: 6" - $20.00, $5.00.

Jumpsy: 1970. (See photo in Series 7, pg. 277.) 14" - $20.00, $8.00. Black: $22.00, $10.00.

Laura Partridge: 1973. 19" - $55.00, $25.00.

Lindalee: 1970. Cloth/vinyl. 10" - $20.00, $9.00.

L.B.J.: 1964. Portrait, 5½" - $25.00, $10.00.

Littlechap Family: 1963. Set of four. $200.00, $60.00. Dr. John: 14½" - $50.00, $20.00. Lisa: 13½" - $40.00, $12.00. Libby: 10½" - $35.00, $10.00. Judy: 12" - $35.00, $10.00.

Mimi: 1972–1973. Battery operated singer. 19" - $40.00, $15.00. Black: $60.00, $20.00.

Orphan Annie: 1967. Plastic and vinyl. 15" - $40.00, $15.00.

Sweet April: 1971. All vinyl baby. 5½" - $15.00, $5.00. Black: 5½" - $20.00, $9.00.

Tippy Tumbles: 1966. 16" - $30.00, $10.00.

Tumbling Tomboy: 1969. 16" - $20.00, $8.00.

SASHA

Sasha dolls were made by Trenton Toys, Ltd., Reddish, Stockport, England from 1965 to 1986, when they went out of business. The original designer of these dolls was Sasha Morgenthaler in Switzerland. The dolls are made of all rigid vinyl with painted features. The only marks will be a wrist tag. All dolls are 16" tall.

Boy or Girl in box: $200.00

Boy or Girl in cylinder: $325.00

Boy: "Gregor" - $200.00.

Girl: $200.00.

Black Boy: "Caleb" - $285.00.

Black Baby: $250.00

Cora: #119, black: $285.00; #111, white: $200.00.

White Baby: $185.00

Sexed Baby: Pre-1979. $265.00

Early Dolls: Tube/sack packaging, girl or boy. $300.00 each.

Limited Edition Dolls: Limited to 5,000, incised #763, dressed in navy velvet. **1981:** $250.00. **1982:** Pintucks dress: $300.00. **1983:** Kiltie Plaid. $300.00. **1985:** Prince Gregor. $350.00. **1986:** Princess. $1,600.00. **1986:** Dressed in sari from India. $1,200.00 up.

16" early dark skinned "Sasha" doll with original packaging tube. The lid made the doll stand. Wears navy blue corduroy dress. $300.00. Courtesy Shirley Bertrand.

Early "Gregor" boy shown with brown paper shipping sack. Sack has pull string on top to close it. Doll was packaged in cardboard tube. $300.00. Courtesy Shirley Bertrand.

First prices are for mint condition dolls; second prices are for played with, dirty, cracked or crazed or not original dolls. Allow extra for special outfits such as "Little Colonel," "Cowgirl," "Bluebird," etc. (Allow 25% to 50% more for mint in box dolls. Price depends upon clothes.)

All Composition:

11" - $725.00, $450.00. 11" Cowgirl: $825.00, $500.00.

13" - $650.00, $400.00.

15-16" - $675.00, $425.00.

17-18" - $725.00, $500.00.

20" - $865.00, $500.00.

22" - $925.00, $550.00.

25" - $1,000.00, $600.00. 25" Cowgirl: $1,200.00, $650.00.

27" - $1,150.00, $650.00. 27" Cowgirl: $1,350.00, $675.00.

Vinyl of 1950's: Allow more for flirty eyes in 17" and 19" sizes.

12" in box - $200.00. Mint, not in box - $165.00. Played with, dirty - $40.00.

15" in box - $325.00. Mint, not in box - $265.00. Played with, dirty - $85.00.

17" in box - $450.00. Mint, not in box - $365.00. Played with, dirty - $95.00.

19" in box - $500.00. Mint, not in box - $450.00. Played with, dirty - $125.00.

36" in box - $1,800.00. Mint, not in box - $1,500.00. Played with, dirty - $800.00.

1972: Reissue from Montgomery Ward. In box - $200.00; Mint, not in box - $165.00; Dirty - $45.00.

1973: Has box with many pictures of Shirley on it. Doll in red polka dot dress. 16" in box - $165.00. Mint, no box - $125.00. Played with, dirty - $45.00.

A beautiful 27" "Shirley Temple" dressed in original "Bright Eyes" dress and has original hair set. 27" - $1,150.00. Courtesy Glorya Woods.

These "Shirley Temple" dolls are made of composition. All are original. Upper: 25" with flirty eyes. Left to right: 19" in original box, 22" in rare "Scotty" dress, another 19" in box, and a 13". 19" in box - $700.00-1,000.00; 25" - $1,000.00; 22" - $800.00; 13" - $650.00. Courtesy Frasher Doll Auctions.

1982–1983: Plastic/vinyl. Made by Ideal. 8" - $25.00, 12" - $30.00.

Shirley Display Stand: Mechanical doll. $2,000.00 up.

"Hawaiian": Marked Shirley Temple (but not meant to be a Shirley Temple.) 18" - $850.00, $400.00.

Japan: All bisque (painted) with molded hair. 6" - $225.00. Composition: 7-8" - $265.00.

German: 1936. 16", marked "GB42." All composition, sleep eyes, open mouth smile. $450.00.

Babies: Marked on head, open mouth with upper and lower teeth, flirty, sleep eyes. 16" - $950.00, $565.00; 18" - $1,000.00, $650.00; 22" - $1,200.00, $700.00; 25" - $1,400.00, $800.00; 27" - $1,600.00, $900.00.

Look-A-Like Dolls: Composition, with dimples. 16" - $200.00; 20" - $350.00; 27" - $600.00. Vinyl: 36" - $800.00.

Shirley Temple Accessories:
Script Name Pin: $18.00-25.00.

Pin Button: Old 1930's doll pin. $90.00. Others - $15.00.

Boxed outfits: 1950's: $35.00 up. 1970's: $30.00 up.

Tagged 1930's dress: $125.00 up.

Purse with name: $12.00-15.00.

Buggy: Made of wood. 26" - $365.00 up; 32" - $425.00 up; 34" - $475.00 up. Wicker: 26" - $450.00 up.

Trunk: $145.00 up. Gift set/doll and clothes: 1950's - $450.00 up.

Statuette: Chalk in dancing dress. 7-8" - $265.00; 4½" - $185.00.

8" "Shirley Temple" that is all painted bisque with painted-on shoes and socks. Original dress is made of crepe paper. Marked "Japan." 8" - $265.00. Courtesy Sandra Cummins.

17" 1958 "Shirley Temple" in original "Heidi" outfit. 17" - $365.00. Courtesy Shirley Bertrand.

12" "Shirley Temple" of 1958. All vinyl and shows a variety of clothes that were available for this doll. You could purchase the doll shown and outfits were boxed extra. You could also buy a dressed/boxed doll.

12" doll only - $165.00. Outfits - $35.00 up. Courtesy Shirley Bertrand.

SIMPLICITY

6½" tall composition style head to make scarves and hats from Simplicity patterns. Called "Miniature Fashions" by Latexture Products, Inc., 17 Rose St. N.Y.C. Original cost was $3.95 and had been marked down to $1.95. Box top covered with red ribbon bows. Mint in box - $100.00. Courtesy of Stan Buler Collection.

STERLING DOLL CO.

29" football and baseball players. Composition heads, hands, and feet with stuffed cloth bodies. Painted features, grinning open/ closed mouths with painted teeth. The football player has cleated shoes. Made in 1935. Marked "Sterling Doll Co." on heads. 29" original - $225.00 each. Redressed - $125.00 each. Courtesy Jeannie Mauldin.

First prices are for mint condition dolls, which could be higher due to the outfit on the doll. Second prices are for soiled, poor wig or not original.

Terri Lee: Composition: $350.00, $100.00. Hard plastic: Marked "Pat. Pend." $285.00 up, $100.00. Others: $265.00 up, $100.00. Black: "Patti Jo." $550.00 up, $250.00. Vinyl: $200.00, $75.00. Talking: $500.00, $185.00. Mint in box: $500.00 up.

Jerri Lee: 16" hard plastic, caracul wig. $300.00, $185.00. Black: "Benjamin." $550.00, $250.00. Mint in box: $500.00 up.

Tiny Terri Lee: 10" - $175.00, $95.00.

Tiny Jerri Lee: 10" - $200.00, $95.00.

Connie Lynn: 19" - $375.00 up, $200.00.

Gene Autry: 16" - $1,600.00 up, $700.00.

Linda Baby: (Linda Lee) 10-12" - $185.00 up, $95.00.

So Sleepy: 9½" - $200.00 up, $100.00.

Clothes: Ballgown - $100.00 up. Riding Habit - $100.00 up. Skaters - $100.00 up. School Dresses - $50.00 up. Coats - $35.00 up. Brownie Uniform - $40.00 up.

Clothes for Jerri Lee: Two-piece pants suit - $100.00 up. Short pants suits - $100.00 up. Western shirt/jeans - $70.00 up.

Mary Jane: Plastic walker, Teri Lee look-alike with long molded eyelids. 16" - $265.00 up.

16" original "Patti Jo" and "Benjamin." "Patti" has painted composition eyes. "Benjamin" has painted rigid plastic eyes. Each - $500.00 up. Courtesy Margaret Mandel.

16" "Terri" and "Jerri Lee." Both are original except Jerri's shoes. "Terri" - $265.00 up; "Jerri" - $300.00. Courtesy Frasher Doll Auctions.

10" "Tiny Jerri Lee" with caracul (lamb's wool) wig, sleep eyes with lashes and original clothes. Guns and belt go with cowboy outfit. 10" - $200.00. Courtesy Frasher Doll Auctions.

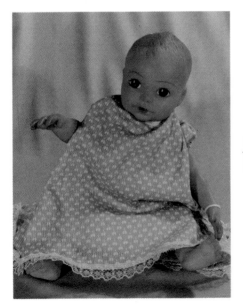

10" "Baby Linda" made of all vinyl with painted eyes and original clothes. $185.00 Courtesy Marie Ernst.

10" "Tiny Terri Lee" that is all original and shows some of the extra outfits that were available for the doll. Original snood and booklet. 10" doll - $175.00; Outfits - $45.00 up. Courtesy Shirley Bertrand.

TROLLS

5" "Troll" and 7" "Troll Giraffe" made of all rigid vinyl with inset plastic eyes. Courtesy Patty Martin.

Trolls: 2½"-3" - $15.00 up; 5" - $20.00-25.00; 7" - $30.00-40.00; 10" - $50.00; 12" - $60.00; 15" - $80.00.

Troll animals: Cow - $65.00; Donkey - $80.00; Ape - $75.00; Turtle - $50.00; Giraffe - $65.00.

3" "Troll" made in 1965. Tag marked "Ughie, Ughie." Inset eyes and original. 3" - $15.00. Courtesy Gloria Anderson.

3" two-headed "Troll" that is all original, 1965. 3" - $20.00. Courtesy Gloria Anderson.

First prices are for mint condition dolls; second prices are for soiled, dirty or not original dolls.

Baby Dollikins: 1958. 21" - $45.00, $20.00.

Baby Trix: 1964. 16" - $20.00, $10.00.

Ballerina: Vinyl. 14" - $25.00, $7.00.

Blabby: 1962. $25.00, $9.00.

Bare Bottom Baby: (See photo in Series 7, pg. 289.) 12" - $25.00, $12.00.

Bob: 1963. 10½" - $20.00, $9.00.

Coquette: 1963. 16" - $30.00, $15.00.

Dollikins: 1957. 8" - $20.00, $8.00; 11" - $25.00, $10.00; 19" - $45.00, $20.00.

Fairy Princess: 32" - $90.00, $40.00.

Freckles: 1960. 32" - $90.00, $45.00.

Freckles Marionette: 30" - $65.00, $30.00.

Grannykins: 1974. Painted on half-glasses. 6" - $12.00, $4.00.

Lucky Lindy: (Lindbergh) Composition. 14" - $350.00, $200.00.

Magic Meg: 1971. Grow hair. 16" - $20.00, $9.00.

Pollyanna: 1960. 10½" - $30.00, $9.00; 17" - $45.00, $15.00; 31" - $100.00, $50.00.

Pri-Thilla: 1958. 12" - $20.00, $8.00.

Purty: 1961. (See photo in Series 7, pg. 289.) Press stomach to make eyes squint. 15" - $30.00, $10.00.

Rita Hayworth: 1948. Composition. 14" - $350.00, $165.00.

Serenade: 1962. Battery-operated talker. 21" - $50.00, $15.00.

Suzette: 1959–1960, 1962. 10½" - $50.00, $25.00; 11½" - $50.00, $25.00; 11½" with sleep eyes: $75.00, $40.00.

Tiny Teens: 1957. 5" - $8.00.

VOGUE DOLLS, INC.

First prices are for mint condition dolls; second prices are for played with, dirty, crazed, messed up wig or not original.

Baby Dear: 1960–1961. 12" - $60.00, $20.00; 17" - $95.00, $40.00. 1964: 12" - $50.00, $20.00. Newborn: 1960. Sleep eyes. $75.00.

Baby Dear One: 25" - $185.00, $85.00.

Baby Dear Two: 27" - $195.00, $95.00.

Baby Wide Eyes: 1976. Very large brown sleep eyes. All vinyl. 16" - $45.00, $20.00.

Brickette: 1960. 22" - $95.00, $40.00. Reissued: 1979–1980. 18" - $65.00.

Ginny: 1948–1949. Composition "Toddles": $265.00 up, $90.00.

Ginny: 1950–1953. 8" hard plastic, strung, painted eyes. $350.00 up, $100.00.

Ginny: 8" hard plastic, sleep eyes, painted lashes and strung. $300.00 up, $100.00.

Ginny: Caracul (lamb's wool) wig. Child, not baby. $400.00 up, $200.00.

Ginny: 1954. Painted lashes, sleep eyes, hard plastic walker. $265.00 up, $95.00.

Ginny: 1954–1957. Hard plastic molded lash walker. $185.00 up, $80.00.

Ginny: 1957–1962. Hard plastic, jointed knee, molded lash walker. $165.00 up, $70.00.

Ginny Hawaiian: 8" brown-black doll. $725.00 up, $365.00.

Ginny Queen: $1,600.00 up, $600.00.

Ginny Crib Crowd: Bent leg baby with caracul (lamb's wool) wig. $650.00 up, $300.00.

Crib Crowd Easter Bunny: $1,400.00 up, $600.00.

Ginny: 1977. All vinyl Internationals. $50.00 up. Other: $35.00 up.

Ginny Exclusives: 1986–1991. **Shirley's Doll House:** Goes Country/Country Fair - $85.00; Black - $65.00; Santa/Mrs. Claus - $70.00; Babysitter: $65.00; Sunday Best (boy or girl) - $55.00. **Gigi and Sherry Meyer's:** Favorite Ginny - $50.00; Clown - $55.00; Cowgirl - $55.00; Prince Charming - $65.00; Cinderella - $60.00. **Little Friends:** Alaska - $60.00. **Toy Village:** Ashley Rose - $55.00. **Enchanted Doll House:** Enchanted Ginny - $50.00.

Ginny Accessories: Ginny Gym: $275.00 up. **Ginny Pup:** Steiff. $165.00 up. **Luggage Set:** $90.00 up. **Shoes/Shoe Bag:** $25.00 up. **Furniture:** Chair, bed, dresser, wardrobe, rocking chair. $55.00 each. **Name Pin:** $55.00.

A strung "Ginny" in original beachwear and shown with very rare vinyl "Freddie the Fish." Replaced shoes. Doll - **$300.00 up**; Fish - **$45.00 up.** Courtesy Shirley Bertrand.

Hug A Bye Baby: 1975. 16" - $35.00, $15.00. Black: $45.00, $20.00.

Jan: 1957. 12" - $125.00, $45.00.

Jeff: 1957. 10" - $65.00, $30.00.

Jill: 1957. 10" - $125.00, $45.00. In box/ballgown - $300.00 up.

Lil Imp: 11" - $65.00, $30.00.

Love Me Linda: 15" - $45.00, $15.00.

Miss Ginny: 1967–1970's. Young lady type. 11-12" - $25.00, $10.00; 15" - $40.00, $15.00.

Star Bright: 1966. 18" - $100.00, $40.00. Baby: 18" - $65.00, $25.00.

Welcome Home or Welcome Home Baby Turns Two: 20-24" - $95.00, $40.00.

Wee Imp: 8", red wig. $400.00 up, $100.00.

8" painted eye "Ginny." All hard plastic with molded hair (never had a wig). Doll wears original, but later outfit. 8" - **$350.00.** Courtesy Kris Lundquist.

Undressed bend knee "Ginny" in her original box with pamphlet. 8" doll only - $185.00. With box - $225.00. Courtesy Carol Turpen.

A very beautiful mint "Ginny" with unusual white eyelashes and eyebrows. In outfit "Easter" #8-6K. 8" - $300.00 up. Courtesy Peggy Pergande.

8" black all vinyl "Ginny" made exclusively for Shirley's Doll House. Doll shop name on life preserver. $85.00 up. Courtesy Shirley Bertrand.

14" tagged Vogue composition doll that is all original. Mohair wig, sleep eyes. $345.00. Courtesy Sharon McDowell.

17½" "Nicole." Head marked "13 EYE/ 9-3/Vogue Dolls, Inc./1965." Dress tag: "Vogue Dolls, Inc./Made in U.S.A." Box: "1980 Vogue Dolls Inc. Sub. of Lesney Products Corp." 18" - $35.00. Courtesy Marie Ernst.

15" "Miss Ginny" older doll with head marked "Vogue Dolls/1974." Tag marked "Malden, Mass." This doll was made before the company was sold to Lesney of England. 15" - $40.00. Courtesy Marie Ernst.

12" "Precious Baby" made of all vinyl with large sleep eyes, rooted hair. Head marked "Vogue/1975." Clothes tag: "Vogue Dolls, Inc./Made in U.S.A." but box is marked "Tonka Toys." (Tonka purchased Vogue molds from Lesney of England.) 12" - $45.00.
Courtesy Marie Ernst.

WOODS, ROBIN

15" "Cathryn" which is one of the early vinyl Robin Woods dolls. All original, 1987. 15" - $400.00.
Courtesy Shirley Bertrand.

14" "Merry Carol," the 1988 Christmas doll. Has painted eyes. $245.00 up. Courtesy Shirley Bertrand.

14" "Scarlett Christmas" of 1988. Carries red bag of presents. Painted green eyes. $200.00 up. Courtesy Shirley Bertrand.

14" "Dickens Boy," a Christmas doll of 1989. He came with the Christmas tree. Painted green eyes. $185.00 up. Courtesy Shirley Bertrand.

14" "Elizabeth St. John," one of the 1989 Christmas dolls. Has very unusual face. Eyes are painted blue. $185.00 up. Courtesy Shirley Bertrand.

WOODS, ROBIN

14" "Mary of the Secret Garden" made in 1989. All original. Painted eyes. $180.00 up. Courtesy Shirley Bertrand.

WORLD DOLL

20" "Ginger Rogers" and "Fred Astaire." Plastic and vinyl, all original. Made in 1986 as part of the Personality Series. Each - $95.00. Courtesy Jeannie Mauldin.

INDEX

INDEX

NUMBERS

Schroeder's Antiques
Price Guide

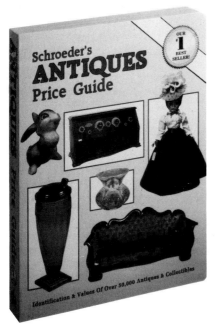

Schroeder's Antiques Price Guide has become THE household name in the antiques and collectibles field. Our team of editors work year around with more than 200 contributors to bring you our #1 best-selling book on antiques and collectibles.

With more than 50,000 items identified and priced, *Schroeder's* is a must for the collector and dealer alike. If it merits the interest of today's collector, you'll find it in *Schroeder's*. Each subject is represented with histories and background information. In addition, hundreds of sharp original photos are used each year to illustrate not only the rare and unusual, but the everyday "fun-type" collectibles as well – not postage stamp pictures, but large close-up shots that show important details clearly.

Our editors compile a new book each year. Never do we merely change prices. Each category is thoroughly checked to spot inconsistencies, listings that may not be entirely reflective of actual market dealings, and lines too vague to be of merit. Only the best of the lot remains for publication. You'll find *Schroeder's Antiques Price Guide* the one to buy for factual information and quality.

8½x11", 608 Pages   **$12.95**

COLLECTOR BOOKS
A Division of Schroeder Publishing Co., Inc.